FRANK DAVIS
Makes Good Groceries!

Also by Frank Davis

The Frank Davis Seafood Notebook
Frank Davis Cooks Naturally N'Awlins
Frank Davis Cooks Cajun, Creole, and Crescent City
The Fisherman's Tackle Box Bible

FRANK DAVIS
Makes Good Groceries!
A NEW ORLEANS COOKBOOK

Frank Davis

PELICAN PUBLISHING COMPANY
GRETNA 2008

The word "Pelican" and the depiction of a pelican are trademarks of Pelican Publishing Company, Inc., and are registered in the U.S. Patent and Trademark Office.

Library of Congress Cataloging-in-Publication Data

Davis, Frank, 1942-
  Frank Davis makes good groceries! : a New Orleans cookbook / Frank Davis.
     p. cm.
  Includes index.
  ISBN 978-1-58980-536-1 (hardcover : alk. paper) 1. Cookery, American--Louisiana style. 2. Cookery--Louisiana--New Orleans. I. Title.
  TX715.2.L68D3834 2008
  641.59763--dc22

                                    2007045368

Printed in the United States of America

Published by Pelican Publishing Company, Inc.
1000 Burmaster Street, Gretna, Louisiana 70053

To my Benny, my littlest grandson and my best food critic,
who just so happens to like everything PawPaw has ever cooked!
Love ya!

Contents

Introduction

Regardless of what it is you're planning to cook, be it a quick throw-it-together lunch for the family or an intricately planned and executed sit-down, white-tablecloth, elegant dinner for eight, it all begins the same way.

As New Orleanians have said for decades upon decades, you first gotta go "make groceries." Let me explain. Everywhere else on this planet that phrase isn't very common. In fact, it's downright misleading. After all, how exactly does one "make" groceries?

It's just New Orleans, you see. It seems that in the Crescent City we have always "made" our groceries. The phrase probably comes from the French term for shopping: *faire des courses,* which literally translates as "make errands." In New Orleans, even today, the two words together—"make groceries"—are patois, slang, jargon, and lingo and they simply mean that the individual proclaiming that phrase is, in fact, doing nothing more than "going grocery shopping."

Why, though, is this so danged important to the formulation and construction and content of this book? Well, it's simple, actually. 'Cuz once you've gotten out and "made your groceries," it then takes only a little effort, skill, and training to transform them into some seriously "good groceries," another slang term used all across Southeast Louisiana (and other regions along the northern Gulf Coast) for a pot or a plate or a bowl of some really fabulously fine eating.

But for that, you first got to have some "good recipes." And that's my thing, as you're about to find out in this cookbook.

Chefs, backyard-barbecue addicts, small-kitchen apartment dwellers who share recipes with other "singles," soccer moms who plan three home-cooked meals a day every day, as well as Uptown socialites who host elegant soirees almost every weekend have all told me that they loved my first three cookbooks and found them all to be instructive and—yes—delicious. Well, if all those comments were in fact true, then these genres will rave over the "good groceries" they're going to find within the pages of my latest culinary literature.

Learning how to cook really good New Orleans groceries, as only talented and trained New Orleanians can, is what this new book is all about. You'll find that the following recipes are nothing less than succulent, savory, delectable, mouth-watering, delicious, slap-your-momma, easy-to-prepare dishes. Each one *you can execute with minimum effort.* Each one is just that simple to do. Oh, and in that long string of adjectives I spouted off a bit ago, did I also say that they're tasty, too?

Well, enough of the culinary chit-chat. It's time you got to thumbing through the pages and picking out the recipes you want to cook first. Be assured that I've formulated them so that anyone and everyone, whether you're a master of the grill, sous-chef of your homestead kitchen, student trying to feed himself in his college dormitory room, or just one of those "I'm-just-now-learning-how-to-turn-my-stove-on cooks," can follow my recipe directions with no guesswork involved. That's because I want you to be able, every time you step up to the range top, to turn out some really *"good groceries!"*

FRANK DAVIS
Makes Good Groceries!

CHAPTER 1

Breakfast Dishes

Frank's Country-Fried Cornmeal Pancakes

If you think a big ol' double stack of good ol' Aunt Jemima conjures up memories of mornings from your childhood, just wait until you whip up a batch of their country-style "cousins in cornmeal." Not only good for breakfast, slathered in butter and dripping with syrup, these old-fashioned hotcakes are also right at home on the lunch or dinner table, as the perfect accompaniment to a pot of smothered cabbage, pinto beans, black-eyed peas, beef and vegetable soup, or whatever else calls for a special cornbread. This, y'all, is it!

1 egg, well beaten	1 tsp. baking soda
2 cups cultured buttermilk	¼ cup margarine or corn oil
⅓ cup all-purpose flour	1 tsp. salt
1½ cups plain yellow cornmeal	

To make country-fried cornmeal pancakes, take a big bowl and a wire whisk and whip together all the ingredients. Note: you want to stir the mixture just until it turns smooth and lump free (*don't over-whip it—you'll make the batter tough*).

When you're ready to cook, heat a heavy, 12-in., nonstick or cast-iron skillet to the point where a drop of water dances off in a sizzle. Then pour in a scant amount of corn oil (or spray the pan with a non-stick coating) and ladle in the cornbread mixture in portions equivalent to the size of coffee-table drink coasters.

Cook them on one side until large bubbles appear in the batter and the bottom side turns golden brown (you can peek at it with the spatula). Then flip them over and continue to cook them on the other side until they stop steaming and the flip side browns, too. I suggest you serve them right away, piping hot from the skillet, slathered in butter and topped with good ol' Luzianna cane syrup, but they're not all that bad after they cool off, either.

They're almost like regular pancakes, only heartier and crispier.

Chef's Note:

1—Use only a good brand of stone-ground cornmeal for this recipe. Do not substitute prepackaged mixes. This is one of those "from scratch" recipes.

2—For the best quality, taste, and texture in the finished pancakes, make every effort to formulate the batter just moments before you cook them. This keeps the baking soda "alive" in the mix and produces lightness instead of flatness.

3—Cornmeal fashioned into flatbreads, muffins, sticks, or even wedges hot from the oven is always a welcomed addition to any table. But when it's pan-cooked in an old-timey, black, cast-iron skillet, it takes on a whole different taste.

Frank's Original Creole Calas

This original recipe dates back to between 1750 and 1800, when the crunchy, tasty rice cakes were sold as breakfast items on the streets of the city by Creole women who wrapped them in towels and carried them in a basket on their heads. Today, they're no longer sold on the streets, but they're still popular among the old-line Creole families of New Orleans, especially at Thanksgiving, Christmas, Mardi Gras, and Holy Communion time.

2 whole eggs, slightly beaten
½ cup granulated or light brown
 sugar
1 tsp. vanilla
1 tsp. cinnamon
½ tsp. apple pie spice
⅛ tsp. nutmeg

¼ tsp. salt
1 cup whole milk
1½ cups self-rising flour
2 cups cold, soft-cooked rice
Vegetable oil for frying
Powdered sugar for dusting
Maple or cane syrup for topping

The recipe is a simple one, created first by making a New Orleans egg custard, then folding in rice. Here's how it's done:

First, you're going to need a large bowl and a wire whisk. Take the bowl, drop in the eggs, sugar, vanilla, spices, and salt, then whip everything together into a smooth and frothy custard (which should take anywhere from 3 to 5 minutes).

Next, pour in the milk and, again using the whisk, whip it thoroughly into the custard. When everything is nice and creamy, begin adding the flour a little at a time and whip it all together until you come up with a silky-smooth batter.

At this point, thoroughly fold the cold rice into the batter, making sure that every grain is uniformly coated. Let the mixture stand for at least 30 minutes so that the flavors "marry." Actually, for intensely flavored calas, you can transfer the premixed batter into an airtight container (a Mason jar works really well) and store it in the refrigerator overnight.

When you're ready to cook, pour about 1 in. vegetable oil into a heavy 12-in. skillet (you want to almost cover the calas as they cook) and heat the oil to high (between 375 and 400 degrees). Then, when the oil reaches the right temperature, drop the calas mixture into the skillet by heaping teaspoonfuls (you want them to form thin 3-in.-wide fritters), fry them for about 1 minute on each side until golden brown and crunchy, and place them on several layers of paper towels to drain.

All that's left is to serve them immediately—piping hot—covered with a generous sprinkling of powdered sugar and a slathering of syrup.

Chef's Note:

1—You can find apple pie spice in the spice section of your supermarket. It is an ultra-fine mixture of cinnamon, nutmeg, allspice, and ginger. Several spice manufacturers prepackage it.

2—To get the ultimate "crunch," first take a 4-qt. Dutch oven or saucepan containing 3 cups water and bring it to a rolling boil. Then stir in 1 heaping cup long-grain rice. When the water comes back to a boil, reduce the heat to simmer, cover the pot, and cook the rice for about 15-20 minutes until it is "softened" (slightly overcooked, but not mushy). Then—without washing the rice!—set the pot into the refrigerator to cool. It is this rice and the starch that becomes a part of it that adds to the crunch when the calas are deep-fried! But plain ol' everyday leftover rice does a halfway decent job, too.

3—Of course, for calas to be eaten when light and crispy, they need to be served as soon as they finish draining. Once they cool and set, they tend to soften, get heavy, and turn greasy. I also recommend that you fry them in only the highest quality vegetable oil.

4—Some recipes call for cooking calas in a lightly greased skillet. I want you to know that this method produces heavy "rice pancakes" rather than light and crispy calas. I suggest you fry them—authentically—in deep fat.

5—If you prefer, you can serve the calas to your guests with a Louisiana cane syrup, maple syrup, or even honey. But traditionally, they are eaten only with a sprinkling of powdered sugar.

Pain Perdu
(Lost Bread or French Toast)

It's what you and I and all of our friends and neighbors have been eating for breakfast in New Orleans and all across the Acadian Triangle for all these years. Depending on where your home place sat, Momma may have called it French toast, or she might have referred to it as Lost Bread, or if you woke up every morning on Bayou Lafourche she told you it was Pain Perdu. But regardless of where it was or what you called it, this has always been and will probably always be one of the primo breakfast foods in the Deep South.

4 eggs, well beaten	⅛ tsp. nutmeg
¾ cup milk or evaporated milk	Pinch salt
1 tbsp. grated orange zest	1 stick butter or margarine, cut
¼ cup fresh orange juice	into 8 pats
2 tbsp. sugar	8 slices stale French bread, 1 in.
1 tsp. cinnamon	thick
½ tsp. vanilla	Powdered sugar for dusting

In a large mixing bowl, whisk together the eggs, milk, orange zest, orange juice, sugar, cinnamon, vanilla, nutmeg, and salt.

Then, in a 12-in. nonstick skillet, melt down 2 pats butter or margarine until it begins to sizzle.

Meanwhile, dip the bread on both sides in the egg/milk coating until thoroughly covered. Then place the slices on a wire rack over a sheet pan for a few minutes to allow the excess coating to drip away.

All that's left is to fry the slices in the butter over a medium or medium-high heat until they turn a richly golden color with weblike markings. This should take about 2 to 3 minutes on each side. Repeat the procedure as often as need to cook all the bread slices. Avoid smashing down on the slices as they cook—this will keep the French toast light and airy.

I suggest you serve the bread immediately from the skillet and dust the slices liberally with powdered sugar.

Chef's Note:
1—Suitable breads for making French toast include French bread, brioche, or challah (egg bread). The trick to creating "perfect" French toast is to get the right staleness to the bread. This is best accomplished

by spreading the slices out on a table overnight. Of course, if push comes to shove, you can always lightly toast the slices before converting them to Lost Bread.

2—French toast can also be served with Steen's Cane Syrup, or a light sprinkling of granular sugar, or 4 tbsp. raspberry preserves creamed together with 4 tbsp. creamy peanut butter. The raspberry-peanut topping is best if spread over the French toast while it is piping hot right from the skillet.

3—One of the classiest toppings for French toast is Orange Crème. It is made by whisking together 1 cup heavy cream, ¼ cup sugar, ⅓ cup orange juice concentrate, and a splash of good brandy. Beat the mixture almost to a froth and serve it slightly chilled. Mmm!

Frank's Homemade Creole Cream Cheese (New, Improved, and Super-Easy Version)

There was a time when the only Creole cream cheese to pass any N'Awlins native's lips was made at Gold Seal Creamery under the direction of the late, great Sam Centanni. But these days, unless you're a shopper at Dorignac's Supermarket or a regular at certain signature restaurants around town, if you want Creole cream cheese for breakfast you best make it yourself at home. And you can—here is the *new and improved easy way* to make your own, based on Sam's original recipe!

1 gal. skim milk
½ cup buttermilk, room
  temperature
½ tablet rennet (or 25 drops
  liquid rennet)
1 pkg. cheesecloth
1 stack drain cups or yogurt
  molds

1 qt. half-and-half (or 2 cups
  half-and-half plus 2 cups
  whipping cream)
Granulated sugar or artificial
  sweetener for sprinkling

Step 1

First, in an 8-qt. stainless-steel stockpot, heat the skim milk to between 80 and 90 degrees (use an instant-read thermometer). You can do this over a very low fire on the stove or simply remove the milk from the refrigerator and allow it to come to the proper temperature if possible. Then, using a stainless steel spoon, stir in the buttermilk. When the milks are well blended, add the rennet and stir the mixture well again.

Step 2

Now set the stockpot aside *at room temperature* for about 12 to 15 hours (*don't place it near a heat source or in the refrigerator*). It's okay to keep it in an air-conditioned room, but be sure to move it away from any direct airflow. Usually, a spot off to the side on a kitchen counter works well.

Keep in mind that once the mixture is placed on the countertop and begins to rest, you must not stir it again (stirring inhibits curd formation). Ideally, the pot should be covered with a layer or two of cheesecloth (you can tape it in place), because air is needed for processing the cheese and the cheesecloth also keeps out interested critters.

Step 3

After the curds have set up, ladle off the whey (that's the watery liquid that rises to the surface of the pot) and discard it. Then scoop out the curds with a stainless-steel spoon, transfer them to the drain cups or yogurt molds, and allow the additional whey to drip away. Since dripping could literally continue for a day or so, I suggest that you put the cups or molds into a large baking pan to catch the liquids. When the curds no longer drip, the cheese is ready.

Step 4

At this point, it is time to scoop the cheese into bowls or plastic tubs or whatever containers you intend to use to store it in. Then immediately cap the containers and refrigerate them for 4 to 6 hours to allow the cheese to set.

Step 5

When the curds have molded, uncap the containers and cover each "cake" with a generous portion of half-and-half or whipping cream or a combination of both. When you're ready to eat, sprinkle the Creole cream cheese liberally with granulated sugar or artificial sweetener and serve with a piece of crispy French bread for dipping.

Chef's Note:

1—The original unaltered recipe from Gold Seal Creamery can be found on page 251 of my Frank Davis Cooks Cajun, Creole, and Crescent City *cookbook. The recipe in this book has been simplified so that the cream cheese can be made quickly and easily in anyone's kitchen.*

2—It is extremely critical that you do not allow the skim milk to get cooler than 70 degrees or higher than 90 degrees at the time you add the rennet. Actually, an even 80 degrees is ideal.

3—Some select specialty cheese stores carry rennet, as do several outlets found on the Internet. Simply go to your favorite search engine (Google, for example) and type in RENNET, CHEESEMAKING. You get lots of sources from which you can buy direct. In New Orleans, though, the locals can find rennet in good supply all the time at Dorignac's Supermarket on Veterans Boulevard. Their brand is made by Junket and is located in the Jell-O and pudding section.

4—If you don't have drain cups or yogurt molds, you can make your own by taking an ice pick and poking a bunch of holes in the plastic tubs that you've saved from grated cheese, crabmeat, dips, or margarine spread. Just make as many holes as it takes to quickly drain the cheese curd. Wide-mouth Styrofoam tubs, particularly the 8- or 10-oz. sizes, also make great drain molds when holes are poked in them.

5—Go ahead and make a big batch of Creole cream cheese when you make it. It will keep beautifully in your refrigerator for at least a month and, according to Crescent City tradition, it makes a great choice for either breakfast or supper.

Ray and Serenia's Famous Mayhaw Jelly

From the quiet backwoods of Bogalusa, where country living is an everyday peaceful way of life, come some of the best down-home delicacies you ever put pass yo' lips! And one of those special treats is old-fashioned mayhaw jelly. Few folks make it better than Ray and Serenia Applewhite, and they were kind enough to share their recipe with me. I hereby do likewise, y'all!

3 qt. water, bottled preferred	5½ cups granular sugar
1 gal. mayhaw berries, washed and sorted	1 tbsp. fresh-squeezed lemon juice
1 box powdered pectin	2 tsp. butter

The procedure for this recipe is simple—bring the water to a rolling boil and stir in all the berries. Then when the water comes back to a boil, cook the mayhaws hard for 30 minutes. When they're done, mash them in the liquid with a potato masher.

Next, using a large sieve, strain the juice from the berry pulp and discard the pulp. Then measure out exactly 4 cups of juice and transfer it to a large pot (an 8-qt. stainless-steel stockpot will do nicely). At this point, while the juice is still hot, stir in the pectin and bring the mixture back to a hard rolling boil, stirring it occasionally. Then pour in all the sugar at once and stir it continuously until the sugar fully dissolves. Finally, add and stir in the lemon juice and butter.

Once again bring the liquid to a full rolling boiling (a boil that rises to the top and cannot be stirred down). The secret here is to boil it hard for exactly *1 minute and 15 seconds* (and stir it constantly). When the time is up, immediately remove the pot from the heat and skim the foam off the top with a metal spoon.

All that's left is to ladle the hot liquid into sterilized jelly jars, leaving about ¼-in. headspace. Then wipe the jar edges with a damp cloth and seal the jars tightly with new lids. The mayhaw jellies will set up (gel) when the jars cool to room temperature.

This recipe will make 6 half-pint jars.

Chef's Note:
1—Try not to make more mayhaw jelly than you'll use in about 6 weeks' time. Once in the jars, the jelly slowly loses its bright cherry-red color, and over a matter of weeks it also loses its fresh mayhaw taste.

2—Strained juice can be kept in the refrigerator for approximately 2 weeks prior to turning it into jelly.

3—Strained juice also keeps well in the freezer for up to a full year!

New Orleans Quick-n-Easy Breakfast Wraps

You need slightly beaten eggs, four different kinds of cheeses, a dab of butter for extra flavoring, and your favorite omelet fillings. Combine everything, roll it up inside a heated flour tortilla, shape it into a genuine "wrap," and you got one of those breakfasts Grandma usta make for the neighborhood kids before school!

2 large eggs
1 tbsp. water
⅛ tsp. Frank Davis Sprinkling Spice or salt and black pepper
1 flour tortilla, 10-in. size
Cooking spray
2 tsp. butter or margarine
⅓ cup cooked and minced breakfast sausage
3 tbsp. shredded Monterey Jack cheese
3 tbsp. shredded Swiss cheese
3 tbsp. shredded cheddar or Colby cheese

1 tbsp. grated Parmesan cheese
2 tbsp. diced red bell pepper
2 tbsp. diced yellow bell pepper
2 tbsp. diced green bell pepper
2 tbsp. thinly sliced green onions
¼ tsp. seeded and minced Jalapeno peppers
¼ cup warm salsa, medium style (or 1 cup diced avocado and tomato with lime juice, chilled)
2 tbsp. minced parsley

The first thing you do is crack the eggs into a quart-size bowl and slightly beat them. Then pour the water over the eggs and gently whisk that around as well. This is also the time when you evenly shake on the Sprinkling Spice (or salt and black pepper).

Then when you're ready for breakfast, place a 10-in., nonstick skillet with sloping sides on the fire and warm the tortilla. When it's heated, remove it from the pan, set it on a plate, and invert a second plate on top of it to keep it warm (and to keep it from drying out). Then spray another 10-in., nonstick skillet with a light coating of cooking spray, turn the heat up to medium high, and quickly melt the butter (*but do not let it burn!*).

Then immediately pour in the eggs and begin pulling their outside edges into the center (this causes them to cook evenly without scorching). Then when a slight "mound" of cooked eggs begins to collect in the center of the pan, begin tilting and rolling the pan to allow the remaining uncooked eggs to run to the outside edge. Then as soon as they *set* and *quit running,* but are still nice and moist, remove them from the heat.

It's at this point that the filling ingredients get sprinkled evenly over the omelet—*first the sausage, then the Monterey Jack, then the Swiss, then the cheddar, then the Parmesan, then the bell peppers, then the green onions, and then finally the Jalapenos.* By the way, it's okay to create in advance a mixture of the cheeses and a mixture of the peppers in order to simplify the procedure.

All that's left to do now is to slide the filled omelet directly out of the pan onto the warm tortilla and roll it into a wrap. The best way to do this is to first fold the bottom of the tortilla up about 1 in. Then fold the left and right sides over about 1 in. Then commence to roll the omelet inside of the tortilla so that the wrap ends with the seam side facing down. *Note: since the eggs will finish cooking inside the tortilla, allow the wrap to "rest" for 1-2 minutes before slicing it in half on a bias (diagonally).*

When you're ready to eat, serve both halves of the wrap on a warm plate alongside salsa or a chilled fresh avocado-tomato relish. Garnish the plate with parsley and top off the presentation with a tall glass of cold milk!

Chef's Note:

1—Adding water to the eggs keeps the omelet light and fluffy. Using milk or cream produces a richer omelet, but a heavier one.

2—The secret to making a "tender" omelet is to cook it over a medium-high heat for a very short period of time (actually until the eggs are still shiny and moist but no longer runny). This takes a little getting used to and demands the undivided attention of the cook. Should focus be diverted away from the eggs and the skillet, even for a short time, the eggs will end up rubbery and scorched!

3—A wooden spoon or rubber spatula is the preferred tool for cooking omelets. And in spite of their marketing label, the least efficient tool is the old metal egg turner.

4—If you prefer a filling other than breakfast sausage, you can substitute ham, prosciutto, cocktail shrimp, baked or grilled oysters, crawfish tails, lump crabmeat, or whatever else your tastebuds desire.

5—These wraps are best done 2 eggs at a time. Leave the 3- and 4-egg omelets to the restaurant cooks, and I heartily suggest you prepare these wraps one at a time without trying to double the recipe.

Great Grandma's Gourmet Grits

Just about every Southerner since Scarlett and Rhett has whipped up a batch of grits at one time or another. And just about everybody on the bayou spices 'em up once in a while with a little cheese and a little bacon. But try this version the next time you fix breakfast. What you end up with is some hominy that's nothing short of gourmet fare!

¾ stick real butter
1 cup minced onions
½ cup minced green bell pepper
1 cup Quaker Quick Grits
½ tsp. salt

4 cups rapidly boiling water
1 cup finely crumbled bacon
1 cup shredded sharp cheddar
   cheese

First, in a heavy saucepan, melt ½ stick butter over medium heat, toss in the onions and the bell pepper, and sauté the mixture until the vegetables soften and just start to brown.

Then, while the seasoning vegetables are cooking, take a 4-qt. Dutch oven and slowly stir the grits—*along with the salt*—into the boiling water. When the water comes back to a boil, reduce the heat to simmer, cover the pot, and cook for about 4 minutes or until the grits reach the consistency you desire (thicker is best for this recipe).

At this point, remove the pot from the heat and stir in the sautéed vegetables, the leftover ¼ stick butter, and all of the remaining ingredients, making sure that they are thoroughly blended into the grits.

Finally, all that's left to do is season 'em up with salt and black pepper to taste (or 1-2 dashes Frank Davis Sprinkling Spice if you got some), tightly cover the Dutch oven, and let the mixture "set up" for about 5 minutes before you serve it. The texture will be creamy and the flavor will be richer than any grits you ever ate!

Chef's Note: Now if you have grits left over, don't throw them away. Put them into the refrigerator and let them get cold. Then cut them into ¾-in. slices, separate them with sheets of waxed paper, and freeze them. The next time you prepare breakfast, just drop the slices into hot butter and pan-fry them to a golden brown along with your eggs, bacon, or sausage. It's a whole different treat!

CHAPTER 2
Appetizers and Snacks

Frank's Cajun-Style Fried Rumaki

It's the best of the Orient combined with the best of the Bayou Country . . . marinated chicken livers dusted in seasoned flour, wrapped in bacon, and deep-fried to a succulent crispness. They're just what you need for your next party *or* elegant meal!

4 cups whole milk	24 round toothpicks
1½ cups diced onions	2 cups corn oil for frying
2 lb. plump chicken livers	1 cup canned chicken broth
24 half-slices lean hickory-smoked bacon	Salt and black pepper to taste
4 cups seasoned all-purpose flour	

First, take a 2½-qt. glass bowl (*do not use metal!*) and mix together 2 cups milk and the onions.

In the meantime, drain the chicken livers and remove any traces of fat that may still be attached. Now drop them into the milk mixture and allow them to marinate for at least 3-4 hours (overnight is even better!).

Then when you're ready to cook, lay out the bacon strips on the countertop. Then take one liver directly from the milk marinade, dust it lightly in the seasoned flour, and wrap it so that it's completely enclosed in a bacon strip. *Note: if you don't dust it in flour first, it'll slip and slide all over the place and you'll never get it to stay inside the bacon!* Then pin the bacon strip in place with a toothpick. Repeat this procedure with each liver. When they're all done, place them momentarily on the countertop on a sheet of waxed paper.

At this point, heat the oil to exactly 325 degrees in a heavy deep-sided skillet. When you're ready to fry, lightly dust the rolled livers in the seasoned flour once again, but be sure to shake off all the excess. Then drop them gently into the oil and fry them on both sides until the bacon turns a golden brown and the flour coating becomes crispy. *Just be sure you don't overcook them, otherwise the bacon will burn.*

When they're ready, set them aside temporarily on a warming platter. Then in a 2½-qt. saucepan, add about 6 tbsp. of the corn oil you used to fry the livers in, mix in about 6-8 tbsp. seasoned flour, and make a light roux. You only need to cook it for a few minutes because you don't want it to brown (you're going to make country-style white-milk gravy here). Now stir in about 2 cups milk plus the canned chicken broth and simmer everything together over *low heat* until the gravy turns silky smooth. At this point, you can season it with salt and black pepper to taste.

When you're ready to eat, all you do is dish up 4-6 of the Cajun-style rumaki bundles for each person and cover them generously with the milk gravy. If you want to make a meal out of these, serve them alongside a big scoop of cheesy grits or mashed potatoes or dirty rice and, maybe, a tossed green salad topped with bleu cheese dressing.

Oooh, cher! Ah-so!

Chef's Note: For best flavor, I suggest you season the flour to taste with my Frank Davis Sprinkling Spice (plus 1-2 dashes Frank Davis Poultry Seasoning). My seasonings can be ordered from my Web site, www.frankdavis.com.

Frank's Almost-World-Famous Buffalo Hot Wings

Nobody really knows the true, coveted, secret recipe for Buffalo Chicken Wings, except for the one person who legend says created it back in 1964 at the Anchor Bar and Grill in Buffalo, New York. That person is Teresa Bellissimo. And last we heard, she wasn't about to give anyone her time-honored formulation. But not to worry. This concoction t'ain't all that bad, and it's about as close to the real thing as anyone outside the Bellissimo family will ever get. So whip up a batch of these real soon and enjoy!

Gourmet Roquefort Wing Dip (Optional):

½ cup high-quality bleu cheese chunks

1 3-oz. pkg. cream cheese, softened

½ cup Blue Plate Mayonnaise

1 tbsp. fresh-squeezed lemon juice

1 tbsp. premium white-wine vinegar

½ cup sour cream

Just in case you want to make your own Roquefort dip instead of using store bought, do this first, because it must chill for at least 3 hours. Put all the dip ingredients into a nonreactive bowl (preferably glass) and combine thoroughly. Then cover with plastic wrap and chill. This keeps well in the refrigerator for about 10 days.

The Wings:

Peanut or vegetable oil for frying   2 cups Frank Davis Chicken Fried
5 lb. chicken wings   Mix

When you're ready to make the wings, in a heavy, high-sided fry pan, heat the oil to 375-400 degrees. Some recipes say you can bake, grill, or broil the wings, but you really don't have "authentic" Buffalo wings unless you deep-fry 'em in small batches. Hot-wing lovers know that this is not a heart-healthy dish!

It is important that you first wash the wings in cold running water. Then with a super-sharp knife, split them at the joints (discard the wing tips), pat them well with paper towels, and air dry them on a rack in the refrigerator. This procedure alone will ensure crispy wings once they are deep-fried.

Next, simply dust them *very lightly* in the chicken fried mix—*do not dip them in an egg wash and coat them with a batter.* The only reason you even want them floured is because the light coating helps to keep the sauce on the wings. I also recommend that if possible you separate the drumettes from the mid-wing sections and fry them separately—the drumettes will take a few minutes longer to cook than the mid-wings.

When you're ready to fix 'em, drop about 15 wings at a time into the hot oil (each wing piece should be submerged in the oil—you want to deep-fry 'em, not pan-fry 'em). Then fry the batch for 12-14 minutes, stirring them occasionally. You can figure they're done when the rapidly bubbling of the oil subsides significantly in the skillet. A couple of batches and you'll get the hang of it!

The Hot Sauce:

1 stick margarine, softened
2 bottles Frank Davis Garlic
   Cayenne Hot Sauce
1 tbsp. premium white-wine
   vinegar

¼ tsp. cayenne pepper
¼ tsp. paprika

In the meantime, while the wings are frying, make the sauce. In a 3-qt. saucepan, first melt the margarine. Then briskly stir in the hot sauce, vinegar, and spices. But once everything is totally combined, remove the pan from the fire right away! Cooked too long over the flame, the sauce will break.

When it's time for the wings to come out of the hot oil, simply lift them out either with a slotted spoon or a pair of tongs and place them immediately on either paper towels or brown grocery bags to drain. Then put them into an extra-large stainless-steel bowl, ladle the sauce over them, and toss them briskly to liberally coat each wing part. The trick to getting them "just right" is to toss them with "just the right amount" of sauce. You don't want them dripping with sauce—you're not marinating them. And the more sauce you use, the hotter they will become.

All that's left to do now is place the wings on a shallow baking sheet, slide them into a preheated 400-degree oven for about 5 minutes or so to bake on the sauce, and then serve them with celery sticks, carrot sticks, and a big bowl of Roquefort dip. This sho' is some fine vittles!

Chef's Note:
1—For the ultimate in Buffalo Hot Wings, try to buy what are called "grinders," extra-meaty, extra-large, unfrozen chicken wings. They are, however, sometimes hard to find.

2—If you don't have any Frank Davis Chicken Fried Mix, you can use all-purpose flour mixed with 1 tsp. kosher salt and 1 tsp. coarse-ground black pepper.

3—If you don't have any Frank Davis Garlic Cayenne Hot Sauce on hand, you can use your favorite bottled hot sauce instead. Just remember to adjust the heat intensity to your taste.

4—The basic formula for hot sauce is x amount of margarine to x amount of hot sauce (with a little BBQ sauce—but not hickory flavored!—tossed in to tone down the heat a little if so desired). But to control the heat intensity of the sauce, simply do the following:

For mild sauce, use equal parts hot sauce and margarine.

For medium sauce, use twice the amount of hot sauce as margarine.

For killer sauce, use three times the amount of hot sauce as margarine.

For kiddie wings, just splash a few drops of the hot sauce into the margarine.

5—If you don't have a large stainless-steel bowl, you can put the wings into a large container with a cover, pour on the sauce, cover the container, and shake it briskly until each of the wings is thoroughly coated.

Microwaved Artichoke

I can't begin to tell you how many dozens of ways there are to prepare the vegetable pride of Sicily—artichokes. Believe it or not, microwaving is one of them (and it yields elegant results, too).

1 fresh artichoke	Dash black pepper
3 tbsp. minced garlic	Pinch dill
1-2 tsp. Frank Davis Sprinkling Spice	1 squeeze lemon
	3 tbsp. extra-virgin olive oil

First, wash the artichoke thoroughly under cool running water, making sure that the water flows between all of the leaves. Then cut off the stem flush with the bottom of the artichoke, and slice off the top third of the artichoke (at this time it's a good idea to peel away the smallest outer leaves, too). When it is fully prepped, place it trimmed side down on a couple of sheets of paper towels (in other words, the stem side should be facing up).

Now put the remaining ingredients in a Tupperware-type bowl that has a lid. Stir everything together until fully blended.

All that's left to do is to place the artichoke facedown in the bowl and cover it with the lid (but leave a slight crack in the seal to allow the excess moisture to vent). Now cook the artichoke for 7 minutes on high.

When the cooking time has elapsed, remove the artichoke from the microwave; but leave the cover on the bowl and let the artichoke stand for an additional 5 minutes.

Chef's Note: When you're ready to eat, pull off the leaves and dip them in an olive oil, balsamic vinegar, black pepper, and grated Parmesan cheese mixture that you make to taste.

Pot-Cooked Artichokes

This is one of the easiest ways to prepare artichokes, y'all.

1½ cups water (or chicken or vegetable stock)
Kosher salt and black pepper to taste
Pinch cayenne pepper

Dash extra-virgin olive oil
Fresh herbs to taste (dill, basil, etc.)
Fresh artichokes
Fresh garlic, cut into slivers

Take a heavy, nonreactive boiling pot with a tight-fitting lid and add the water or stock. Now season the "pot liquor" with salt, pepper, cayenne, oil, and herbs.

Now trim the chokes. You do this by cutting off the stems flush with the bottoms and slicing off the thistle ends (about ¼ of the way down from the top). At this point, take time to stick garlic slivers between most of the leaves.

Now, with the pot liquor boiling, place the artichokes right side up into the water, cover the pot tightly with the lid, reduce the heat to simmer, and steam the chokes for 30-40 minutes, depending upon their size. They are done when the leaves pull away from the globes easily.

When they're done, drain them and cool them slightly. Pot-boiled artichokes can be eaten immediately or refrigerated and eaten later. I personally like to dip the leaves in a sauce of drawn butter and lemon juice (1 stick melted butter plus the juice of 1 lemon).

Chef's Note: Do not cook artichokes in aluminum or cast-iron cookware. These metals will discolor the chokes. Stainless steel is preferred.

Sicilian Stuffed Artichokes

This preparation is the ultimate favorite!

3 large artichokes	2 tsp. coarse-ground black
12 oz. grated Parmesan cheese	pepper
4 large garlic cloves, minced	½ cup extra-virgin olive oil
2 cups Italian breadcrumbs	Lemon juice

First, cut the stems and tops off the artichokes.

Now, in a large stainless-steel bowl, mix together the cheese, garlic, breadcrumbs, and pepper. Then place each artichoke down into the bowl of breading, spread the leaves with your thumbs, and stuff each layer of leaves—*from the inside out*—with the mixture.

At this point, place the artichokes right side up in a nonreactive pot with a lid that has about 2 in. water in the bottom. Then drizzle the oil and lemon juice equally over the tops of the chokes.

All that's left to do is to cover the pot, set the fire on simmer, and steam the artichokes for about 45 minutes or so, checking occasionally that the water has not completely evaporated. The chokes are done when the leaves can be pulled off easily.

Chef's Note: To make a richer bread stuffing, pour just enough olive oil into the breadcrumb mixture to give it a slightly moist, crumbly consistency.

Mary Clare's Baked Artichokes with Garlic and Sausage

If you'd like one of the easiest, no-hassle methods of fixin' artichokes (that you don't have to keep monitoring minute to minute), you'll like this one that my wife, Mary Clare, fixes for me as a special snackin' treat. I'm guessing this could be your favorite way to eat these bad boys!

4 medium to large artichokes
1 lemon
8 large cloves garlic, minced
¼ cup extra-virgin olive oil
½ cup grated Romano cheese
2 tsp. Frank Davis Vegetable
  Seasoning

½ lb. bulk Italian or N'Awlins hot
  sausage
½ cup chicken stock
½ cup dry white wine

First off, prep your artichokes. Then before you begin cooking, take a melon baller and scoop out the thistle-like center of each choke (along with the inedible purple-tinged leaves). Follow this procedure by thoroughly rubbing down the cut portions of the artichokes with the lemon to keep the chokes from turning black. Oh, yeah—and in the meantime, preheat the oven to 350 degrees.

Next, mix together the garlic and oil. Then meticulously fold in all of the Romano cheese and the vegetable seasoning. When the mixture is fully blended, spread the artichoke leaves apart and—*with a teaspoon*—put a little of the mixture in between the leaves of each artichoke (as well as in the scooped-out center). When the chokes are filled, roll a wad of sausage about the size of a golf ball between your palms until it is perfectly rounded. Then pack it tightly into the hollowed-out center of an artichoke (it is okay to overstuff the artichoke center slightly). Repeat for the other artichokes.

All that's left to do at this point is to put the artichokes into a baking dish, pour the stock and wine in the bottom, cover the dish securely with aluminum foil, and bake the artichokes for approximately 1 hour (or until the leaves can be pulled off easily).

These you can serve warm or at room temperature.

Chef's Note: Use only a good dry white wine when cooking artichokes. Artichokes have the tendency to make wine taste sweeter, so a naturally sweet wine would not be very compatible with the characteristics of the artichoke.

Frank's Snacking Artichokes

Poached artichokes dipped in their own special sauce might just be the perfect ultra-light meal for those hot and humid summer evenings in Southeast Louisiana, while still providing all the low-fat nutrition your body needs. Give 'em a try.

The Chokes:

4 large artichokes, trimmed at
   the stem
2 qt. bottled water

1 tbsp. salt
1 tsp. red pepper flakes

First, take a large stockpot (with a lid) capable of holding all 4 artichokes and bring the water to a rapid boil. Then while the water is at a full boil, stir in and completely dissolve the salt. Then whisk in the red pepper flakes.

At this point, place the artichokes down into the pot. Note that the water will stop boiling. But immediately when the boil returns, lower the fire, put the lid on the pot, and simmer the chokes slowly for about 1 hour (or until an ice pick easily pierces the leaves and heart through and through).

When the chokes are done, remove them from the pot and set them on a platter on the countertop so that they can cool to room temperature.

When the artichokes are cool enough to handle, pull apart the leaves and place them on a platter. Then scrape away the burr from the artichoke hearts, cut the hearts into bite-size chunks, and set them aside on a dish.

The Dippin' Sauce:

¾ cup extra-virgin olive oil
2 tbsp. balsamic vinegar
6-8 cloves roasted garlic,
   mashed to a paste
4 whole anchovies, mashed to a
   paste

⅓ cup grated Romano cheese
½ tsp. Frank Davis Sicilian
   Seasoning
½ tsp. fresh-cracked black pepper
¼ cup toasted breadcrumbs
   (optional)

While the artichokes are cooling, it's a perfect time to make the sauce you'll be dipping the leaves into. In a large stainless-steel bowl (or in a food processor or drink blender), beat together the oil, vinegar, garlic, anchovies, cheese, Sicilian seasoning, and pepper. In fact, it's probably more accurate to say "emulsify" the mixture to a creamy consistency.

Just before you serve a bowl of the dipping sauce to your family or friends, you can sprinkle the sauce lightly with the breadcrumbs if you wish, in order to give the dip a richer Italian flavor.

Chef's Note: This recipe is ideally served as an appetizer or snack. Simply take a stack of leaves—they can be hot or cold—and plunge them one at a time into the dipping sauce before placing them into your mouth. Then scrape away the artichoke pulp (and the sauce) from the leaves with your teeth.

N'Awlins Artichoke Appetizer Dip

This is lagniappe, y'all!

1 cup Blue Plate Mayonnaise	Dash Worcestershire sauce
1 cup grated Parmesan cheese	Garlic salt to taste

Very simply, mix all the ingredients together. Then chill briefly and serve as an all-around artichoke dip.

Frank's Snacking Edamame

The next time you feel the snacking urge coming on, before you reach for the beer nuts, pretzels, potato chips, nachos, cheese balls, popcorn, cakes, cookies, or ice cream, check the freezer to see if you have any edamame on hand. If you do, you got yourself a great snack. If you don't, head out to the Asian food store and pick up a frozen 1-lb. bag of these Japanese soybeans. Then you're gonna boil them and prepare their own special dipping sauce!

	2 tsp. kosher salt or 1 tsp. Frank
1 lb. frozen edamame	Davis Sprinkling Spice for
6 cups water	sprinkling (optional)
1 tsp. salt	

Preparation of these super-healthy and exceptionally tasty beans is probably amongst the easiest in the world. Very simply, you bring the water and 1 tsp. salt to a rapid boil in a large saucepan or wok. Then you drop in the entire contents of the package of beans—while they're still frozen.

The water will immediately stop boiling. But when boiling resumes, cover the pan and cook the edamame for exactly 6 minutes. At the end of the allotted time, immediately drain the beans and serve them (either hot or at room temperature).

If you care to, you can scatter a little kosher salt or sprinkling spice over the hot shells and toss them in the bowl a couple of times, thereby adding a little more seasoning to the dish. Most fans of edamame, however, also dip the shells in an Asian dipping sauce.

The Dippin' Sauce:

4 tbsp. soy sauce	3 slices pickled ginger
2-3 drops sesame oil	½ tsp. wasabi paste

All you do is put all of the sauce ingredients in a small bowl or ramekin and mix thoroughly. It's just that easy! Oh, and you can make a couple of batches of it, too, because it keeps well in the fridge for at least a couple of weeks.

Chef's Note: The rich, green, nutty-flavored beans pop out of the shells very easily. To eat them, you can either shell them first so that you can eat them with a fork or (and this is the most popular way) you can pop the entire hull into your mouth and use your teeth to split the shell seam and extract the beans.

Sicilian Frittatas

In Italy, frittatas (thick omelets) are traditionally served cold for lunch. Wives make them early in the morning and wrap them up, and the men take them with them and slice them into wedges for the midday meal. I'm gonna teach y'all how to cook these the authentic way!

4 tbsp. extra-virgin olive oil or
  sweet cream butter
1 small onion, minced
6 eggs
⅛ tsp. Frank Davis Sicilian
  Seasoning
Salt and coarse-ground black
  pepper to taste

6 tbsp. water
¼ cup freshly grated Parmesan
  cheese
1 small jar Sal & Judy's Marinara
  Sauce, warm

These are what are called your "baseline ingredients." Regardless of the kind of frittata you make, you will have to start with these ingredients. The primary "signature ingredients"—shrimp, crabmeat, calamari, sausage, pork, chicken, spinach, sundried tomatoes, mushrooms, pasta, more cheese, or whatever else you like—are added once the baseline is in place.

So let's say you wanted to make an Italian sausage frittata. All you'd need to add to the baseline is Italian sausage (of course, you could drop in any combination of things you like with the sausage). And this is how the recipe would come together.

In a 10- or 12-in. nonstick skillet, heat the oil or butter until it begins to sizzle. Then drop in—and sauté—the onions over medium-high heat until they just begin to caramelize (turn a light brown). Then when the onions are ready, put in your Italian sausage and cook it until it too begins to brown slightly.

Of course, while all this is happening, you should crack the eggs in a large mixing bowl, sprinkle on the Sicilian seasoning, salt, and pepper, pour in the water, and sprinkle on the Parmesan. Then whip the eggs to a froth! And when the Italian sausage is a beautiful golden brown, pour in the whipped eggs, lower the fire to medium, agitate the pan until the eggs settle evenly, and cook them for 4-6 minutes or until they begin to brown slightly around the perimeter.

When the bottom side of the frittata is done, place a dinner plate upside down in the skillet. Then flip the skillet and the frittata over into the plate, put the skillet back on the fire, slide the frittata off the plate back into the skillet, and cook the other side of the frittata for another 4 minutes or so. When it's ready, serve it hot or cold, sprinkled over the top with a little extra Parmesan and sloshed with a little warm marinara sauce.

Chef's Note:

1—How big a frittata can you make? One as big as you can flip over onto a plate without making a mess in the kitchen.

2—You can make spaghetti frittatas, sundried tomato frittatas, spinach frittatas, chorizo frittatas, salami frittatas, anchovy frittatas . . . in fact, I can't imagine a signature ingredient you could not fashion into a frittata. Salmon, shrimp, crabmeat, prosciutto, ham, garlic, eggplant, potato, green onion, whew!—the list goes on.

3—Never add milk to a scrambled-egg mix! Milk tends to toughen the egg. Instead, add 1 tbsp. bottled water for every egg you whip. The water expands the egg and makes it light. Just a little secret I thought you'd want to know.

Mid-City Banana and Peanut Butter Sandwich

If you were born in the Crescent City, if you grew up here, if you've always lived here, you've no doubt had all four of the famous New Orleans sandwiches on the following pages. If you haven't, then I'm sorry . . . but there's just no way you can honestly call yourself Naturally N'Awlins until you've savored each one of them! This traditional neighborhood sandwich from Mid-City can be done one of two ways: (1) you can fix the banana au naturel right out of the peel, or (2) you can slice and pan-fry the banana in margarine first. My version has the margarine, but either way, it's a great sandwich and reminiscent of your childhood.

1 tbsp. margarine
1 ripe banana, peeled and
   sliced lengthwise

2 slices Sunbeam, Merita, or
   Bunny bread
¼ cup creamy peanut butter

In a heavy skillet, heat the margarine until it sizzles. Then, place the banana slices into the pan and quickly fry them on both sides, flipping them gently with an egg turner so that they don't break apart in the middle (if you're good at it, you should be able to get 3 slices out of 1 medium banana).

While the bananas are frying, lay out the bread on the countertop and evenly and thinly spread the peanut butter on both slices (the peanut butter needs to be soft to do this; otherwise you'll rip the bread every time!). Then when the bananas are ready, take the egg turner, lift all the strips from the pan one at a time, place each on top of one slice of bread, and cover the bananas with the other slice of bread to form the sandwich.

All that's left is to press down on the sandwich with your hands, thereby wedging the bananas into the peanut butter and sealing the edges of the bread. And presto! An ol'-fashioned banana and peanut butter sandwich like we made as kids! Of course, I don't have to tell you that this calls for cold chocolate milk, right?

Variation: If you ever end up with a couple of bananas that are super overripe (you know, the black mushy ones!), peel them, place them on a dinner plate, smush them all up with a fork, and make yourself a sandwich by spreading the ripe banana on one slice of bread and peanut butter on another slice of bread and smashing the 2 slices together. This we always called a "Peanut Butter and Banana Quickie."

Momma's Tomato and Mynaze Sandwiches

I remember lots of days as a kid when twelve o'clock rolled around and we had no luncheon meat for sandwiches (and couldn't afford any either). But nobody was gonna go hungry! Momma called us inside, even let us invite our friends, and whipped up some of the tastiest Old New Orleans sandwiches I ever ate: tomato and mynaze.

4 slices Holsum, Merita, or
  Tip-Top bread
½ cup Blue Plate Mynaze
  (Mayonnaise)

1 large Creole tomato from the
  backyard garden
Salt and black pepper to taste

With the bread laid out on the countertop, slather the mynaze liberally on each slice. Then with a really sharp knife, cut the tomato into rounds about ¼ in. thick. When the slicing is done, place several rounds on 2 slices of bread (it's okay to overlap the rounds), sprinkle them liberally with salt and pepper, and top with the other 2 slices of bread, thereby creating 2 sandwiches (they're so good you gotta have 2!).

Chef's Note: We usta make a variation of this sandwich using green tomatoes that Momma would slice, dip in egg, coat with breadcrumbs, and pan-fry! But that's another recipe for another time.

Tuesday Red Bean Sandwich

Monday has always been red beans and rice day in N'Awlins. And usually there is just a little bit of the red beans left over in the refrigerator come Tuesday morning. Well, when I was growing up, that was the main ingredient of the sandwich you brought with you to school every Tuesday for lunch. Remember how it was made?

1 French bread heel	1 small bowl cold red beans
1 tbsp. margarine	

First take the heel of the French bread (some folks call it the toe) and dig out the soft bread inside the outer crust. Then, "butter" the inside of the heel. It is important that you distribute the margarine evenly.

When the "cone" is properly prepared, take the red beans—*cold and straight from the refrigerator*—and begin to pack them into the French bread cone with a tablespoon, forcing them in tightly as you stuff. Then when the bread is filled to capacity, smooth off the top and wrap the cone tightly and securely with plastic wrap or waxed paper.

On Tuesdays in New Orleans, lunchtime was like having "ice cream."

Chef's Note: I remember that a few guys who ate red bean sandwiches at school always had them hot. They musta known the cafeteria ladies or something. Mine was always traditional—cold and creamy. And every now and then Momma hid a piece of pickled meat down in the middle for me!

That Famous Fried Potato Po' Boy

It was the sandwich that fed New Orleans during the Great Depression. Martin Brothers Restaurant is said to have been the originator; but Herschtel's on St. Claude also made and served them by the thousands! They were a foot long and cost 15 cents. The story goes that workmen would buy one, have it cut in half, eat one half for their lunch, and bring the other half home to the wife for supper. Real restaurants that maintain New Orleans traditions still serve them today.

Vegetable oil for frying
2 medium white potatoes, thinly
   sliced into strips or rounds
12-in. loaf French bread

½ cup Blue Plate Mayonnaise
½ cup roast-beef gravy
Salt and black pepper to taste

First, take a frypan, fill it with enough oil to cover the potatoes when you drop them in, and bring it up to 350 degrees. Then drop in the potato strips (or rounds) and deep-fry them until they turn a golden brown.

In the meantime, while the potatoes are cooking, slice the French bread down the middle, separate the top from the bottom, and liberally slather both with mayonnaise.

Then, when the potatoes are done, remove them from the frypan, drain them on several thicknesses of paper towels, and arrange them on one half of the French bread. And you need to be generous, too—*don't skimp on the spuds.*

Then, right before the time when you're ready to put the lid on the sandwich, take a ladle and pour roast-beef gravy over the potatoes, sprinkle with salt and pepper, and serve up the treat piping hot.

Chef's Note: It's okay these days to dress the potato po' boy with lettuce and tomato if you want to; but the original was comprised of nothing but fried potatoes, mayonnaise, and gravy, something the old-timers referred to as a "wish sandwich." You ate the potatoes, but you wished you had some meat!

Superbowl Crabmeat Dip

This dip and the other "super dips" that follow should be set out for your family and friends come Superbowl Sunday. And with nothing more than a food processor, you can make them all with little or no effort. Oh, yeah—and they really don't have to be served just at Superbowl time . . . they're mouth-wateringly fantastic every day of the football season and all year long.

3 pkg. cream cheese, 8-oz. size
1 tsp. Frank Davis Hot Sauce
⅓ cup half-and-half, as needed
1 tsp. Minor's Lobster or
   Chicken Base
1 tsp. Frank Davis Seafood
   Seasoning
½ cup minced yellow onions
1 tsp. minced garlic

½ cup thinly sliced green onions
⅓ cup minced parsley
1 lb. fresh claw crabmeat, flaked
Salt and coarse-ground pepper
   to taste
Dash sweet paprika
1 large bag tortilla chips for
   dipping

Into the work bowl of your food processor, drop in the cream cheese (it works best if you allow the blocks first to come to room temperature and then break them into small chunks). Then add in the hot sauce, half-and-half, lobster base, and seafood seasoning and turn the machine on. Ideally, you want to "cream" the mixture to a silky-smooth consistency (but don't make it watery). About 1-2 minutes at full speed should do nicely.

Next, transfer the cream-cheese base to a large mixing bowl. Then with a rubber spatula fold in the onions, garlic, green onions, parsley, and crabmeat, mixing everything until fully and uniformly blended. At this point, taste the mixture and adjust the salt and pepper if necessary.

Finally, place the finished dip into a serving bowl, sprinkle the top lightly with paprika, cover tightly with plastic wrap, and stash in the refrigerator for at least 3 hours for the flavors to "marry" before serving. The dip is best if served chilled with crispy tortilla chips.

Chef's Note:

1—The lobster and chicken base, while ordinarily available only to restaurateurs, is sold to the public at a number of specialty food centers.

2—Only a food processor will produce the consistency necessary for the dip. A blender will not mix thoroughly enough.

3—The flavor of this dip is far more intense with claw crabmeat than any other kind.

4—For a little extra tartness, spoon about ⅓ cup sour cream into the finished dip.

Superbowl Shrimp Dip

4 tbsp. butter	½ cup minced yellow onions
2 lb. raw shrimp, peeled, deveined, and patted dry	1 tsp. minced garlic
	½ cup thinly sliced green onions
3 pkg. cream cheese, 8-oz. size	⅓ cup minced parsley
1 tsp. Frank Davis Hot Sauce	½ cup shrimp drippings
¼ cup half-and-half	Salt and coarse-ground pepper to taste
1 tsp. Minor's Lobster or Chicken Base	Dash sweet paprika
1 tsp. Frank Davis Seafood Seasoning	1 large bag tortilla chips for dipping

First, in a 12-in. nonstick skillet, heat the butter to sizzling over a high flame. Then a few at a time drop in the shrimp and sauté them until they turn pink all over—*but do not overcook them or they'll turn rubbery!* When they're done, remove them from the skillet, let them cool, and then chop them into small pieces.

Meanwhile, into the work bowl of your food processor, drop in the cream cheese (it works best if you first allow the blocks to come to room temperature and then break them into small chunks). Then add in the hot sauce, half-and-half, lobster base, and seafood seasoning and turn the machine on. Ideally, you want to "cream" the mixture to a silky-smooth consistency (but don't make it watery). About 1-2 minutes at full speed should do nicely.

Next, transfer the cream-cheese base to a large mixing bowl. Then with a rubber spatula fold in the onions, garlic, green onions, parsley, shrimp, and shrimp drippings. Then mix everything until fully and uniformly blended. At this point, taste the mixture and adjust the salt and pepper if necessary.

Finally, place the finished dip into a serving bowl, sprinkle the top lightly with paprika, cover tightly with plastic wrap, and stash in the refrigerator for at least 3 hours for the flavors to "marry" before serving. The dip is best if served chilled with crispy tortilla chips.

Chef's Note: The shrimp flavor in this recipe is far more intense with butter-sautéed shrimp as opposed to poached or boiled shrimp. Just take care to control the amount of pan drippings you add to the cream-cheese base—you don't want the mix runny. For other helpful tips, see the Chef's Note for Superbowl Crabmeat Dip above.

Superbowl Crawfish Dip

2 lb. crawfish tails, chopped
3 pkg. cream cheese, 8-oz. size
1 tsp. Frank Davis Hot Sauce
⅓ cup half-and-half
½ tsp. Minor's Lobster or
   Chicken Base
1 tsp. Frank Davis Seafood
   Seasoning
½ cup minced yellow onions

1 tsp. minced garlic
½ cup thinly sliced green onions
⅓ cup minced parsley
Salt and coarse-ground pepper
   to taste
Dash sweet paprika
1 large bag tortilla chips for
   dipping

First, place the crawfish in the food processor. Then, using the pulse device, continually start and stop the blades quickly to mince the tails (just be sure you don't overprocess, though—you do not want the crawfish pureed). When they're ready, remove them from the processor's work bowl and transfer them to a large mixing bowl.

In the meantime, put the work bowl back on your food processor (*do not clean away the crawfish fat from the walls of the bowl*). Then drop in the cream cheese (softened and broken into small chunks), add in the hot sauce, half-and-half, lobster base, and seafood seasoning, and turn the machine on. Ideally, you want to "cream" the mixture to a silky-smooth consistency (but don't make it watery). About 1-2 minutes at full speed should do nicely.

Next, transfer the cream-cheese base to a large mixing bowl. Then with a rubber spatula fold in the onions, garlic, green onions, parsley, and crawfish. Then mix everything until fully and uniformly blended. At this point, taste the mixture and adjust the salt and pepper if necessary.

Finally, place the finished dip into a serving bowl, sprinkle the top lightly with paprika, cover tightly with plastic wrap, and stash in the refrigerator for at least 3 hours for the flavors to "marry" before serving. The dip is best if served chilled with crispy tortilla chips.

Chef's Note: The crawfish flavor in this recipe becomes intense only after resting in the refrigerator for several hours. Try to give it time to develop. For other helpful tips, see the Chef's Note for Superbowl Crabmeat Dip above.

Superbowl Ham-N-Cheese Dip

3 8-oz. pkg. cream cheese
1 tsp. Frank Davis Hot Sauce
⅓ cup half-and-half
½ tsp. Minor's Chicken Base
1 tsp. Frank Davis Sprinkling
   Spice
½ cup minced yellow onions
½ tsp. minced garlic
½ cup thinly sliced green onions

⅓ cup minced parsley
¾ cup diced ham
¾ cup diced Colby or mild cheddar cheese
Salt and coarse-ground pepper
   to taste
Dash sweet paprika
1 large bag tortilla chips for
   dipping

First, place the work bowl and blades onto your food processor. Then drop in the cream cheese (broken into small chunks) and add in the hot sauce, half-and-half, chicken base, and sprinkling spice. Then turn the machine on. Ideally, you want to "cream" the mixture to a silky-smooth consistency (but don't make it watery). About 1-2 minutes at full speed should do nicely.

Next, transfer the cream-cheese base to a large mixing bowl. Then with a rubber spatula fold in the onions, garlic, green onions, parsley, ham, and cheese. Then mix everything until fully and uniformly blended. At this point, taste the mixture and adjust the salt and pepper if necessary.

Finally, place the finished dip into a serving bowl, sprinkle the top lightly with paprika, cover tightly with plastic wrap, and stash in the refrigerator for at least 3 hours for the flavors to "marry" before serving. The dip is best if served chilled with crispy tortilla chips.

Chef's Note: The ham and cheese flavor in this recipe becomes intense only after it rests in the refrigerator for several hours. Try to give it time to develop. For other helpful tips, see the Chef's Note for Superbowl Crabmeat Dip above (but don't try any sour cream in this one).

Superbowl Roasted Chicken Dip

3 8-oz. pkg. cream cheese
1 tsp. Frank Davis Hot Sauce
⅓ cup half-and-half
½ tsp. Minor's Chicken Base
1 tsp. Frank Davis Poultry
    Seasoning
½ cup minced yellow onions
1 tsp. minced garlic
½ cup thinly sliced green onions

⅓ cup minced parsley
2-3 cups minced roasted chicken
    (de-skinned)
Salt and coarse-ground pepper
    to taste
Dash sweet paprika
1 large bag tortilla chips for
    dipping

First, place the work bowl and blades on your food processor. Then drop in the cream cheese (broken into small chunks) and add in the hot sauce, half-and-half, chicken base, and poultry seasoning. Then turn the machine on. Ideally, you want to "cream" the mixture to a silky-smooth consistency (but don't make it watery). About 1-2 minutes at full speed should do nicely.

Next, transfer the cream-cheese base to a large mixing bowl. Then with a rubber spatula fold in the onions, garlic, green onions, parsley, and chicken. Then mix everything until fully and uniformly blended. At this point, taste the mixture and adjust the salt and pepper if necessary.

Finally, place the finished dip into a serving bowl, sprinkle the top lightly with paprika, cover tightly with plastic wrap, and stash in the refrigerator for at least 3 hours for the flavors to "marry" before serving. The dip is best if served chilled with crispy tortilla chips.

Chef's Note:

1—The chicken flavor in this recipe becomes intense only after it rests in the refrigerator for several hours. Try to give it time to develop.

2—For a little extra flavor, whip in some of the drippings from the roasting pan and top the dip with a sprinkling of bacon bits.

3—As a variation, the chicken can be processed along with the cream cheese to produce a creamy (instead of chunky) chicken dip.

Superbowl Spinach-N-Artichoke Dip

Fresh spinach
Chicken or vegetable stock for
  poaching
Marinated artichoke hearts
3 8-oz. pkg. cream cheese
1 tsp. Frank Davis Hot Sauce
⅓ cup half-and-half
½ tsp. Minor's Roasted Bell
  Pepper or Chicken Base
1 tsp. Frank Davis Vegetable
  Seasoning

½ cup minced yellow onions
½ tsp. minced garlic
½ cup thinly sliced green onions
⅓ cup minced parsley
Salt and coarse-ground pepper
  to taste
Dash sweet paprika
⅓ cup real bacon bits, crispy
1 large bag tortilla chips for
  dipping

First, cook down the spinach in a saucepan with just enough chicken or vegetable stock to create a scant amount of poaching liquid (but do not boil it!). You want to end up with 1 cup of poached spinach. About 4-5 minutes cooking time should do. Then while the spinach is on the stove, drain the artichoke hearts and mince them to make 1 cup. When everything is ready, set it aside until you prepare your cream-cheese base.

To do that, place the work bowl and blades on your food processor. Then drop in the cream cheese (broken into small chunks) and add in hot sauce, half-and-half, bell pepper or chicken base, and vegetable seasoning. Then turn the machine on. Ideally, you want to "cream" the mixture to a silky-smooth consistency (but don't make it watery). About 1-2 minutes at full speed should do nicely.

Next, transfer the cream-cheese base to a large mixing bowl. Then with a rubber spatula fold in the onions, garlic, green onions, parsley, spinach (squeezed dry and chopped to make 1 cup), and artichokes. Then mix everything until fully and uniformly blended. At this point, taste the mixture and adjust for salt and pepper if necessary.

Finally, place the finished dip into a serving bowl, sprinkle the top lightly with paprika and bacon bits, cover tightly with plastic wrap, and stash in the refrigerator for at least 3 hours for the flavors to "marry" before serving. The dip is best if served chilled with crispy tortilla chips.

Chef's Note: The spinach and artichoke flavor in this recipe won't really intensify until after the dip rests in the refrigerator for several hours. Try to give it time to develop. For other helpful tips, see the Chef's Note for Superbowl Crabmeat Dip above.

Frank's Mamacita-Approved Guacamole

If you grew up in New Orleans dearly loving alligator pears, you probably ate them right out of the peel with a splash of lemon juice, a little garlic hot sauce, and a sprinkle of salt and black pepper. Well, you can add this here recipe for real guacamole, which couldn't be any better if your name was Manuel Ortega Poncho Fernando Hernandez Carlos Jose Raoul Garcia Martinez!

⅓ cup freshly minced onions
3 green chili peppers, minced
1 small Creole tomato, seeded and minced
3 ripe alligator pears, chopped

1 tbsp. minced cilantro
2 tbsp. fresh lemon juice
1 tsp. salt
½ tsp. black pepper
Dash ground cumin

In a large bowl, mix together the onions, peppers, and tomatoes until thoroughly blended. Then, *using a fork,* slightly mash the alligator pears into a semi-chunky paste and fold it into the vegetable mixture.

At this point, *gently fold* in all the remaining ingredients until thoroughly blended . . . *but do not overstir and do not overcream the alligator pears.* Whatever you do, do not turn the mix into a soupy sauce (unless, of course, you plan to use it for a delicate salad dressing—see below)!

Finally, cover the mixture, put it into the refrigerator, and chill it about 4 hours before serving it with tortilla chips or nachos.

Chef's Note:
1—First of all, if you're not from here and you never had a New Orleans mawmaw, you probably know alligator pears by their other name . . . avocados.

2—With that out of the way, you need to know that this mix is good not only as a guacamole dip or as a topping for fajitas or tacos, it makes an excellent salad dressing (as previously mentioned) as well as a unique sauce for baked chicken or grilled shrimp.

CHAPTER 3

Soups, Stews, and Gumbos

Frank's Corn and Crabmeat Bisque

Fresh corn cut off the cobs, succulent white lump crabmeat, rich heavy cream, and the perfect blend of authentic New Orleans spices—when they all come together harmoniously, they make one of the tastiest bowls of corn and crabmeat bisque you ever savored!

6-8 ears fresh corn
3 qt. water or seafood stock
1¼ sticks butter
¼ cup all-purpose flour
1 cup minced onions
½ cup minced celery
½ cup minced green bell
   pepper
½ cup minced carrots
4 cloves garlic, minced
1 qt. heavy cream
2 tsp. salt or Frank Davis
   Seafood Seasoning

½ tsp. white pepper
¼ tsp. cayenne pepper
¼ tsp. black pepper
½ tsp. dried thyme
1 tsp. basil
½ tsp. dill
¼ cup minced flat-leaf parsley
1 lb. lump or claw crabmeat,
   picked through for shells
1-2 cans creamed corn
   (optional)
½ cup sliced green onions
Dash paprika for garnish

First, take the corn on the cob and a sharp paring knife and slice off all the kernels from each ear. Then, using a tablespoon, scrape each ear in a large bowl to extract the "corn milk" from the hulls in the cobs. When they've all been done, add the kernels and set the bowl aside.

Next you need to make your corn stock. You do this by dropping the scraped cobs into a large pot filled with the water or seafood stock. Then bring the liquid to a rapid boil, but immediately reduce it to simmer. Cover the pot, and let the stock develop for about 45 minutes to 1 hour. When the stock has finished steeping, remove the corn cobs and discard them. Then set the stock aside momentarily.

While all this is happening in the stockpot, take a heavy 5-qt. Dutch oven with a lid (I find that aluminum or porcelain-glazed cast iron works best), melt down the stick of butter over low heat, whisk in the flour, and make a light French roux (under no circumstances should you allow the roux to brown). After the raw taste has been cooked out of the flour (which should take about 6 minutes), drop into the mixture all the seasoning vegetables—the onions, celery, bell pepper, carrots, and garlic—and fold them in thoroughly.

At this point, it's time to begin building your bisque.

To the roux in the Dutch oven add the cream, stir in the corn kernels and corn milk, and begin pouring in the stock (you'll want your bisque not too thick but not too thin either—you don't have to use all the stock). Be sure to stir the mixture constantly as the stock is added so that the butter roux takes on a creamy, smooth, silky consistency. It's also time to sprinkle in the seasonings and spices—the salt, peppers, thyme, basil, and dill. Then cover the pot and begin simmering the bisque over a low to medium-low flame, stirring occasionally to ensure that the cream and roux aren't scorching on the bottom of the pot. Ideally, you want the bisque to cook for about 40 minutes.

Finally, about 10 minutes before you're ready to eat, gently fold in the parsley and crabmeat, taking care not to break the lumps apart too much. This is also the time to adjust the thickness of the bisque if it is not to your liking, and the easiest way to do that is to add creamed corn. (*By the way, creamed corn can also be substituted for the cream, to reduce the caloric or cholesterol value of the bisque.*) You should also adjust the seasonings at this time—you may need to add a little more to taste after the addition of the crabmeat.

Then when you're ready to serve, gently swish in the remaining butter and ladle out generous portions of the bisque in deep soup bowls, garnished with a sprinkling of green onions and a dash of paprika for color. Present a stack of buttered multigrain crackers alongside! This is an authentic touch of the Crescent City that very few can pass up!

Chef's Note:

1-You can use any kind of seafood stock as long as it is made from shellfish—shrimp, crabs, crawfish, lobster, etc. Do not use fish stock unless you're making fish bisque.

2—If you opt to use my seafood seasoning, you might want to leave out the cayenne and black pepper, along with the thyme and basil. Of course, this is purely a matter of taste, and you should taste a bisque as it cooks to give it a personal touch.

3—Be aware that combining a roux with heavy cream will give you a thickened base as it cooks, so you will need to thin it with stock to get the smoothness you want. Ideally, a good bisque has the final consistency of a rich melted ice cream or a somewhat-thinned pancake batter. Whatever you do, don't turn it into a "soup"!

Cajun Shrimp and Crabmeat Soup

This is not a bouillabaisse, not a gumbo, not a chowder, not a bisque, and not a stew—but a bowl of pure Creole goodness nonetheless. Think of it as a rich vegetable soup to which we've add two ingredients we all love so dearly—shrimp and crabmeat! I mean, how can you go wrong with a combination like that? By the way, this makes a perfect N'Awlins holiday appetizer!

1 large red bell pepper
1 large green bell pepper
2 carrots
1 small onion
4 cloves garlic
3 green onions
3 cups water
4 cans Swanson's chicken broth, 10¾-oz. size
12-oz. can Rotel diced tomatoes with chilies
1 cup chopped celery
½ tsp. basil

⅛ tsp. dried thyme
¼ tsp. turmeric
2 bay leaves
¼ tsp. red pepper flakes
1 tbsp. Frank Davis Seafood Seasoning
3 lb. fresh shrimp, peeled and deveined
2 lb. claw crabmeat
Sea salt and black pepper to taste
¼ cup chopped fresh parsley
1 lemon, cut into wedges

First prep all your ingredients—wash and cut the peppers, peel and dice the carrots and onions, mince the garlic, and thinly slice the green onions. Then bring to a rapid boil in a 6-qt. saucepan the water and broth. When the liquid is at a rolling boil, drop in the peppers, carrots, tomatoes, onions, garlic, green onions, celery, basil, thyme, turmeric, bay leaves, red pepper flakes, and seafood seasoning. Then reduce the heat and simmer the mixture *uncovered* for 30 minutes.

In the meantime, thoroughly rinse the shrimp under cool running water.

Then increase the heat under the saucepan to medium high and, when the soup base once again begins to boil, drop in the shrimp and cook them hard for exactly 2 minutes. At that point, reduce the fire to low, gently stir in the crabmeat, and allow the soup to simmer for about 10 minutes uncovered. Then just before you're ready to serve, add salt and pepper, if necessary.

All that's left is to ladle out the soup into heavy crockery bowls, garnish with a sprinkling of the parsley, and spritz on a few drops of lemon juice. I'd have just a bit of French bread on the side in case I'd want to do a little soppin'.

Chef's Note:

1—Yes, use the liquid in the Rotel can! Do not discard it! It becomes part of the soup!

2—If you can't find fresh or frozen crabmeat where you shop, it's okay to substitute 3 cans king crabmeat (drained, with the cartilage removed). Just do not substitute surimi (artificial crabmeat).

3—This soup can be made days in advance and reheated when you're ready to serve it.

Amanda's Holiday Seafood Chowder

For practically every holiday that comes along you can bet that some-one either in the family or at the office is going to request that my daughter, Amanda Clare Landry, concoct her traditional Holiday Seafood Chowder. It has got to be one of the easiest recipes you ever fixed, but it is also one of the tastiest recipes you ever ate. But be fore-warned—you could very well decide that you don't want to serve her chowder just for holidays, 'cuz it might turn out to be something you whip up a couple of times a week!

2 cups minced onions	1½ cans evaporated milk
2 cups coarsely chopped mush-rooms	1½ cans low-fat milk
4 cloves garlic, minced	1 lb. mild Mexican Velveeta Cheese, cubed
1 stick butter or margarine	2 pkg. frozen chopped broc-coli, cooked and drained
1 can Campbell's Cream of Mushroom Soup	1 lb. crawfish tails with fat
1 can Campbell's Cream of Chicken Soup	2 tsp. Frank Davis Seafood Seasoning or Sprinkling Spice
1 can Campbell's Cream of Celery Soup	½ cup minced flat-leaf parsley for garnish

First, in a heavy aluminum 4-qt. Dutch oven, sauté the onions, mushrooms, and garlic in the butter until the mixture wilts and turns clear. It is important that you stir the pot almost continuously to cook the moisture out of the mushrooms and to keep the garlic from scorching.

When the seasoning veggies are ready, immediately stir in all the soups and milks. All you do is stir, stir, and stir some more until the chowder base is heated all the way through and barely begins to bubble.

Now at this point, drop in the cheese and slowly stir it, too, until the cubes completely melt. Then drop in the broccoli, along with the crawfish tails and fat. And again—yep—you got it! Stir everything until the chowder is thoroughly heated—actually, hot and bubbly this time!

Then, just minutes before you're ready to eat, give the dish its final seasoning—sprinkle on either the seafood seasoning or sprinkling spice. All that's left is to ladle out the chowder into preheated deep soup bowls, garnish with parsley, and serve either with garlic rounds or hot French bread.

Warning! You'll probably find yourself making this every time it turns cold!

Chef's Note:
1—Like red beans, jambalaya, étouffée, and a number of other dishes, this recipe is always better the next day. The only problem with that philosophy is that there's rarely any left over to be eaten the next day!

2—This chowder is probably a prime example of what constitutes a true convenience dish. Essentially, most ingredients in this recipe are "ready to eat" as is, which means there is relatively little actual cooking to do—most of it involves simply "combining and heating."

3—Just because the recipe is easy to do doesn't mean it can't be creative! Be open to making substitutions to create additional tastes. For example, substitute crabmeat for crawfish tails; or put in both crabmeat and crawfish tails; or leave out the crabmeat and the crawfish tails and use chopped shrimp instead; or use chopped chicken or grilled sausage or just plain veggies with no meat! You decide, because whatever you come up with will be unbelievably good!

4—Oh, yeah—you can make the recipe "Cajun spicy" just by spiking the dish about halfway through the cooking process either with cayenne pepper or red pepper flakes.

5—If you prefer to use fresh broccoli (which is my choice), just cut the florets from the main broccoli stalk and drop them into boiling water for about 2 minutes (don't overcook them!). Then when they come out, chop them into small pieces and add them to the chowder as I've indicated. This is the method to use if you'd like to serve additional broccoli as a side dish to the chowder.

6—For a different variation, instead of using butter or margarine to sauté the onions and mushrooms, substitute about 12 oz. lean bacon, cut into small pieces before cooking. Sauté the onions and mushrooms in both the drippings and the bacon pieces to intensify the flavor of the chowder.

Frank's Cream of Redfish Soup

A nice light butter roux, the perfect blend of seasoning vegetables, spicy Rotel tomatoes folded into cream-style corn, tender diced potatoes, slivers of sautéed mushrooms, meticulously trimmed redfish fillets, and a base of half-and-half—that's what all goes into my Cream of Redfish Soup! And you ain't never tasted anything this good in your life.

1 stick + 3 tbsp. butter
½ cup all-purpose flour
2 cups minced onions
1 cup minced celery
¾ cup minced green bell pepper
6 cloves garlic, minced
1 cup thinly sliced mushrooms
4 red potatoes, peeled and
    diced
3 pt. half-and-half
1 can Campbell's Cream of
    Shrimp Soup (10¾ oz.)
10-oz. can Rotel tomatoes
    (undrained)

1 can creamed corn (15 oz.)
2-3 lb. trimmed redfish fillets
1 bay leaf
1½ tsp.-1 tbsp. Frank Davis
    Seafood Seasoning
½-1 tsp. salt (optional)
4 tomatoes, seeded and diced
    for garnish
¾ cup thinly sliced green onions
    for garnish
½ cup minced parsley for garnish
Stack of multigrain wheat
    saltines

First, take a large soup pot or 5-qt. nonstick Dutch oven, drop in the stick of butter, and heat it over a medium flame until it fully melts (but don't let it burn). Then, a little at a time, with a wooden spoon, begin whisking in the flour until it becomes velvety smooth. This is going to take a little while, so don't go to rushing it! The trick is . . . *you don't want the flour to brown at all! You want to make nothing but a white butter roux.*

When the roux smoothes (which should happen in about 5 minutes), drop in the onions, celery, bell pepper, garlic, mushrooms, and potatoes. The introduction of the vegetables into the pot does two things—(1) it softens the vegetables in the hot roux, and (2) it reduces the temperature of the roux so that it cannot brown.

Immediately after the vegetables and roux are thoroughly combined, it's time to begin adding the ingredients that will make this dish a soup—the half-and-half, cream of shrimp, Rotel tomatoes, and creamed corn. Just pour these into the mix and begin stirring everything into the roux. At this point, it's also time to begin dropping in the fish fillets a few at a time so that they can incorporate into the cream base and release their liquids into the soup. Finally, flip in the bay leaf, reduce the fire to low, and simmer the dish until all the individual flavors marry (which should take 45-50 minutes).

Now note a couple of things here: (1) plan to stir the mixture every 10 minutes or so to keep the cream base from sticking to the bottom of the pot and scorching, and (2) don't worry about breaking up the redfish—you're supposed to break it up into "flakes."

During the last 10 minutes of cooking time, taste the soup and add the seafood seasoning and salt if needed—the other ingredients may contain enough salt and pepper to suit your taste. You can start off by adding a small amount of seasoning, then increase it as necessary. It's always easy to add a little more; it's very difficult to take any of it out! Remember, the dish should be spicy, but it should never burn your lips and tongue.

When you're ready to eat, drop in the remaining 3 tbsp. butter and very gently fold it into the soup to give it a sheen. Then ladle out the finished product into soup bowls and garnish with a sprinkling of the diced tomatoes, sliced green onions, and minced parsley. All that's left to finish off the presentation is a stack of buttered multi-grain saltine crackers.

Chef's Note:

1—If you wish to avoid using white flour, simply substitute whole-wheat flour for the all-purpose flour.

2—Be careful not to cook the soup "hard" once the half-and-half is added. Hard-boiling will cause the milk and the cream to separate, thereby curdling the cream base. My best advice is to barely simmer the soup from that point on. And it's okay for you to use a little more or a little less half-and-half in the soup, depending upon the taste and thickness you desire.

3—Be sure all the bloodline is trimmed off of the redfish fillets. Trimmed, the fish will give the soup a very delicate flavor; untrimmed, or carelessly trimmed, it will impart a "fishy" taste once it begins cooking.

4—If you can't find my seasonings where you shop, you can order them by going to my Web site—the address is www.frankdavis.com.

Frank's Back-a-Town Chicken Soup

Since I can only come close to being Jewish when I beg my agent's mother to temporarily adopt me during the High Holidays, this might not be authentic "Jewish penicillin." But when the rabbi at one particular temple on West Esplanade Avenue tasted my chicken soup, he commented, "Mmm—not bad for a gentile!" You wanna try it already?

1 medium chicken, split in half
10 cups bottled water
2 ribs celery with leaves
1 onion, quartered
3 cloves garlic, minced
5 whole black peppercorns
6 sprigs parsley
2 bay leaves
2 tsp. Frank Davis Poultry
   Seasoning
2 tsp. kosher or sea salt
1 tsp. coarse-ground black
   pepper

1 cup broken vermicelli,
   uncooked
2 whole eggs, beaten
Juice of 1 lemon
1 cup chopped parsley for
   garnish
1 cup sliced green onions for
   garnish
1 carrot, shredded
Multigrain saltine crackers,
   buttered

Start off by putting the chicken into a stockpot or other large heavy pot with a lid and covering the chicken with the water (*tap water can be used, but you won't get the smooth mellow flavor you do from bottled water*). Now cut the celery into pieces, add it to the pot along with the onion, garlic, peppercorns, parsley, and bay leaves, and bring the pot to a gentle boil. *Note: you don't want the stock to boil rapidly or the soup will turn out murky and cloudy.*

At this point, reduce the heat to low and skim away the foam that has accumulated on the top of the stock. Then cover the pot halfway and simmer the stock for about 90 minutes. When the cooking time is done, remove the lid from the pot and cool the stock slightly.

Next, remove the chicken from the pot and set it aside momentarily. Then using a fine-mesh sieve, carefully strain the stock, discard the seasoning debris, and immediately return the clear stock to the stockpot. *For a lean version of the soup, take a ladle and skim as much chicken fat as possible from the surface of the stock.* Then while the stock is still warm, go ahead and stir in the poultry seasoning, salt, and pepper. Adjust to your taste if desired.

In the meantime, remove the chicken meat from the bones and chop it up into bite-size pieces. Then add as much of the chopped meat to the stock as you wish (depending upon how rich you want the soup to be). Any remaining chicken can be set aside in your refrigerator for other uses (like, maybe, a big bowl of New Orleans chicken salad, for example—mmm!).

Anyway, return the fire to low and then stir in the vermicelli—you want to allow it to simmer in the stock for approximately 15 minutes to become al dente.

Now here's the secret to really good chicken soup. Beat the eggs with the lemon juice. Then temper the eggs (by adding small amounts of the hot stock to the beaten eggs a little at a time to bring up the temperature of the eggs without curdling them). Then rapidly pour the egg mixture into the stockpot with the soup and whisk it in well.

When you're ready to eat, ladle the soup out into deep bowls and garnish with a generous sprinkling of chopped parsley, sliced green onions, and shredded carrot. A stack of buttered multigrain crackers and glasses of chilled white wine will top off the presentation!

Chef's Note:

1—To produce a totally fat-free version of this chicken soup, allow the stock to come to room temperature. Then cover the pot and place it in the refrigerator overnight. The next day the fat will have congealed into a "cake" on the surface of the soup. Simply lift it up and toss it out, leaving you with "defatted" chicken stock.

2—You can substitute other types of pasta for the vermicelli if you choose, but vermicelli is traditionally used in chicken soup.

Frank's Creole Sour-Cream Potato Soup

Some folks think that soup is one of those "throw-'em-together" dishes, where you take a whole bunch of ingredients left over in the 'frigerator and throw 'em together in a pot. Well, that might be soup for some, but if you want a great soup—especially potato soup—it requires specific methodology that's anything but haphazard! Like this home-style potato soup, for example—it's truly gourmet!

1 cup minced hickory-smoked
   bacon
1 cup minced Canadian bacon
1 medium white onion, minced
3 cloves garlic, minced
5 lb. medium-size red potatoes,
   peeled and diced
8 cans chicken broth
½ cup heavy cream
½ cup sour cream
½ cup thinly sliced green onions
2 tsp. Frank Davis Vegetable
   Seasoning

1 tsp. white pepper
1 lb. "B" creamer potatoes,
   boiled and peeled
2 cups whole milk
¼ stick butter
¼ cup minced flat-leaf parsley
2 cups Durkee's French-Fried
   Onions
1 cup shredded cheddar
   cheese
1 loaf hot buttered French
   bread

First, take a heavy, porcelain-coated cast-iron or Teflon-coated aluminum 5-qt. Dutch oven and place it on the stove over medium-high heat. Then drop in the bacon and Canadian bacon and cook them together—*stirring constantly*—until the bacon begins to brown. When it does, add to the pot the onions, garlic, and red potatoes and cook the mixture over medium heat for about 10 minutes. You want the potato chunks to begin softening, and the pre-frying also tends to sweeten them and make them richer.

At this point, pour in the chicken broth and slowly cook the potatoes, still over medium heat, until they fully soften and begin to fall apart. Remember, you're not "boiling" them—essentially you're only poaching them, and just until they "cream" in the stock. If you cook them at a hard boil they'll turn grainy and won't give you a smooth consistency for a soup. By the way, you may want to skim off some of the starch bubbles that float to the top as the potatoes cook.

When all the potato pieces have practically liquefied, take a hand-held mixer and run it around inside the pot to fully puree them and thicken the stock. Don't worry about chopping up the bacon—it's just there for flavor anyway. Now whisk into the soup (with a wire whip) the cream and sour cream, making sure to fully incorporate them into the starch. This is also the time you want to drop in the green onions, vegetable seasoning, and pepper and stir them into the mixture as well. Then reduce the fire to low and simmer the soup for about 30 minutes, stirring frequently to ensure that the potatoes don't stick to the bottom and scorch.

While the soup is simmering, cut the creamer potatoes into small dice and set them aside. Then after the allotted cooking time, test the soup for thickness. If it is too thick for your liking, simply thin it out with a little milk. If it's too thin, simply cook it slowly—*uncovered*— until the appropriate amount of liquid evaporates. When you're happy with the texture, stir in the potatoes, butter, and parsley, allow the ingredients to simmer in the stock for another 5 minutes or so, and then ladle it out into oversize soup bowls.

I've found that the best way to serve it to savor optimum flavor is to top every bowl with a sprinkling of fried onions and a handful of cheddar cheese. Of course, you jus' gotta have a big piece of buttered French bread on the side for dipping and sopping!

Chef's Note:

1—For a creamy-smooth potato soup, be sure to use only fresh, hard red potatoes. White potatoes are too grainy.

2—Good, rich, homemade chicken stock makes the best base for potato soup. But if you decide to go with the canned broth, before you add any extra salt, taste the soup! You may find that there is already enough in the canned broth to your liking (to say nothing of how much sodium might be in the bacon).

3—The creamer potatoes you add when the soup base is done should be left in diced form to give the soup definition and character. They also add a variance of texture to the finished dish.

Frank's Naturally N'Awlins Baked Potato Soup

No doubt you've many a time savored a big bowl of hot potato soup. But on a really cold night in January, have you ever spoon-sipped from a piping-hot bowl of "baked" potato soup? With all the fixin's? Well, that's what this recipe is all about. Take your time and follow the directions to the letter and you'll end up with a very simple concoction that can only be described as "comfort food that's truly gourmet"!

8 medium baking potatoes
½ stick butter
4 heaping tbsp. all-purpose
  flour
1 medium yellow onion, minced
6 cloves garlic, minced
3 qt. whole milk + 1 qt. whole
  milk or half-and-half
2 tsp. Frank Davis Vegetable
  Seasoning
2 tsp. salt
1 tsp. white pepper
⅔ cup thinly sliced green onions

⅓ cup minced flat-leaf parsley
¾ cup instant mashed potatoes
¾ cup sour cream
1 cup shredded cheddar
  cheese
1 cup minced cooked hickory-
  smoked bacon
1 cup minced ham (optional)
Parsley or green onions for
  garnish (optional)
Dash paprika for color (optional)
Multigrain crackers

First, take the potatoes, scrub them under cold running water with a vegetable brush, pat them dry with paper towels, and wrap them individually with aluminum foil. Then place them into a preheated 400-degree oven on the center rack and bake them for about 1 hour or so, or until a toothpick easily pierces a potato. When they're cooked, remove them from the oven and allow them to cool to room temperature for at least 2 hours (actually, potatoes that are allowed to sit in the refrigerator overnight provide the best texture for baked potato soup).

In the meantime, take a heavy, porcelain-coated cast-iron or Teflon-coated aluminum 8-qt. Dutch oven or oval roaster and place it on the stove over medium heat. Now drop in the butter, and when it fully melts and begins to sizzle, begin whisking in the flour—*technically, you want to make a true French roux, which is nothing more than flour and butter combined over low heat so that the flour cooks but does not brown.*

After about 5 minutes or so, drop in the onions and garlic. Then begin stirring in the initial 3 qt. milk a little at a time, dissolving the

French roux and converting it into a smooth milk-base gravy. Now lower the flame and simmer the contents of the pot while you get the potatoes peeled and shredded.

To do this, take a sharp paring knife and gently "scrape the peel" off the baked potatoes (don't try to peel them as you would peel an apple—you remove too much potato this way and you eliminate the top layer of starch, which you need in the soup). When all the potatoes are ready, run them through a cheese grater or shredder one by one to transform them into what is commonly referred to as "shoe-string cut." Then add the potatoes to the pot, pour in the remaining milk or half-and-half, and stir everything together completely. Now once again cook the mixture over medium heat, this time for about 10 minutes—*but be really careful that the milk doesn't stick to the bottom of the pot and scorch!* The end objective is to cause the baked potato chunks to soften further (which tends to sweeten them and make them richer).

At this point, it's time to season the soup. Whisk in the vegetable seasoning, salt, and pepper. I recommend "overstirring" as the seasonings are added, to ensure that they blend in uniformly. This is also the time when you want to drop in the green onions and parsley. Then once more, reduce the fire to low and simmer the soup for about 20 minutes this time, again stirring occasionally to ensure that the potatoes and the creamy stock do not stick to the bottom and scorch.

Then after the allotted cooking time, test the soup for thickness. If it is too thick for your liking, simply thin it out with a little water, chicken stock, or milk. If it's too thin, sprinkle in as much of the instant potato flakes as are necessary to adjust the consistency to your taste. The best approach here is to spoon in the flakes a couple of tablespoons at a time and stir them in completely, thickening the base a little at a time as you go.

Finally, when you're happy with the texture, ladle out the piping-hot, creamy mixture into oversize soup bowls and top them with everything you'd put on a baked potato—a dollop of sour cream, a sprinkling of ham or bacon or both, a pile of cheddar, maybe a little extra parsley or green onions, and even a dash of paprika. All that's left then is to bring out a stack of crispy multigrain crackers and pig out—especially if it's cold out!

But then, again, it doesn't have to be!

Chef's Note:
1—For a creamy-smooth potato soup, be sure to use only fresh, hard

russet potatoes that have been baked to perfection then chilled in the refrigerator for at least 2 hours (this keeps them from crumbling).

2—Good, rich, homemade chicken stock can also be added to the soup base in place of some of the milk. In fact, for a richer, more intense flavor, you can make the French roux with the bacon drippings instead of the butter and cook the bacon and ham right along with the milk base instead of adding them at the end of the preparation. Of course, if you decide to use canned broth, be sure to taste the blend for salt before you add any extra salt. You may find that there is already enough in the canned broth (to say nothing of how much sodium might be in the bacon).

3—Be sure to watch the pot as the soup simmers—you don't want the potato pieces to disintegrate. And overcooking will certainly do that, thereby ruining the texture of the dish.

Frank's Pasta, Shrimp, and Potato Soup

Take a rich, full-flavored broth, spice it up with chilies and tomatoes, float in a pound of mushrooms, some ditalini pasta, tender diced potatoes, and more shrimp than you'd ever need to make the dish, and you end up with a pot of soup that's nothing short of Naturally N'Awlins!

4 tbsp. butter or bacon
   drippings
2 tbsp. extra-virgin olive oil
2 cups vegetable mirepoix
2 cups sliced mushrooms
1 cup halved baby carrots
1 large onion, coarsely chopped
⅓ cup coarsely diced celery
8 cloves garlic, minced
½ cup dry white wine
12-oz. can Rotel diced tomatoes
   with chilies
6 Roma tomatoes, peeled,
   seeded, and chopped
⅓ cup minced parsley
2 cups diced cooked red
   potatoes

2 cups cooked ditalini pasta
2 cups drained black beans
1 bunch green onion tops, thinly
   sliced
8-10 cups canned chicken
   broth
⅓ cup julienned basil
¼ cup fresh oregano
½ cup sliced fresh chives
2 bay leaves
¼ tsp. red pepper flakes
1 tbsp. Frank Davis Seafood
   Seasoning
5 lb. fresh Louisiana shrimp
¼ cup chopped parsley for
   garnish

Start by combining the butter (or bacon drippings) and oil in a 10-qt. stockpot over medium-high heat. Then drop in the seasoning vegetable mixture, mushrooms, carrots, onion, celery, and garlic. At this point, stir, stir, and stir some more! Ideally you want to sauté all of the vegetables until they clear and soften nicely. Cook them easy and try to keep them from browning too much, especially the garlic.

Now add to the pot the wine, Rotel tomatoes, and Roma tomatoes and stir everything together once again. Then add the parsley, potatoes, pasta, beans, green onions, and chicken broth. Stir again!

It is imperative at this stage of the game that you now bring the pot of soup to a rolling boil. But once it boils, *immediately* reduce the fire to medium low and stir in the basil, oregano, chives, bay leaves, pepper flakes, and seafood seasoning. Then lower the flame even more and simmer the soup uncovered for about 20 minutes to fully reheat the pasta and potatoes and marry all the flavors.

While all this is going on, peel and devein the shrimp and rinse them thoroughly under cool running water.

Then increase the heat under the pot to medium high, and when the soup once again begins to boil, drop in the shrimp, stir them in well, and cook them hard for exactly 2 minutes—*but no more!* At that point, reduce the fire to low once again and allow the soup to simmer for a final 10 minutes—*uncovered*—until piping hot. Then just before you're ready to serve, adjust the seasoning to your taste, if necessary.

All that's left is to ladle out the soup into heavy crockery bowls and garnish with a sprinkling of parsley. I like to have just a little hot French bread on the side to do a little soppin'.

Chef's Note:

1—A mirepoix *is a proportionate mix of onions, celery, green bell pepper, carrot, parsley, garlic, and green onions diced to a rather fine consistency. You can make your own at home or buy it precut in the produce section of most major supermarkets. It will keep in your refrigerator for at least 7 days and will eliminate a lot of "prep" work.*

2—Yes, use the liquid in the Rotel can! Do not discard it! It becomes part of your soup!

3—If you can't find Frank Davis Seafood Seasoning where you shop, you can order it from my Web site: www.frankdavis.com.

4—This soup can be made days in advance and reheated when you're ready to serve it. It also freezes well.

5—This soup is not very thick. Its consistency is more along the lines of a flavored broth or bouillabaisse. To attain a thicker consistency, use uncooked diced potatoes and ditalini pasta and cook them in the soup until the potatoes and pasta are tender (about 25 minutes). The natural starches in the potatoes and pasta will give the soup further body. Just remember to increase the final seasonings to make up for the change.

Frank's Classic N'Awlins Neighborhood Corn Stew (with Shrimp)

Served over steamed rice, this is one of those recipes that hardcore gourmets will rave about for a long, long time. Over the years it has been prepared numerous ways in the faubourgs of the Crescent City. But only by using fresh ingredients do you capture the succulence that originally came to us a long time ago from a shrimp boat down on the bayou! Of course, you don't need to be a shrimper to make this stew for your family.

2 tbsp. Canola or vegetable oil
6 strips bacon, coarsely chopped
6 ears fresh white or yellow corn
1 stick butter or margarine
1 large white onion, minced or grated
2 ribs celery, minced
⅓ cup diced green bell pepper
2 cloves garlic, minced
2 tbsp. all-purpose flour
6-oz. can tomato paste
1 small can tomato sauce
12-oz. can Rotel diced tomatoes with chilies

2 bay leaves
1 qt. vegetable or homemade shrimp stock
1 tbsp. Frank Davis Seafood Seasoning
Salt and cayenne pepper to taste
2 lb. medium shrimp, peeled, deveined, and chopped
6 cups cooked buttered rice
1 bunch green onions, thinly sliced
1 bunch parsley, minced

First thing you do is take a 5-qt. Dutch oven or oval roaster that has a tight-fitting lid, heat it over a medium flame, pour in the oil, drop in the bacon, and gently fry down the bacon until it becomes semi-crisp.

While that is happening, take a really sharp knife, cut the kernels .

of corn off the cobs, and soak them briefly in cold water to plump them up (this should take 10 minutes or so). Then, when the bacon is rendered out, drain the kernels really well, drop them into the roaster, increase the heat to high, and stir-fry them until they just begin to toast on the edges.

At that point, take a slotted spoon, quickly remove the corn and bacon from the pot, place them into a large bowl, and allow them to cool for a while.

After the corn is out of the pot, drop in the butter, heat it to a sizzle, and sauté the onion, celery, bell pepper, garlic, and flour until the veggies soften slightly. When that happens, stir in the tomato paste and fry down the entire mixture until the paste starts to darken. Then add in the tomato sauce, Rotel tomatoes (with their liquid), bay leaves, and vegetable stock (or shrimp stock) and stir everything together until you get a nice, smooth consistency. It's at this stage that you now season the pot either with seafood seasoning or salt and cayenne pepper, depending upon your preference. Then immediately reduce the fire to medium high and bring the gravy to a gentle boil (stir continually at this point to keep the gravy from sticking to the bottom of the pot and burning).

It's now time to put the corn kernels and bacon back into the pot, mix them into the stew completely, and cover the pot. Then immediately reduce the heat to low and let the corn simmer for about 1½ hours or until the corn kernels puff. *Oh—peek inside the pot only if you absolutely must!*

Finally, just about 20 minutes before you're ready to eat, drop in the shrimp, which should be chopped into small segments if you had to settle for extra-large shrimp (like an 11-15 or 16-20 count). Then after stirring one more time to equally distribute all the ingredients in the stew, let the pot simmer once more for about 10 minutes until the shrimp turn a solid pink and slowly release all of their essence into the stew—*do not, however, overcook them or they will become tough and rubbery.*

To serve, I suggest that you put a little more than ½ cup rice into the center of a warm plate and ladle a generous amount of corn stew over the top. All that's left before you dive in is to garnish each dish with the green onions and parsley. Enjoy this stew while it's piping hot. I'd serve freshly baked, hot, crusty rolls on the side for dippin'.

Chef's Note:
1—If you can't find good fresh corn on the cob at your supermarket, it's perfectly okay to buy a couple of bags of fresh-frozen corn

and use them instead. *Just try to avoid doing this dish with canned corn—you lose the crispness in the can.*

2—*For a really intense corn flavor, after cutting the kernels from the cob, take the back of the knife and scrape it down the length of the cob to extract the "corn milk." Fold that into the pot when the kernels are added.*

3—*You can make your own shrimp stock by gently boiling the washed shrimp heads and shells in about 1 gal. bottled water for about ¹/₂ hour. Then strain the stock.*

4—*Maquechoux is an altogether different recipe from corn stew. Corn stew is believed to be a Cajun/Creole dish, born on the bayou and introduced to the city. Maquechoux is an American Indian dish, using maize, tomatoes, and cream.*

Momma's Original Corn Stew
(With Rose Rice and Grilled Sausage)

When I was growing up in Mid-City, we had Momma's Corn Stew at least once a week. In fact, everybody in my old neighborhood had corn stew at least once a week! It was what the folks called "fillin' food." Mixed with a pile of rice, it filled you up—*fast and cheap!* Of course, it always had great flavor, and it still does today. So have you planned anything yet for supper *tonight?*

½ gal. water	2 bay leaves
2 lb. smoked sausage	1 tsp. basil
8 oz. thick-sliced bacon	2 tsp. Frank Davis Vegetable
3 tbsp. bacon drippings	Seasoning
1 cup vegetable mirepoix	1 tbsp. all-purpose flour
½ lb. portabello mushrooms,	if needed
diced	1 cup vegetable or chicken
10 ears yellow corn, shucked	stock as needed
and washed	Salt and black pepper to taste
2 cans Rotel diced tomatoes	6 cups cooked rose-flavored or
with chilies, 12-oz. size	brown rice

The first thing you want to do is bring the water to a rapid boil in a heavy aluminum oval roaster on top of the stove. Then set a link of sausage on the countertop, place a pair of cooking chopsticks directly alongside the link (you'll use it as a block to keep from cutting all the way through), and begin making partial slices along the entire length of the sausage about every $1/8$ in. or so. Repeat the same procedure with all the links.

Then when they've all been partially sliced, gently place them into the boiling water, reduce the fire to medium low, and poach them for about 15 minutes—*this gets rid of a great deal of internal fat in the links and gets them ready for the grill.*

In the meantime, in a 5-qt. Dutch oven that has a lid, fry the bacon over medium heat until the fat renders out. Remove all but 3 tbsp. bacon drippings. Then drop in the vegetable mirepoix and mushrooms and smother them in the bacon drippings until the mixture wilts, softens, and begins to brown slightly. While the veggies are cooking, take a sharp knife and slice the kernels off the ears of corn (also be sure to scrape away the "corn milk" from the cobs with the back of the knife). Then add the corn and "milk" to the Dutch oven, stir in the Rotel tomatoes, drop in the bay leaves and basil, and season with the vegetable seasoning.

At this stage of the recipe, with the fire on medium high, continue to stir the mixture around and around in the pot, sprinkling in the flour as you go, to thicken as needed. When all the ingredients are thoroughly mixed, lower the flame, cover the pot, and simmer the stew for about 40 minutes (stirring occasionally) until the kernels turn tender and a creamy base forms. If for one reason or another you find that you need a little extra liquid, pour in scant amounts of chicken stock until the consistency reaches the thickness you desire. Be careful not to add too much, however; *you don't want corn soup!* This is also the time to adjust the salt and pepper content to your taste.

Finally, about 10 minutes before you're ready to eat, place the sausage links on a hot grill. Gently roll them back and forth, searing the sliced edges really well (but without scorching them). Then when they're sizzling from one end to another, serve them piping hot alongside a plate of steamed rice covered with a couple of hearty ladlefuls of spicy corn stew.

It's just like the good old days in the 'hood!

Chef's Note:
1—I've used regular New Orleans smoked sausage in this recipe.

But the dish will turn out equally as tasty if you substitute Polish kielbasa, Creole hot sausage, or even Italian sausage or green onion sausage in its place.

2—If you decide that you want to make your corn stew meatless, instead of using bacon drippings to sauté the mirepoix, use butter or margarine. You will also want to use vegetable instead of chicken stock.

3—If you are avoiding eating corn, 3 lb. fresh green beans cut into segments make a nice alternative. The rest of the recipe is the same, except you may have to cook the stew a tad bit longer.

4—If you can't find rose-flavored rice where you shop, you might want to substitute either jasmine rice or popcorn rice in its lieu. And, of course, brown rice is the perfect variety to use for certain diets. The choice is yours.

Honey Ham and Green Bean Stew

Here's one of those "everything in one pot" dishes. You smother down the seasonings, then you smother down the ham, and then you smother down the beans. And when all the flavors come together and reach their mouth-watering intensity, you simply spoon it out over a bowl of rice and dig in! Mmm!

3 tbsp. vegetable oil
6 strips hickory-smoked bacon
⅓ cup vegetable mirepoix
2 tsp. minced garlic
2 lb. honey ham, diced
1 hambone
2 bay leaves
1 tsp. basil

1 can chicken broth
4 lb. green beans, trimmed
2 tsp. salt
1 tsp. black pepper
Frank Davis Vegetable Seasoning
    to taste
6 cups cooked rice

Start by taking a heavy, anodized, aluminum, 5-qt. Dutch oven and heating the oil to sizzling over a medium-high fire. Then drop in the bacon, Creole Seasoning Mix, and garlic and sauté everything together, until the seasonings are fully wilted and soft.

Next, drop in the ham and hambone and stir them into the seasoning vegetables. When the ham pieces begin to show a hint of "brown" (caramelization) around the edges, stir in the bay leaves, basil, and broth. Then reduce the fire to medium and simmer the ingredients in the pot for about 10 minutes to marry the flavors.

At this point, add the beans to the Dutch oven and meticulously fold them into the pot mix, making sure that each bean is coated with the seasonings. Now sprinkle in the salt, pepper, and vegetable seasoning, toss again, put the lid on the pot, reduce the heat to low, and simmer for 30-40 minutes. It is necessary that you check the cooking process every 5 minutes or so to "re-toss" the beans and distribute them in the pot to ensure even cooking. The beans are done when they become tender *but not so soft that they fall apart.*

When you're ready to eat, fill a soup bowl with about ½ cup rice and ladle the beans (along with some of the pot liquor and a generous helping of ham) over the top. With a couple slices of hot, buttered sourdough bread and a tall glass of iced tea, this becomes one of those "stick-to-your-ribs" meals that you'll fix for your family over and over again.

Chef's Note:

1—If you can't find the prechopped mirepoix at the grocery where you shop, you can make your own by mincing and mixing together onions, celery, green bell pepper, carrot, parsley, garlic, and green onions in a proportion that suits your individual taste. The usual ratio, however, is 1 cup onions, ³/₄ cup celery, ½ cup pepper, ½ cup carrot, 2 tbsp. parsley, 4 cloves garlic, and ¹/₃ cup green onions.

2—Most supermarkets no longer carry hambones, but "ham stores" (such as Honey Baked) usually keep them for their customers.

3—Both snap beans and regular green beans can be used in this stew. Just be careful not to select the kind of pole beans with strings in them!

4—To get the most intense flavor out of the beans, once they're cooked, remove from the fire the pot you cooked them in and let them "fade" into the residual heat. This causes the steam trapped inside the Dutch oven to "sweat" the beans and the ham, further increasing their delicateness.

5—They will keep well in the refrigerator for about 6 days and are always better "the next day."

Mother-in-Law's Homemade Sicilian Stew

My sweet little Sicilian mother-in-law, Nina Scalia Bruscato, taught me how to cook this dish back in the 1960s, and it has been a weekly tradition at my house ever since. But don't let its simplicity fool you! It's rich, robust, and tantalizing, whether you're Sicilian or not! Oh, yeah—and for one reason or another, the kids love it too!

¼ cup extra-virgin olive oil
2 cups minced yellow onions
6 cloves garlic, crushed
2 lb. lean chuck roast, bias sliced
1 lb. lean pork, small cubed
2 cans whole tomatoes, 303 size

3 bay leaves
2 tsp. Frank Davis Sicilian Seasoning
Salt and black pepper to taste
2 lb. fresh green beans
2 lb. "B" creamer potatoes, peeled
1 cup grated Parmesan cheese

In a heavy aluminum 5-qt. Dutch oven that has a lid, heat the oil on medium high and sauté the onions—stirring constantly—until they wilt (this should take about 5 minutes). Then toss in the garlic, stir it around briskly, and cook it down for about 3 minutes (but be extra careful not to let the garlic burn or it will taste bitter).

Now, when the onions and garlic are sautéed, turn up the fire to high. Then stir in the beef and pork a little at a time (be sure to keep them briskly moving in the pot!) and cook the meats quickly until they brown slightly and you can no longer see any red coloration (this should take another 5 minutes or so).

At this point, chop the tomatoes into small pieces or run them briefly through a food processor and add them to the pot. This is also when you add the bay leaves and Sicilian seasoning. Now mix everything together well, put the lid on the pot, turn the fire down to low, and *simmer* the meat and tomatoes for at least 45 minutes.

Finally, after the allotted cooking time, season the stew with salt and pepper. Then, drop in the beans and potatoes, stir them uniformly into the mixture, turn the fire up to medium, cover the pot again, and cook once more for 30 minutes to 1 hour (depending upon the tenderness of the vegetables). Just watch carefully that the pot doesn't boil!

When you're ready to eat, spoon out heaping portions of the stew into soup bowls, sprinkle liberally with cheese, and serve it all up with either Italian bread, French bread, or cornbread.

Chef's Note: Broad Italian green beans are best for this recipe—they tenderize quicker than string beans and lend a more authentic flavor. But if you must use regular green beans, make certain you buy the "stringless" variety.

Mary Clare's Mouth-Watering Trowittagetta Chikin Stew
(A Really Easy Gourmet Creation!)

This old-fashioned New Orleans stewed chicken doesn't require particular procedures. True, the recipe appears to have lots of ingredients, but as the name implies, it's all thrown together, which makes it so simple even a child could do it.

8 skinless, bone-in chicken thighs
3 skinless chicken breasts or 12 white-meat chicken strips
7 tbsp. extra-virgin olive oil
2 tbsp. butter
½ cup all-purpose flour
1 cup diced yellow onion
3 ribs celery, diced
2 tsp. fresh garlic, chopped
½ cup diced green bell peppers
4 cups canned chicken broth
¾ cup white wine (Pinot Grigio preferred)
1 cube chicken bouillon (dissolved in the wine)

2 large tomatoes, peeled and chopped
14-oz. can small-diced tomatoes
3 bay leaves
1 tsp. Frank Davis Poultry Seasoning
2 tsp. Frank Davis Sprinkling Spice
6 medium red potatoes, peeled and quartered
2 cans cut green beans, washed and drained
Salt and black pepper to taste
¼ cup minced parsley for garnish
Shredded Parmesan cheese for topping

First, roll the chicken thighs and breast pieces in 4 tbsp. oil. Then sauté them a few pieces at a time in a 12-in. skillet (just don't overcrowd them). When they have all seared, remove them to a platter for a while.

In the meantime, drop into the skillet the butter and remaining oil. Then slowly sprinkle in the flour and whisk it into a dark roux. When it reaches the right color, drop in all the seasoning veggies to halt the cooking (keep in mind that the residual heat will cook the veggies).

At this point, pour in the broth, wine (with the bouillon cube dissolved in it), tomatoes, canned tomatoes, bay leaves, poultry seasoning, and sprinkling spice. Hold off on adding any salt and pepper at this stage (there may be enough salt in the broth and sprinkling spice to satisfy your taste—and you can always adjust the salt and pepper to your taste later).

Then bring the stock to a boil *but quickly reduce the heat and simmer it for about 20 minutes so that it can develop full flavor.* Now drop in all the chicken pieces and cook them over a low heat for about 45 minutes to 1 hour (or until they become tender—just try to keep from overcooking them so that the meat doesn't fall off the bone). Then, about 30 minutes before the chicken is done, add the potatoes, stir them into the mix gently, and cook them over low heat until fork tender.

Finally, gently fold in the beans until uniformly distributed and simmer until everything is heated through. Now adjust for your salt and pepper if necessary.

When you're ready to eat, serve the stew piping hot in deep soup bowls alongside a pan of buttered Southern cornbread. Then sprinkle each bowl with parsley and a handful of Parmesan.

Chef's Note:

1—If you decide to use chicken drumsticks instead of thighs, be sure to skin the drumsticks before adding them to the stew. Otherwise the stew will end up too oily.

2—The seasoning veggies do not have to be minced for this dish. Because this is a "stew," you want them to have somedefinition.

3—Even though the stew contains potatoes and your mawmaw told you that you should never serve two starches in one meal, it's perfectly okay with me if you want to ladle this over a pile of steamed rice.

4—This is another one of those dishes that gets richer and better tasting "the next day."

5—And before you start writing and calling and e-mailing, there is no special recipe for the pan of cornbread! Simply follow the directions on the back of the package of the brand you buy. Then when you take the pan out of the oven, brush it liberally all over with lots of melted butter.

Carnival-Time Chilly Chili

If you think all of the dishes we traditionally cook for Mardi Gras are great, wait till you brew up a batch of this "Chilly Chili." And if you plan to take it with you and eat it out along the parade route, you might want to bring extra for all the new friends you're gonna make!

3 lb. lean coarse-ground beef
¼ cup extra-virgin olive oil
8 oz. mushrooms, sliced
2 medium onions, chopped
1 cup diced green bell pepper
6 cloves garlic, minced
12-oz. bottle chili sauce (hot or mild)
10-oz. can Rotel tomatoes with chilies (undrained)
8 oz. tomato sauce
½ cup chicken stock
1 tbsp. chili powder
1 tbsp. Worcestershire sauce
1 pkg. 2-Alarm Chili Mix (3⅝ oz.)

1 tbsp. ground cumin
2 tsp. Frank Davis Beef Seasoning
2 cans black beans, washed and drained
½ tsp. salt
¼ tsp. black pepper
2 tbsp. minced parsley
8 cups cooked long-grain rice
1 cup thinly sliced green onions for garnish
4 cups shredded sharp cheddar cheese
1 box multigrain crackers, buttered

First, in a large skillet, fry down the beef over medium-high heat until it crumbles and is no longer pink. Then, while it is still hot, pour off and discard any excess rendered-out fat. Set the skillet aside for a while.

In the meantime, take a large Dutch oven that has a lid, heat the oil, and sauté the mushrooms a handful at a time until they are wilted and tender. Then drop in the onions, bell pepper, and garlic and sauté that mixture until it softens.

When the veggies are ready, stir in the chili sauce, Rotel tomatoes, tomato sauce, stock, chili powder, Worcestershire, chili mix, cumin, beef seasoning, beans, salt, and black pepper . . . *along with the browned beef.* Then mix everything together well and stir, stir, and stir again!

When the contents of the pot are homogenized, bring them up to high heat—*but without boiling!* Then immediately reduce the fire to low, put the lid on the pot, and simmer the recipe for about 1 hour, stirring occasionally to keep the mixture from sticking to the bottom of the pot. (It is also a good idea to taste the chili from time to time as it cooks and make whatever seasoning adjustments you desire.)

Then when you're ready to eat, quickly whisk in the parsley, heap the chili in single servings over scant bowls of rice, sprinkle with green onions and cheese, and serve with buttered crackers.

This version is fit for Mardi Gras royalty!

Chef's Note:

1—You can eliminate a maximum amount of fat from the chili if you drain the browned beef in a colander.

2—I suggest you don't cook the chili in a regular black cast-iron pot—the tomatoes will tend to give it a slightly "rusty" taste. Anodized aluminum or heavy commercial stainless steel is best.

3—The quantity of liquid in this recipe should be ideal already, but if you find that a little more is needed, you can go ahead and pour in tad extra chicken stock. On the other hand, if you find the chili too soupy, you can stir in 1-2 tbsp. prepared roux to thicken it slightly. All this is nothing more than a matter of preference.

4—If you'd prefer not to put black beans in the chili, you can substitute ranch-style or pinto beans in their place or you can leave out beans completely. But here's the Rule of Thumb—main-dish chili always has beans; hotdog chili never has beans. But it's your call, 'cuz it's your chili!

Frank's Crab Plus Crabmeat Gumbo

This is not one of those gumbos where the main ingredient is lightly passed over the top of the pot just to give it a name! This gumbo is fully loaded with not only lots of good stuff but with lots of cracked blue crab and claw crabmeat as well. Ladle this over a bowl of steamed rice, podnuh, and you got yourself some real New Orleans home cookin'!

¼ cup vegetable oil
⅓ cup all-purpose flour, as needed
2 cups vegetable mirepoix
2 dozen gumbo crabs
4 qt. bottled water
2 qt. concentrated chicken broth
1 tsp. basil
4 bay leaves
2 cans Rotel diced tomatoes (undrained)
2 medium overripe tomatoes, seeded and diced

2 slices lemon zest
⅓ cup minced parsley
1 tsp. red pepper flakes
4 tsp. Frank Davis Seafood Seasoning
1 tbsp. Frank Davis Seafood Boil
1 lb. unpeeled shrimp, heads off
2 lb. claw crabmeat
8 cups cooked long-grain rice
¾ cup thinly sliced green onions for garnish
1 jar filé powder
Buttered saltine crackers

First, in a heavy gumbo pot or stockpot that has a lid, heat the oil over a medium-high heat just to the point of it beginning to smoke. Then, with a wire whip in one hand and the flour in the other, begin sprinkling and whisking the flour into the hot oil to make a roux.

Now here's the trick—*never stop whisking once!* Continue to swirl the two ingredients together as you add the flour, to prevent them from scorching and burning. Then, when the roux takes on the consistency of a heavy pancake batter, stop adding flour—*at that point it will be all you'll need.* But keep whisking and cooking the roux until it becomes a rich dark-brown color.

When that happens, immediately toss in the vegetable mirepoix. This action reduces the temperature of the roux and serves to thoroughly combine the veggies and the roux. At the same time take the pot off the fire to stop the cooking process. Set it aside temporarily so that you can prepare the gumbo crabs. Wash them (precleaned with top shell removed) under cool running water, taking care to pick away all the debris from the belly section and gills. Then with a sharp knife split them into right and left halves and set them aside.

When the roux has cooled down sufficiently (remember, you never want to add liquids to a hot roux!), put the pot on a high fire and add half the water and half the broth. Then immediately stir everything together well to blend in the flour and create a smooth "gumbo base." Continue to pour in additional liquids a little at a time (first the broth, then the water) as the base develops and thins out— *keep in mind that you want the final gumbo stock to mirror the consistency of melted ice cream.*

Now, when the stock reaches this stage, it's time to drop in the basil, bay leaves, Rotels, fresh tomatoes, lemon zest, parsley, red pepper flakes, crab halves, seafood seasoning, and seafood boil and stir them all together well. Then put the lid on the pot, lower the fire to simmer, and allow the gumbo to cook for 30 minutes (stirring periodically). *Note: depending upon how well the roux turned out, you may need to stir in additional small amounts of either broth or water as the dish simmers so that it doesn't thicken too much.*

Then after the allotted cooking time, and about 10 minutes before you're ready to eat, you're going to drop in the shrimp, along with the claw crabmeat, and stir everything together one more time. Then, after putting the lid back on the pot and making sure that the fire is still set at low, let the gumbo simmer once more for 10 minutes, before it's served in deep soup bowls over a mound of steamed white rice.

I like it best adorned with a sprinkling of both green onions and filé powder and dished up next to a stack of buttered saltine crackers. Mmm—talk about mouth-watering! This is its true definition!

Chef's Note:

1—If you can't find the packages of vegetable mirepoix where you shop, you can always chop up a couple of cups of an onion, celery, green bell pepper, garlic, green onion, and parsley mix. Just blend it in amounts to your liking.

2—Because of the delicateness of crabmeat, bottled water is preferable in this gumbo, as it lacks a harshness likely to be found in everyday tap water. After all, if you're striving to showcase the unique flavor of crab, you want to keep the base as neutral as possible.

3—You can use either homemade or canned chicken broth in this gumbo. If you decide to use your own, just be sure to defat it before adding it to the pot. By the way, for a thinner gumbo, you can add 1-2 cups more of either water or chicken stock.

4—The easiest way to strip off a slice of lemon zest (and you really don't want to make crab gumbo without it!) is to use a potato peeler. It gives you just the "zest" and leaves the pith on the lemon.

5—The unpeeled shrimp actually accent the subtleties of the crab-meat. And like with the crab halves, all you do is just pick them out of the gumbo bowl with your fingers and eat them very informally (which is the way we do dishes like this down South anyway).

6—Finally, if claw crabmeat is a little pricey where you live, it's okay to use only 1 lb. instead of 2 in this gumbo. Just don't, whatever you do, substitute imitation *crabmeat! It's nothing but a formed fish paste and will dissolve into a gooey mess in your gumbo!*

7—Crab gumbo contains no okra. Instead, filé powder (finely powdered sassafras leaves) is used as a topical thickener in this recipe. And of course, the filé should always be added at the table as a condiment, never put into the pot on the stove.

8—Oh, yeah—like all gumbos, this one too is unbelievably better the next day (or so I'm told, since the pots I always cooked up never made it to the next day).

Mary Clare's Chunky Shrimp and Noodle Gumbo

This is kinda like a stew, similar to a bisque, thicker than a soup, and lighter than a chowder. Combine shrimp and noodles in a rich sauce in Bayou Country, and like it or not, you got yourself a gumbo!

2 cups coarsely diced onions
1 cup coarsely diced celery
2 tsp. minced garlic
2 tbsp. extra-virgin olive oil
16-oz. can diced tomatoes
4 cups shrimp, fish, or chicken stock
½ cup white wine
2 bay leaves
1 tsp. red pepper flakes
2 tsp. salt

2 tsp. Frank Davis Bronzing Mix
3 lb. peeled and deveined shrimp (26-30 count)
1 lb. broad egg noodles (cooked al dente)
3 tbsp. cornstarch + ½ cup chicken broth
½ cup sliced green onions
¼ cup minced parsley
¾ grated Parmesan cheese

In a high-sided fry pan or oval roaster that has a tight-fitting lid, sauté the onions, celery, and garlic in the oil over a medium-high fire until the vegetables soften and clear. Then, without reducing the heat, stir in the tomatoes and cook them into the mixture until thoroughly blended. *Hint: to get the tomatoes to impart a light and delicate flavor, I suggest you chop them into small pieces as they cook.*

At this point, add the stock, wine, and bay leaves and season the resultant courtbouillon with the pepper flakes, salt, and bronzing mix. Then reduce the flame to low, cover the pot tightly, and simmer the base for about 20 minutes to get the flavors to marry.

Then when the flavors have combined, toss in the shrimp along with the noodles and stir the entire pot once again—*but this time very gently*. Remember that both the shrimp and the noodles will be ready to eat in just a matter of minutes, so be careful that you don't overcook (about 5 minutes should be all it takes!)

Finally, just before you plan to serve the gumbo, increase the heat to high and stir in the cornstarch mixture a little at a time. When the "sauce" thickens slightly and glazes the pasta as well as the shrimp, the recipe is right! All that's left at this stage is to sprinkle on the green onions, parsley, and cheese and fold everything together once more.

The dish is best when ladled out into deep soup bowls surrounded by either sesame-studded bread sticks or hot buttered French bread right from the oven.

Chef's Note:
1—Don't overcook the shrimp. The moment they turn a rich pink, they're done! Overcooking makes them tough and rubbery.
2—The worst thing you can do to this dish is thicken the liquid to resemble a heavy sauce. The stock should barely have body, and only enough of it to coat the shrimp and pasta. Let's put it this way—if you're satisfied that what you have is a "chunky thick soup," you're right on!

Mike Keefe's Turkey Andouille Gumbo

So what do you do with turkey leftovers after Thanksgiving? Turkey soup? Turkey a la king? Turkey tetrazzini? Turkey sandwiches? Turkey pizza? Turkey tacos? Turkey tamales? Well, since this is New Orleans, how 'bout a good turkey and andouille gumbo? Before my old friend Mike Keefe passed away, he shared with me his longtime secret family recipe! I know he would have wanted you to have it.

1 roasted turkey carcass
3 qt. water
2 cups canned chicken broth
Kosher salt, black pepper, and
    cayenne pepper to taste
2 lb. andouille sausage, coarsely
    diced
3 tbsp. bacon drippings or veg-
    etable oil
¼ cup all-purpose flour
1 large onion, medium diced
2 ribs celery, medium diced
1 green bell pepper, coarsely
    chopped

2 tbsp. minced parsley
4 cloves garlic, minced
2 cans Rotel diced tomatoes,
    10-oz. size
3 bay leaves
1 tsp. basil
2 tsp. ground thyme
1 tsp. Frank Davis Poultry
    Seasoning
1 pt. fresh-shucked Louisiana
    oysters, with liquid (optional)
6 cups cooked long-grain or
    brown rice
1 jar filé powder

Start off by taking an 8-qt. stockpot and gently simmering the turkey carcass in the water and broth with salt, black pepper, and cayenne pepper until the turkey meat begins to fall off the bones, which should take about 2 hours total. If necessary, add more broth to the pot to compensate for any liquid that evaporates.

When the simmering time is done, remove the carcass from the pot, let it cool slightly, and pick off every bit of the remaining meat from the bones. In the meantime, continue to simmer the stock until you reduce its volume by about one-fourth (this serves to concentrate the flavors of the finished gumbo).

Meanwhile, in a 12-in. nonstick skillet, begin sautéing the sausage, stirring occasionally to render out its excess fats. Then when the sausage is thoroughly browned, remove it from the skillet and set it aside. But immediately combine the bacon drippings with the sausage drippings and begin whisking in the flour to make a roux (one the color of peanut butter will do nicely). When the roux is ready, to stop it from browning further, drop in the onions, celery, bell pepper, parsley, and garlic and fold them into the roux well. Then remove the skillet from the fire and set the mixture aside to cool.

At this stage, add the tomatoes to the turkey stock, along with the picked turkey meat, andouille, bay leaves, basil, and thyme, and simmer everything together on a low fire for about 15 minutes, stirring frequently. Then begin adding the roux a little at a time, briskly whisking it into the stock as you go. (Mike was quick to recommend that you dissolve some of the roux in small amounts of the hot stock in a separate measuring cup to keep it from "lumping" in the gumbo—in cooking, this process is called "tempering.")

Finally, when everything is blended and the gumbo is thickened to your liking, stir in the poultry seasoning, and simmer the gumbo on low for another 30 minutes or so, stirring occasionally. If you decide to include the oysters in your recipe, drop them in (along with the oyster liquid) about 10 minutes before serving. The idea is to get the oysters to "just curl," not overcook.

When you're ready to eat, liberally ladle the gumbo, piping hot, over big bowls of steaming hot rice and generously sprinkle it with filé. A couple of toasty French-bread pistolettes right out of the oven make a nice accompaniment.

Chef's Note:
1—Take time to remove all the turkey debris from the stock. Often bits of rib bones settle in the bottom of the stockpot. These should be removed before serving the gumbo.

2—The proper consistency of the gumbo is that of a semi-thick soup. Remember, this is a Cajun-style gumbo. You don't want it to have a thick stew consistency—that's New Orleans and Creole style.

3—Like red beans and jambalaya, this dish is always better the next day! Unfortunately, it goes so fast it never stays around that long!

CHAPTER 4

Meats

Genuine N'Awlins Chicken-Fried Steak
(With Real Homemade Mashed Potatoes)

Chicken-fried steak is probably the most comforting of all the comfort foods. It's made in the country, it's made at the neighborhood corner café, and it's made in your mawmaw's kitchen back-a-town. And when it's served up with real, homemade mashed potatoes (creamed, we call 'em!), you got yourself something really special, yeah!

The Chicken-Fried Steak:

2 lb. cube steak, trimmed of fat
1½ cups all-purpose flour
¼ tsp. garlic powder
¼ tsp. onion powder
½ tsp. paprika
1 tsp. salt
½ tsp. freshly ground black
   pepper

2 cups cultured buttermilk
1 pt. EggBeaters
1 tsp. hot sauce
2 cups Frank Davis Chicken Fried
   Mix
2 cups shortening

The first thing you want to do is cut the steaks into serving-size pieces. Then tenderize each piece by pounding it to ¼-in. thickness with a meat maul.

Then make the dredging mix by combining the flour, garlic powder, onion powder, paprika, salt, and pepper, taking care to mix everything well. *Note: if you'd like your steak to turn out super spicy, go ahead and sprinkle a touch of cayenne into the flour mixture right about now.*

Set up 3 shallow baking pans side by side on the countertop. Fill the one on the right with the dredging mix. Fill the middle pan with the buttermilk, EggBeaters, and hot sauce, blended together. Then finally fill the third pan with the Frank Davis Chicken Fried Mix (or a second pan of seasoned flour).

When you're ready to cook, dredge a steak in the first pan and coat it evenly. Then lift it out and shake off the excess flour. Next, dip the floured steak into the buttermilk, carefully coating both sides yet allowing the excess to drip off. Then place the steak into the chicken-fried mix, once again coating it well and shaking off all the excess. Repeat the process with all the steaks, and as each one of them is done, place it on a sheet of either waxed or parchment paper. At this point, chill the steaks for about 15 minutes in the refrigerator before cooking them.

To fry them, heat the shortening to medium high (365 degrees) in a large high-sided skillet. Then with a long-handled fork or a chef's meat hook, fry 2-3 steaks at a time until they brown nicely on both sides, turning them only once (cooking time is 3-5 minutes, depending upon the thickness of the meat). Repeat the process with the remaining cutlets.

When you remove them from the skillet, transfer them to a plate lined with paper towels and drain them briefly. Then set them aside on a wire rack in a 200-degree oven to keep them warm and crispy while the rest of the meal is being prepared. In the frying pan, save ¼ cup of the pan drippings to make the gravy.

The Mashed Potatoes:

6 large white or russet potatoes	¾ cup heavy cream
1 gal. salted water	Salt and black pepper to taste
1 stick salted butter	Sour cream for garnish

First, using a potato peeler like a soldier on K.P., strip away the outside peel from the potatoes and cut them into medium dice. Then place the pieces into a bowl of cold water to keep them from turning a yucky brown.

In the meantime, while you're prepping the spuds, bring the water to a rolling boil. Then drop in the taters; but as soon as the water comes back to a boil, reduce the heat to low to create a true "simmer." This will allow the potato chunks to "poach" gently and retain their starchy creaminess (figure this will take about 25 minutes).

Then when they are tender (a fork or ice pick will pierce the pieces easily), drain off the hot water and transfer them to a large mixing bowl.

At this point it's time to season and flavor the chunks. First drop the butter into the bowl and, with a potato masher, work it completely into the pieces until fully melted. Next, a little at a time, pour in the cream and thoroughly incorporate it into the buttered tubers. And finally, sprinkle in the salt and pepper, once again using the potato masher to distribute the seasonings evenly throughout the bowl.

When you're ready to eat, spoon out a generous helping of the creamy taters next to a crispy, crunchy chicken-fried steak and crown the pile with a dollop of sour cream.

The White Country Gravy:

¼ cup reserved pan drippings
2 tbsp. butter
¼ cup all-purpose flour
1 cup warm milk

1 cup chicken stock
1 qt. milk, as needed
Salt and freshly ground pepper
   to taste

Heat the pan drippings over a medium flame, along with the butter. By the way, be sure to keep the browned bits (the dregs) in the pan—this is where the flavor intensity of the gravy will come from.

When the dregs have been scraped off the skillet and stirred into the drippings and butter, go ahead and whisk in the flour (and, yes, it's okay to use some of the leftover seasoned flour from the dredging pan). When the full measure is in the drippings, cook and stir the roux mixture for 1-2 minutes until lump-free. Then very slowly add the warm milk and the stock, stirring constantly until everything is uniformly blended.

At this point, bring the gravy base to a boil, but immediately reduce the heat and cook until the resultant gravy is thickened (now's the time to whisk in more milk if you want to thin out the gravy a tad). Of course, take special care to stir the mixture continually until it turns smooth and silky.

All that's left then is to season the gravy with salt and pepper and ladle it over the hot, crispy steaks and mashed potatoes. Incidentally, white country gravy is supposed to be thick, but if thinner gravy is more to your liking, simply add more milk.

Chef's Note:

1—The Texans claim to have originated chicken-fried steak. The country folk from Oklahoma to West Virginia say it was all their idea. And the New Orleans Creoles insist the recipe originally came from them. Who knows who did it first? One thing is for certain, though—we all agree they's some doggone good groceries!

2—If you can't find cube steaks already cut, tenderized, and packaged in the meat department of your supermarket, you can always buy a 2-lb. piece of boneless beef top loin and slice it crosswise into 8 (4-oz.) cutlets. Then, using a glancing motion, pound each cutlet thin with a moistened maul or the side of a heavy cleaver. Of course, if push comes to shove, t'ain't nothing wrong with using a couple big ol' ½-in.-thick round steaks either (you might want to ask your butcher to run 'em through his tenderizing machine, though).

3—Three disposable aluminum pans placed side by side make ideal breading trays. And after they've been used, they can be emptied out, crumpled up, and placed in the recycle bins, with no cleanup required.

4—While many recipes call for a traditional egg wash (3 eggs + 1 cup milk) when prepping chicken-fried steak, I've found that EggBeaters (which are little more than liquefied egg whites) and buttermilk work a whole lot better to produce a crispiness in the finished steak.

5—If you don't have a chef's meat hook but would like to get one, they can be obtained from www.cookperfect.com.

Precise, Never-Fail Directions for Making a Roux!

First of all, you can never ever make too much roux. Whatever you make and don't use can be placed in an airtight plastic container or Mason jar and stored in the refrigerator for weeks.

Secondly, in spite of all the things you've heard from the so-called experts over the years, there is no true formula for making roux (not if you want it to come out perfect every time, anyway!). Besides, I don't want you relying on a formula anyway. Do this instead:

1—Take ¹/₄, or ¹/₃, or ¹/₂ cup oil (you always start with some quantity of oil—makes no difference how much) and put it into a heavy pan.

2—Have about 1 cup all-purpose flour ready on the side.

3—Heat the oil over medium-high heat, just short of it starting to smoke. When the oil has reached the right temperature, begin sprinkling the flour into it a little at a time, *whisking it constantly as it goes in.* This will allow the flour to begin cooking right away and keep lumps from forming.

4—Keep sprinkling more and more flour into the oil until the mixture reaches the consistency of a heavy pancake batter. *That's the precise amount of flour you need—right there!* That's the trick—that's the texture you want. That makes a perfect roux. When it gets to that texture, stop adding flour .... *but continue to whisk!*

5—The roux will turn from white to pale tan to light tan to beige to light brown to peanut-butter color to medium brown to dark brown to black. Watch it closely as it goes through this metamorphosis ... *but never stop whisking.* If you stop for even a moment, the roux will burn, you'll have to throw it out, and you'll have to start all over again!

6—When it reaches the color you want, drop in about 1 cup mixed chopped seasoning (onions, celery, green bell pepper, garlic, green onions, and parsley) and take the pot off the fire. The roux will now stop cooking and stay the color it is, and the moisture from inside the veggies will cool it down. *Never add liquid to a hot roux—it explodes!*

Once you got your cooled roux, it's then just a matter of adding as much of it as you need to whatever liquid you're going to use to make a gravy—chicken stock (homemade or canned) is by far my favorite base liquid, but you can also use wine, beer, juice, a variety of canned soups, and even water.

At this point, to make a gravy, you take as much stock as you'll need for your guests and bring it to a rolling boil. Then begin spooning (and whisking) in the roux a little at a time, dissolving it in the stock as it goes. After about 5 minutes of cooking, reduce the heat to medium low and continue to stir—the stock and roux will thicken and be instantly transformed into a silky, smooth gravy. All you do then is season it with either salt and pepper or any Frank Davis pre-mixed seasoning that you desire.

Did you follow that? If you did, you can now make the perfect roux. And with that you can make a rich, lump-free gravy anytime you want one!

Old-Style New Orleans Brocioloni

Everybody's Italian mawmaw, especially those who lived in the old New Orleans neighborhoods, cooked these stuffed, rolled, Sicilian round steaks at least once a week. And while there must be a dozen or so variations to this dish around town, this one I believe comes closest to the simplicity and taste of the Old Country!

2 round or flank steaks, about
  1 lb. each
2 tsp. Frank Davis Beef
  Seasoning
4 cloves garlic, minced
½ lb. button mushrooms, minced
½ cup chopped basil
½ cup minced parsley
2 green onions, thinly sliced
1 tsp. black pepper
2 cups Italian seasoned
  breadcrumbs
1½ cups grated Parmesan
  cheese

¾ cup shredded mozzarella
1 tsp. Frank Davis Sicilian
  Seasoning
½ cup beef broth
2 eggs, beaten
4 hardboiled eggs, chopped
¼ cup olive oil + 4 cloves garlic,
  crushed
4 qt. warm tomato gravy
6 cups cooked elbow pasta
Parmesan or Pecorino Romano
  cheese for garnish

First, place the steaks on the countertop and carefully remove the small bone with a very sharp knife. Then position the steaks between 2 sheets of either parchment paper or plastic wrap and, with a meat maul, pound them out until they are no more than ¼ in. thick (this makes them easy to roll). Now pin the bone hole in each steak shut with a couple of toothpicks and season the meat liberally with the beef seasoning.

Meanwhile, in a large bowl, thoroughly combine the garlic, mushrooms, basil, parsley, green onions, pepper, breadcrumbs, Parmesan cheese, mozzarella cheese, Sicilian seasoning, beef broth, and eggs to form the steak stuffing. Add extra beef broth a little at a time if necessary just until a moist but crumbly consistency is achieved.

At this point you can do one of two things: (1) you can either spread out a thin layer of the stuffing over the steak and roll it up lengthwise in "jellyroll" style, or (2) you can mound a generous amount of the stuffing right down the middle of the steak and wrap the meat lengthwise around it. Whichever method you choose, be sure to include a liberal sprinkling of chopped eggs with the stuffing before you roll the steaks. When the roll is wrapped tight, tie the steak closed with several pieces of butcher twine (or skewer it together with toothpicks).

Now take a heavy 12-in. skillet, heat the oil and garlic mixture to sizzling, and brown the rolled steaks well on all sides. All that's left to do then is to take the rolls, submerge them in tomato gravy in a large pot, bring everything to a gentle boil, reduce the fire, and simmer the brocioloni for about 45 minutes or until they become "fall-apart tender."

When you're ready to eat, lift the rolls out of the gravy and onto a serving platter, snip away the twine (or remove the toothpicks), and cut the steaks into serving-size slices on a bias. Remove the toothpicks you used to close the bone holes. For each serving, dish out several slices of the brocioloni (as well as the tomato gravy it simmered in) on top of a plate of elbow pasta. Then top off everything with a generous handful of either Parmesan or Romano cheese.

Chef's Note:

1—Ideally, you want to use a very thinly cut veal or beef round steak with the smallest bone-in you can find. When the bone is removed, patch up the hole with toothpicks and lay the steak flat in order to stuff it. If you can get your butcher to custom cut the steaks for you, the thinner they will be and the better the brocioloni will come out.

2—If you don't have my beef seasoning handy, you can order it from my Web site (www.frankdavis.com) or substitute about $\frac{1}{2}$ tsp. coarse-ground black pepper and about $\frac{1}{2}$ tsp. kosher salt in its place.

3—You can either make a tomato gravy from scratch or use one of the commercial gravies on the market and doctor it up (by adding a little extra onions, garlic, parsley, Sicilian seasoning, canned chicken broth, and a splash of red wine).

Prime Beef Short Ribs

Most of the time when you order BBQ ribs out (and usually even when you cook them at home), you get pork ribs, either the sparerib kind or the more tender "baby backs." But even though you have to order them special, there's a whole lot to be said for "beef ribs," especially when they're spiced up like those in the recipe below and served next to a plate of hot, buttery grits. You gotta go fix some of these right away!

12+ meaty beef ribs, trimmed into riblets	2 cups tomato catsup
2-4 qt. lightly salted water	½ cup dark brown sugar
4 tbsp. margarine	3 tbsp. white wine vinegar
2 cups diced onions	1 tbsp. Worcestershire sauce
1½ cups minced carrots	2 tbsp. Dijon mustard
½ cup thinly sliced green onions	1 tsp. chili powder
½ cup diced celery	2 bay leaves
¼ cup minced green bell pepper	½ tsp. lemon zest
2 cloves garlic, minced	Frank Davis Beef Seasoning or salt and black pepper to taste

First lay out the beef ribs on a cutting board and, with a sharp paring knife, trim away as much of the excess fat as possible. Then place them onto a shallow-sided cookie sheet and broil them quickly on both sides until they turn a toasty brown.

At this point, immediately transfer the ribs to a stockpot containing just enough water to cover them and boil them for 30 minutes at a slow roll. Then, with a pair of tongs, remove them from the stock, place them side by side in a deep-sided baking dish, and set them aside momentarily—*but don't throw away the stock.* Continue to cook it at a slow boil until only 2 cups are left in the pot (this is called reduction—it concentrates the flavor and makes the stock rich).

Meanwhile, in a heavy, 12-in., high-sided skillet, heat the margarine and sauté the onions, carrots, green onions, celery, bell pepper, and garlic until they soften. Then one ingredient at a time, stir in the catsup, sugar, vinegar, Worcestershire, mustard, chili powder, bay leaves, and lemon zest. Now cook the sauce over low heat for about 20 minutes (but you want to stir it frequently to keep the sugar from burning).

When the sauce is ready, skim the fat off the reduced beef stock. Then gradually stir into the sauce enough of the beef stock (maybe ½ cup) to give you the consistency you desire. *But don't dilute it too much, because it will thin automatically as the natural beef juices render out of the ribs as they bake.*

Finally, season the sauce with either beef seasoning or salt and pepper, ladle it liberally over the ribs, cover the baking dish with aluminum foil, and place it in a preheated 350-degree oven for 1½-2 hours.

After the allotted cooking time—and when the ribs are fall-off-the-bone tender—serve them piping hot with a plate of buttery grits and a cold crisp salad, along with a hot loaf of homemade beer bread. Ain't no doubt about, you got y'self an encore meal you'll want to fix at least twice a week.

Chef's Note: If you just want to make BBQ sauce, put together just the sauce portion of this recipe and you got a winner, podnuh. It will go great over pork ribs, steaks, brisket, chicken, and wild game.

Frank's Backyard Barbecued Beef Ribs

Lots of folks won't barbecue beef ribs because they say they're too tough and fatty. Well, if you follow this recipe to the letter, you'll end up with some of the best-tasting, tenderest beef riblets you ever had. This technique will make you proud . . . I promise!

1 gal. water
3 cans Campbell's Beef Broth
1 square cotton cheesecloth
   (6x6 in.)
½ large onion
½ cup diced celery
2 cloves garlic, crushed
¼ cup parsley sprigs

2 bay leaves
1 tsp. red pepper flakes
1 tsp. basil
12 beef ribs
1 tbsp. Frank Davis Beef
   Seasoning
2 cups commercial barbecue
   sauce

First, combine the water and broth in a large stockpot that has a lid and bring the mixture to a rapid boil. Then, in the cheesecloth, fold up and tie tightly the onion, celery, garlic, parsley, bay leaves, red pepper flakes, and basil. This is called a "bouquet garni," and it is used to flavor the stock without all the individual ingredient pieces floating free in the liquid and sticking to everything. Now drop the bouquet garni into the stock and boil it for about 10 minutes to develop the flavors.

While the stock is cooking, prepare the ribs. First, with a paring knife, remove the silverskin from the backside of the entire rib rack. (Unless you do this, the seasoning won't penetrate the backside of the meat; but worse yet, your ribs will end up tough and chewy because the silverskin is tough and chewy.) Simply separate the silverskin from one corner of the rack with the knife blade, then peel the skin off with your fingers, much as you would peel away the backing on a decal. If you do it right, it comes off easily in one big sheet.

Next, with a sharp knife, cut away the excess fat from the meat. Take your time—this is the step that removes all the greasiness from the finished riblets.

Finally, cut between each of the bones so that every rib separates into individual riblets. Then cut the riblets into 2-in. pieces and drop them into the boiling stock. When they're all in, wait for the water to come back to a boil. Then immediately reduce the heat to low and allow the riblets to simmer—*covered*—for about 30 minutes (but no longer—the meat will then begin to fall away from the bones!). Oh—if you notice any scum rising to the surface of the stock while the beef is cooking, skim it off. But if you've trimmed the ribs properly, there shouldn't be much.

After the allotted time, take a strainer spoon and remove the riblets from the stock, place them in a shallow pan, and allow them to cool down. Then, while they're still slightly moist, sprinkle them all over with the beef seasoning. All that's left now is to place them on your preheated barbecue pit and brush them liberally with the barbecue sauce.

Finally, grill them about 5-10 minutes on the grate (just long enough for the sugar in the barbecue sauce to start to caramelize) and your beef riblets are done. And they're "fall-off-the-bone tender"—and greaseless!

I suggest you serve them piping hot right from the pit, alongside creamy baked potatoes topped with butter and sour cream and a big bowl of barbecue-baked beans. Whew! This'll turn any meal into a three-day holiday!

Chef's Note:

1—The poaching step not only tenderizes the beef and melts away all the excess fat, it also flavors the inside of the meat. The barbecue sauce then caramelizes on the outside, giving the riblets the distinctive barbecue taste.

2—Under no circumstances should you throw away the poaching stock! Chilled in the refrigerator and defatted, it makes a base for one of the best-tasting, richest soups you every had. All you have to do is add vegetables!

3—To make a good bowl of barbecue-baked beans, drain 2 cans

Bush's Pork-N-Beans, cook down in ¹/₂ stick butter ¹/₂ onion and ¹/₂ green bell pepper that have been minced, mix everything together in a glass baking dish, stir in about ¹/₄ cup brown sugar, cover tightly with aluminum foil, and bake for 20 minutes covered and 5 minutes uncovered in a preheated 350-degree oven. Oooh, yeah!

N'Awlins Creole-Braised Sirloin Beef Tips

Think you can't enjoy a great beef dish just because you've been told to eat "heart healthy"? Well, I'm here to tell you not only that you can, but it can also be nothing less than gourmet! Here's a good old N'Awlins Creole rendition you're gonna love!

2 tsp. vegetable oil (or cooking spray)	1 small yellow onion, minced
½ tsp. freshly ground black pepper	3 medium tomatoes, peeled and crushed
2 tsp. Frank Davis No-Salt Seasoning	½ cup canned sliced mushrooms
½ tsp. Adolph's Unseasoned Meat Tenderizer	1¼ cups low-sodium beef broth
2 lb. lean sirloin beef tips, defatted and cubed	½ cup dry cocktail sherry
4 cloves garlic, crushed and minced	1 tbsp. light soy sauce
	2 tbsp. cornstarch
	¼ cup cold water
	6 cups cooked rice
	¼ cup minced parsley

First thing to do is to place a large nonstick skillet that has a lid on the stovetop, add the oil to it, swoosh it around, and bring it up to medium-high heat. In the meantime, sprinkle the pepper, no-salt seasoning, and tenderizer on the meat. (For best results, I suggest you then tightly wrap the cubes with plastic film and place them in the refrigerator for about 30 minutes to "cure.")

Then, when the oil is sizzling, drop the beef cubes into the skillet and sear them on all sides, turning them often until they become well browned. At this point, stir in the garlic, onion, tomatoes, and mushrooms and stir-fry the mixture until the onions clear and the tomatoes render out their juices.

Now add in the broth, sherry, and soy sauce and bring all of the ingredients to a gentle boil. Then immediately reduce the heat to medium low, cover the skillet, and simmer the ingredients for about 1¹/₂ hours or until the beef cubes are tender.

After the allotted cooking time, take a small bowl, combine the cornstarch with the cold water, and whisk the mixture together until slick and smooth. Then a little at a time, slowly pour the cornstarch blend into the skillet, stirring constantly as it's added. All that's left is to continue to cook and stir the contents of the skillet until the resultant gravy thickens.

When the beef tips are tender enough to be easily pierced with a fork, scoop out several ladlefuls over each plate of steaming hot rice and garnish the top with a sprinkling of parsley. If it has simmered for the right amount of time, the beef ought to literally fall apart.

By the way, you're looking at right around 180 calories, 5-7 grams of carbohydrates, and only about 5 grams of fat, only 2 of which are saturated. In other words, your cardiologist should have no problem with you chowing down on this dish!

Frank's Slap-Yo-Momma Boiled Brisket

Instead of baking, broiling, grilling, or barbecuing your brisket, try fixin' it this way. It's the epitome of simplicity, the flavor is phenomenal, and—if that don't beat all!—it's good for you and healthy too! Of course, once you go slathering on the creamed horseradish sauce and drizzling melted butter all over the potatoes and green beans that come with it . . . well, forget I even brought it up!

6-8 lb. beef brisket, trimmed
1 gal. bottled water
3 tbsp. pickling spice
1 tbsp. black peppercorns
1 tbsp. salt
4 bay leaves
3 small onions, peeled and
    quartered
6 cloves garlic, peeled
4 ribs celery, chunked
⅓ cup minced parsley
10 medium-size red potatoes,
    peeled and halved

6 carrots, peeled and chunked
2 small cabbages, coarsely
    chopped
1 bunch broccoli, coarsely
    chopped
2 lb. fresh green beans, trimmed
⅔ cup creamy horseradish
¼ cup heavy cream
Salt to taste
12 hot buttered Pee Wee
    French bread rolls

First, wash the brisket thoroughly under cold running water. When all of the "slick" has been removed from the surface (and you can feel the difference on your hands once it's gone), set the brisket aside so that you can prepare the poaching stock.

Start by pouring the water into a large oval roaster that has a lid and setting it over a medium-high flame. Then drop in the pickling spice, peppercorns, salt, bay leaves, onions, whole garlic cloves, celery, and parsley and stir everything together completely. When the water comes to a boil, reduce the fire and allow it to simmer for about 15 minutes (covered) so that a flavored poaching stock develops.

When the simmering time is up, place the brisket into the roaster, cover it again, and allow it to cook over a low heat—actually a very gentle bubble—for 4-5 hours until tender. It will be necessary to skim the stock occasionally to remove the "beef scum" that forms periodically. When doing this, though, it's also a good idea to check the level of the poaching stock for evaporation—ideally you want the liquid to just barely cover the meat.

I suggest you remove the lid from the roaster about a half-dozen times during the total cooking time to taste the stock, adding whatever it needs as the cooking process continues. Depending on the quality of the beef, it could take extra salt, or pepper, or onions, or whatever. Let your personal preference be the determining factor.

Now, to make a complete one-dish meal (actually, a one-pot meal is probably more like it!), add the potatoes, carrots, cabbage, broccoli, and green beans to the oval roaster on top of the brisket during the final 30 minutes of cooking. Then replace the cover and allow the veggies to simmer until they become tender crisp.

When you're ready to eat, serve the beef and vegetables piping hot together. To do this easily, first remove the vegetables from on top of the brisket and place them into a large glass bowl. Then with 2 large meat forks (because the brisket will be so tender at this point it will fall apart if you try to use only 1), lift the beef from the roaster and place it on a cutting board. For best results, carve it into thin slices across the grain while it is still hot.

To make a creamed horseradish sauce, whisk together with a wire whip the horseradish and cream, along with a tad extra salt.

Finally, place several slices of meat into each serving bowl, top them with an assortment of poached veggies, and pour on a ladleful of the pot liquor. A hot buttered roll, 1 tbsp. or so creamed horseradish sauce, and a frosty glass of iced tea rounds out the meal.

Chef's Note:

1—For this recipe, you can choose either a plain brisket from the meat department of your supermarket or opt for the preseasoned "corned beef"-style brisket. Whichever one you choose, be sure to wash it thoroughly under cool running water before putting it into the poaching pot (especially if you selected one that has been pre-cured).

2—Make sure you trim away as much of the fat from the brisket as possible before placing it into the poaching stock.

3—If you buy a preseasoned brisket—corned beef style—reduce the amount of salt you put into the poaching stock. You might also want to cut back slightly on the pickling spice.

Frank's Beefy Mirliton Casserole

Most New Orleanians take the time to stuff their mirlitons with shrimp. But if you occasionally want to take the easy way out, you can turn these delectable vegetable pears into a one-pan casserole made with all our traditional Creole seasonings and some really choice ground beef. Try making this on one of those laid-back days.

4 medium-large mirlitons
3 tbsp. butter or margarine
1½ lb. lean ground sirloin
1 medium onion, minced
⅔ cup minced celery
4 cloves garlic, minced
1 tbsp. minced parsley
¼ tsp. ground thyme
¼ tsp. ground rosemary
½ tsp. basil

1 tsp. salt
¼ tsp. cayenne pepper
¼ tsp. black pepper
2 tsp. Frank Davis Vegetable Seasoning
1½ cups seasoned breadcrumbs
1 egg, well beaten
1 cup breadcrumbs + ¼ cup butter, melted

Start by taking the mirlitons and gently boiling them in lightly salted water until a fork or ice pick will pierce them all the way through (without using excessive force). Then remove them from the water and set them aside to cool.

Meanwhile, in a 4½-qt. cast-iron or heavy aluminum Dutch oven, melt the butter or margarine over medium heat. Then sauté the beef, onion, celery, and garlic until the meat loses all traces of pink and the vegetables become wilted and tender (about 5 minutes). About 2 minutes into the sautéing process, reduce the fire to low and, while the vegetables are simmering, peel and dice the mirlitons (be sure to discard the center seedpod).

At this point, turn up the fire to high and toss the pulp into the Dutch oven. Then stir the stuffing mixture until the ingredients are completely blended. When the consistency is just right, remove the pot from the fire.

Now is the time to add the herbs and spices—the parsley, thyme, rosemary, basil, salt, peppers, and vegetable seasoning. Blend them well into the pulp mix. Then begin stirring in the dry breadcrumbs a little at a time. When they've all been added, if you find the mix to be too moist, add a little more crumbs, because if the mixture is too wet it won't firm up during the baking process.

All that's left is to stir in the egg (but do it quickly, otherwise the residual heat from the stuffing will cause it to "scramble") and turn the mixture out into a buttered, 10x14 glass baking dish.

Finally, generously sprinkle the casserole with the buttered breadcrumbs, slide the pan into a 300-degree preheated oven, and bake it for about 25 minutes or until the topping turns golden brown.

This casserole actually needs no accompaniment, but if you feel like you need a little something extra, a cold crisp garden salad tossed with balsamic vinaigrette will fill the bill!

Chef's Note: For you folks up north who know not of mirlitons, they're also known as chayotes or vegetable pears.

Frank's Gourmet Hamburger Steaks with Gravy and Baby Taters

A couple years back, I shared my secret recipe for authentic Salisbury steaks with my TV audience. Well, I guess it's about time that I share its down-home kissing cousin . . . the hamburger steak. Serve this up with the rich brown gravy it makes, a fistful of smothered onions, a plate of taters, a chunk of crusty hot French bread, and your favorite salad, and you will have just created a meal that's mighty hard to beat!

2 lb. lean ground beef (bone-less chuck or sirloin recom-mended)
½ tsp. kosher salt or 1 tsp. Frank Davis Beef Seasoning
¼ tsp. coarse-ground black pepper
⅔ cup minced onions
½ cup thinly sliced green onions
2 tsp. minced garlic
½ cup water

⅓ cup breadcrumb/oatmeal mixture
1 egg, slightly beaten
2 egg yolks
6 tbsp. unsalted butter
3 tbsp. dry red wine
1 pkg. brown gravy mix
1½ cups canned beef broth
1 medium red onion, thinly sliced

In a large bowl, combine the beef, beef seasoning, pepper, onions, green onions, garlic, water, breadcrumbs, beaten egg, and egg yolks. Then hand-mold the meat mixture into 6 oblong steaks that are ³/₄ in. thick (be careful not to overwork the meat or it will become rubbery!).

Meanwhile, in a large skillet that has a lid, heat 3 tbsp. butter over medium-high heat (but take extra care not to let it burn).

Now add the steaks and brown them gently on both sides until the insides are just barely pink or no longer pink. Transfer them to a warming platter and temporarily set them—*uncovered*—in a 150-degree oven. Now add the remaining butter and the wine to the skillet and gently simmer the mixture until most of the liquid has evaporated.

All that's left now is to whisk together in the skillet the gravy mix and the beef broth and bring it to a simmer (along with the pan drippings) until the gravy is smooth and velvety. Then nestle the hamburger steaks back into the skillet, top them with red onions, ladle on the brown gravy, cover the pan, and smother the steaks over low heat for about 30 minutes until they are fall-apart tender.

The Baby Taters:

Small "A" creamer potatoes
Water or chicken broth
Minced parsley for garnish

Thinly sliced green onions for
garnish

To make baby taters you need to head out to your local farmer's market and hand-pick some of the smallest "A" creamer potatoes you can find (I like them ping-pong-ball size). Then simply slow-poach them in either water or chicken stock until you can pierce them easily with an ice pick.

When you're ready to eat, serve up the steaks with a half-full plate of baby taters, cover it all in gravy, garnish the baby taters with a little parsley and green onions, and dig in!

Chef's Note: To formulate your breadcrumb/oatmeal breading mix, simply take equal parts of toasted French-bread crumbs and old-fashioned oats (which you've processed lightly in a blender) and mix them thoroughly. You can season them and even add grated or shredded Romano or Parmesan cheese. In an airtight plastic container, the mix will keep nicely in the refrigerator for 2-3 weeks.

Frank's Old-Fashioned Homemade Hamburgers

The sad fact is, you have a hard time finding a good old-fashioned hamburger these days! No matter where you go, they always seem to taste like cardboard. So here's my age-old secret family recipe from my childhood days on Tonti Street, when a hamburger was as pure a comfort food and as simple as it could get. Fix some and remember!

¼ cup vegetable oil
1 large onion, minced
1 lb. ground round or ground
  sirloin
Salt and coarse-ground black
  pepper to taste
4 tbsp. softened margarine
4 sesame-seed hamburger buns
8 tbsp. real mayonnaise

4 tbsp. yellow mustard
4 tbsp. catsup
½ cup dill pickle slices
1 medium onion, sliced in rings
1 large tomato, thinly sliced
1 cup shredded lettuce
Ruffled potato chips on the side

First, heat a seasoned griddle or 12-in. nonstick fry pan to about 350 degrees and coat it with the oil. Then, begin sautéing the minced onions, using a spatula to toss them over and over, until they wilt and begin to turn a light honey brown. Now position them in 4 equal portions on the griddle or pan.

In the meantime, separate the ground meat, also into 4 evenly divided portions, and very gently shape them into ovals using your hands. Then, place the 4 portions of ground meat directly on each pile of onions, and push the meat down into the onions with a spatula. In other words, you're forming the hamburger as you go.

At this point, take your time and shape the meat into patties (2 spatulas make this easy to do) and, with the edges of the spatulas, chop the onions into the meat, releasing the onion juices as you cook. Then when each of the hamburgers has cooked on one side, flip it over and cook the opposite side. Ideally, you want to have them come out crusty brown on the outside and finished all the way through.

Finally, in the last few minutes before you're ready to eat, sprinkle each burger with salt and pepper. All that's left is to lightly butter and toast the insides the hamburger buns, dress them with mayo, mustard, catsup, pickles, onion rings, tomatoes, and lettuce, and serve them each with a piping-hot burger as the main ingredient.

It's shades of the good ol' days, especially when served with a stack of crispy chips!

Chef's Note: The best hamburgers are formed right on the hot griddle or fry pan. Burgers get tough and heavy when they're pounded out by hand ahead of time. And under no circumstances should you salt ground round or ground sirloin until the last minute before it's served. Pre-salting draws out all the juices and makes the meat chewy.

Mexican Meatloaf and Cheesy Polenta

Premium ground chuck, medium-hot taco sauce, sweet buttermilk, both Monterey Jack and sharp cheddar cheeses, and chopped cilantro go into this meatloaf *español.* Unlike other meatloaves, this one is not only spicy—it's ultra moist and fall-apart tender and goes exceptionally well with cheesy polenta.

The Meatloaf:

1 lb. ground chuck	1 cup medium-hot taco sauce
1 lb. ground pork	2 large eggs, slightly beaten
2 cups shredded Monterey Jack/cheddar cheese blend	2 tbsp. chopped cilantro
	1 tbsp. minced jalapenos
1 cup plain breadcrumbs	1 tsp. kosher or sea salt
⅔ cup buttermilk	Flour as needed for thickening

Start off by preheating the oven to 350 degrees. Then lightly grease either a small Bundt pan or a 9x5-in. loaf pan and set it aside.

In the meantime, place the ground beef and ground pork into a large mixing bowl. Then in a second mixing bowl thoroughly combine the cheeses, breadcrumbs, buttermilk, taco sauce, eggs, cilantro, jalapenos, and salt. When all the ingredients are uniformly combined, pour them over the beef and pork and, with your hands, work them gently into the meat mixture. Note: make every effort not to overwork the ground meat or it will turn out heavy and dense instead of light and fluffy. When everything is blended, stop mixing!

At this point, transfer the meat mixture to the baking pan you've prepared. Then bake the meatloaf for 1 hour or until it is no longer pink in the center (about 150 degrees on a meat thermometer). When it's done, remove it from the oven, drain off the drippings into a saucepan, and cool the loaf in the pan on a wire rack for about 10 minutes.

To make the gravy, bring the drippings to a boil. Then reduce the heat to medium low and whisk in just enough flour (about 2 level tbsp. is a good place to start) to cause the drippings to thicken after they cook for about 5 minutes or so.

When the loaf is cool enough to handle, remove it from the baking pan, slice it into serving sizes, and top the slices with the rich gravy.

The Polenta:

¼ cup extra-virgin olive oil
6 tbsp. unsalted butter
½ head garlic, roasted
2 cups whole milk
2 cups vegetable stock
¼ cup chopped cilantro
2 tbsp. diced green chilies
¾ cup coarse-ground yellow
  cornmeal

¾ cup canned white corn
Salt and freshly ground black
  pepper to taste
2 cups shredded Monterey
  Jack/cheddar cheese blend
¾ cup grated Parmesan cheese

Start off by heating the oil and butter in a large nonstick saucepan that has a lid (a glass Dutch oven will also do the job nicely). Next, smash and cream the roasted garlic, add it to the saucepan, and sauté it ever so slightly until incorporated into the butter and oil.

At this point, whisk in the milk, vegetable stock, cilantro, and green chilies and bring everything to a boil. Then, in small amounts at a time, add the cornmeal slowly, stirring it continuously to keep it from lumping (I prefer using a wire whisk to get the cooking process started, then switching to a chef's spoon later).

When all the cornmeal is in the pan, stir in the corn, reduce the heat to low, and bring the polenta to a gentle simmer. Now cover the pan and let the mixture simmer for about 20 minutes—*but stir it briskly every few minutes to keep it from scorching and sticking to the pan.* You'll know when it's done because the mixture will become creamy and thick.

All that's left is to remove the pan from heat, add salt and pepper, and stir in the cheeses. Polenta is best when served immediately. Oh, yeah—and be sure to ladle on some of the meatloaf gravy for a little extra zip!

Frank's Mawmaw-Style Cabbage Rolls

If you've lived in New Orleans all your life, you've no doubt eaten your share of cabbage rolls! But these are not just your everyday cabbage leaves stuffed with meat and rice. Mawmaw showed me a long time ago that what makes cabbage rolls special is the combination of seasonings along with the stir-fried cabbage that you mix into the stuffing. If you want a recipe a skosh above the average, try this . . . and enjoy!

1 large head green cabbage	1 tbsp. Worcestershire sauce
1 medium head red cabbage	1 cup concentrated beef stock
1 qt. boiling water	2 cups cooked rice
½ stick margarine	Salt and black pepper to taste
2 tsp. red wine vinegar	(or Frank Davis Beef
1 lb. lean ground beef	Seasoning)
1 lb. lean ground pork	2 cans tomato sauce, 15-oz. size
1 large onion, minced	10-oz. can Rotel tomatoes
6 green onions, thinly sliced	2 tsp. Frank Davis Vegetable
6 cloves garlic, minced	Seasoning
2 ribs celery, minced	¼ cup grated Parmesan cheese
½ tsp. thyme	½ cup shredded provolone
1 tsp. basil	cheese

First, pull off 8-10 large cabbage leaves (you can mix the green and red cabbage to give the dish added color). Then, with a sharp utility knife, meticulously thin out the thickened base of the cabbage leaves. Then place them in the boiling water for about 5 minutes until tender. *But do not overcook them or they will tear apart when you try to stuff them!* When they're ready, lay them out on paper towels and allow them to drain.

Meanwhile, shred the remaining cabbage (both red and green). Then, in a 12-in. skillet, melt the margarine and stir-fry the cabbage. About halfway through the cooking process, add the wine vinegar and cook until most of the pungent aroma is gone. When done (and it should take 8-10 minutes), set the mix aside to cool.

Next, using another 12-in. skillet, sauté the ground beef and pork together until lightly brown. Then toss in the onion, green onions, garlic, celery, thyme, basil and Worcestershire sauce. Continue cooking until the vegetables have wilted. Then, using a strainer, drain off all the excess fat.

Now place the meat mixture back into the skillet, stir in the stir-fried cabbage and the beef stock, and simmer the meat mix until most of the stock evaporates.

At this point, remove the skillet from the heat, mix in the rice, and season with salt and pepper. Then fill each cabbage leaf with about ¼ cup of meat stuffing and roll it up, folding the sides tightly over to the center. When they're all done, place the rolls into a lightly oiled casserole dish.

Then, in the same skillet you used to sauté the meat mix, simmer the tomato sauce and Rotels together, along with the vegetable seasoning, until the mixture turns hot and bubbly and thickens slightly. All that's left is to ladle the sauce over the cabbage rolls, sprinkle them with Parmesan and provolone, and bake them uncovered at 350 degrees for 45 minutes-1 hour.

Chef's Note:

1—As a special technique, I like to bake the rolls lightly covered with a sheet of aluminum foil for the first 30 minutes, then finish the process by baking them uncovered for the last 30 minutes. This produces a moister cabbage roll.

2—I suggest you serve the rolls with a crisp garden salad and a side of crunchy buttered cornbread. Incidentally, any extra stuffing you have left can be simmered into the tomato sauce mixture.

3—These cabbage rolls can be baked in advance and kept in the refrigerator for up to 4 days before serving. They can be reheated in the oven or in the microwave. And they freeze well too!

Frank's Spanish Pan Pies

Start off by browning the ground beef, sautéing the veggies until they're wilted, folding the ground meat into the veggies, and combining and blending in the seasonings. Then begin layering the meat mix and the Spanish blend, preheat the oven, pour on the cornbread batter, and bake until golden brown. This is a hard recipe to beat— Spanish or no Spanish!

Cooking spray
2 lb. ground beef (ground
   chuck preferred)
1 large onion, chopped
1 bunch green onions, thinly
   sliced
1 small green bell pepper,
   chopped
⅓ cup minced parsley
2 tsp. minced garlic
2 cans sliced mushrooms
1 can green chilies, minced
2 tsp. mild chili powder
2 pkg. taco seasoning
1 medium-size jar smooth
   picante sauce
8-oz. can enchilada sauce
8-oz. can taco sauce

1 can cream of chicken soup
1 tbsp. ground cumin
1 tsp. salt
1 tsp. black pepper
¼ cup minced cilantro
2 cans black beans, drained
2 cans garbanzo beans, drained
1 tub cottage cheese
1 lb. grated or shredded
   cheeses
2 pkg. Mexican-style cornbread
   mix, 6-oz. size
2⅔ cup milk
4 eggs
Shredded lettuce for garnish
1 tub sour cream for garnish
Shredded cheese for garnish
   (optional)

Start off by liberally spraying a 5-qt. Dutch oven with cooking spray. Then drop in the ground beef and fry it down over high heat until it becomes thoroughly browned. When it's done, take a slotted spoon, remove the beef from the pot, and set it aside for a while.

Next, in the same pot you used to brown the beef, combine and sauté in the drippings the onions, green onions, bell pepper, parsley, and garlic until the mixture softens (which should take about 4 minutes). Now add the ground beef back to the wilted seasoning vegetables and stir everything together well.

At this point, fold into the meat mix the mushrooms, green chilies, chili powder, taco seasoning, picante sauce, enchilada sauce, taco sauce, soup, cumin, salt, and pepper. Now simmer this mixture very gently over medium-low heat for about 10 minutes, taking time to stir occasionally.

When you're ready to build the "pies," take 2 anodized or Teflon-coated 12-in. skillets (they will need to have oven-safe handles since they'll go into the oven) and spray them liberally with cooking spray. Then begin layering into each skillet all of the ingredients in small batches—meat mixture on the bottom, followed by a sprinkling of cilantro, followed by a thin layer of black beans, followed by a thin layer of garbanzo beans, followed by a thin layer of cottage cheese, and finally by a thin layer of shredded cheese. Then repeat the layers once more in the same order and set the pans aside to "compact and settle" for about 10 minutes while you make the cornbread crown.

Prepare the cornbread batter according to package directions (usually the mix plus $1^1/_3$ cups milk plus 2 eggs, for each package). When fully blended, pour the mixture evenly over the 2 pans of casserole ingredients. Then slide them into a preheated 450-degree oven and bake them uncovered for 30-35 minutes or until the cornbread crown is richly browned.

All that's left now is to place a handful of shredded lettuce on each dinner plate, spoon out the Spanish Pan Pie over the lettuce, drop a hearty dollop of sour cream right on the top, maybe sprinkle with a little extra shredded cheese while still piping hot, and dive in!

Chef's Note:
1—This dish need not be done in skillets. It comes out just as pretty and just as appetizing in a couple of baking pans. And if you're doing this for a church potluck, you can even make 'em in the disposable aluminum kind.

2—This dish is at its best when eaten right out of the oven as soon as it is baked. But it's also pretty tasty the next day when popped into the microwave right out of the fridge.

3—It is not uncommon to have extra filling ingredients left over after building the pan pies. If you find this to be your case, simple combine everything together in a bowl, cover tightly with plastic wrap, and stash in the refrigerator. Then a couple of days later, heat up a half-dozen or so taco shells, dice up a couple of ripe tomatoes, shred a little extra lettuce, and use the "extras" you saved as taco filling.

4—Feel free to either double or halve the recipe. The ingredients listed above will serve 10-12 folks. You can reduce that to 6 by cutting the recipe in half.

Franco's Sloppy Giuseppes

You've heard of "Sloppy Joes," haven't you? Probably grew up on them, right? Well, in my old Italian neighborhood of New Orleans, we never ate Sloppy Joes—we always had "Sloppy Giuseppes." And they were the best! Here's a recipe just like MawMaw usta fix when I was just a kid!

2 lb. ground beef, 86 percent lean
¼ cup extra-virgin olive oil
8 oz. sliced mushrooms
1 cup chopped onions
⅔ cup chopped green bell pepper
1 rib celery, diced
2 tbsp. minced garlic
12-oz. bottle chili sauce
8 oz. tomato sauce
½ cup chicken stock

1 tbsp. brown sugar
1 tsp. chili powder
1 tbsp. Worcestershire sauce
2 tsp. Frank Davis Sicilian Seasoning
½ tsp. salt
¼ tsp. red pepper flakes
2 tbsp. minced parsley
2 pkg. sesame-seed sandwich buns, slightly toasted
4 cups shredded mozzarella

First, in a large skillet, fry down the ground beef over medium-high heat until the meat crumbles and is no longer pink. Then, while it is still hot, pour off and discard any excess rendered-out fat. Set the skillet aside for a while.

In the meantime, take a large Dutch oven, heat the oil, and sauté the mushrooms until they are wilted and tender. Then drop in the onions, bell pepper, celery, and garlic and sauté that mixture until it softens.

When the veggies are ready, stir in the chili sauce, tomato sauce, chicken stock, brown sugar, chili powder, Worcestershire, Sicilian seasoning, salt, and pepper flakes. At this point, add the beef and mix everything together well. Then simmer the pot on very low heat for about 10 minutes, stirring occasionally.

When you're ready to eat, quickly whisk in the parsley, heap some beef mixture over the bottom half of each sandwich bun, sprinkle each with a handful of cheese, and top with the top half of the bun.

Chef's Note:
1—If you prefer, you can first brush both bun halves with mayonnaise, then slather on the meat mix, then "dress" with the cheese, and

top with a thin tomato slice and a torn lettuce leaf. It's what Giuseppe calls "lagniappe."

2—To do a complete "sit-down meal," simply boil a pot of pasta in advance, cool it down, toss it with extra-virgin olive oil, and stash it in the fridge in a large zipper bag. Then when you're ready to eat, all you have to do is zap the pasta and the meat sauce in the microwave, toss 'em together, plate 'em up, and cover each plate with a handful of mozzarella (or even shredded Parmesan). Mangia!

Acadian Boeuf Boulettes
(Old-Time Cajun Meatballs)

If you always thought that meatballs were the exclusive property of Italians, wait until you try this Acadian recipe. These tender beef boulettes, spiced and seasoned to perfection and suspended in a rich brown gravy, are guaranteed to please even the most discriminating gourmands. Served over fluffed rice, with a side of buttered mixed veggies and a piece of crusty French bread to sop up the sauce, Acadian Boeuf Boulettes are destined to become a family favorite.

The Meatballs:

3 lb. lean ground chuck
1 cup minced onions
½ cup minced celery
½ cup minced green bell
  pepper
4 cloves garlic, minced
¼ cup minced parsley
3 eggs

¾ cup French-bread crumbs
1 tbsp. Worcestershire sauce
1 cup whole milk
2 tbsp. Frank Davis Beef
  Seasoning
1 tsp. coarse-ground black
  pepper

First, take a large mixing bowl and put all the ingredients into it. Then work everything together with your hands—a spoon won't give you a uniform mix. Ideally, you want to take your time and create a pliable mixture—not dry, yet not too wet either. Actually, when you can pick out a wad of meat and easily roll it into a boulette the size of a ping-pong ball without it sticking to your hands, you got it right.

When all the boulettes have been formed, place them side by side without touching onto a shallow cookie sheet that's been coated with a cooking spray or lined with a piece of parchment paper. Then slide them into a preheated 450-degree oven to brown. This should take 12-15 minutes. Just don't overcook them. *(Alternative method: if you'd prefer not to bake them you can place the meatballs, a few at a time, into a hot nonstick pan and fry them on top of the stove, rolling them around and around as they sear, until they turn a toasty brown color—which is how the Cajuns do it.)*

The Gravy:

½ cup vegetable oil
½ cup all-purpose flour
1 cup minced onions
½ cup minced celery
½ cup minced green bell
    pepper
4 cloves garlic, minced
⅓ cup minced parsley

4 bay leaves
4-6 cups chicken stock
1 tsp. Kitchen Bouquet
2 tbsp. Frank Davis Beef
    Seasoning
12-oz. can Rotel diced toma-
    toes with chilies
¾ cup thinly sliced green onions

In the meantime, using a 5-qt. Dutch oven, heat the oil to high, but don't let it smoke. Then with a wire whip, stir in the flour and continue to cook it over medium-high heat, stirring constantly, until you form a smooth, dark roux. When the mixture reaches the color you want, remove the pot from the burner and whisk in the seasoning vegetables—*onions, celery, bell pepper, garlic, and parsley*—to flavor the roux and cool it down.

At this point, begin whisking the chicken stock into the roux to form a gravy, stirring it in thoroughly to get the consistency you desire (you may or may not want to add all of the stock). *One word of caution here: if you pour the stock into the pot before the roux has had a chance to cool down, it could splatter and burn you seriously.* This is also the time when you add the bay leaves to the pot.

Now finish up the gravy by stirring in the Kitchen Bouquet, beef seasoning, and tomatoes (including the liquid they came packed in).

Next, remove the browned meatballs from the oven (or the fry pan) and with a pair of tongs submerge them in the gravy. Take care to leave in the pan the excess fat that renders out during the browning stage—*you don't want that in your gravy.* Then reduce the heat under the Dutch oven to low and simmer the meatballs for about 1 hour. This gives the various flavors a chance to marry and serves to tenderize the meat.

When they're done, skim off what little oil floats to the surface during the simmering and serve the meatballs piping hot over a bowl of steamed rice and with a side of buttered mixed veggies. Top off the presentation by garnishing with a sprinkling of green onions.

Chef Note:

1—It's the milk that produces a light and tender meatball. Add as much to the meat mixture as you need (a little at a time) to get a pliable texture that holds the meat and breadcrumbs together.

2—Because you don't want oily gravy, I don't suggest you use regular ground beef in this recipe. Lean ground chuck, round, or sirloin are your ultimate choices.

3—But regardless of what kind of ground beef you use, there will be some oil floating on the gravy once the dish is cooked. To adequately defat it, skim off the excess with a spoon. To completely defat it, refrigerate the meatballs and gravy for several hours, then lift off the solidified fat when it floats to the surface.

4—To get a richer flavor in the gravy, if you're not concerned about fat calories, use the meatball pan drippings instead of vegetable oil to make your roux.

5—Now don't go t' stirrin' the gravy once you put the meatballs in it! You'll break them all up and your dish will resemble a "messy chili." Just let them simmer! They'll be okay!

6—Now don't labor over how to fix the mixed veggies. You simply buy 1 can Veg-All, 1 can whole kernel corn, and 1 can baby lima beans. Then you drain each can of its packing liquid, pour everything into a large bowl, sprinkle with salt and pepper (or a little Frank Davis Vegetable Seasoning), and top with several pats of butter. Heat the mixture either on top of the stove in a skillet or in the microwave in a glass bowl and serve it hot along with the rice and boulettes.

Frank's Classic New Orleans Grits and Liver!
(With Smothered Onions in Brown Gravy!)

When MawMaw made "liver and onions" in New Orleans, this is what you got! Well, maybe not exactly, 'cuz frankly it's not going to be as tantalizingly tasty as this recipe! That's because I got a couple of little tricks I use in the preparation. So let's do this—from this moment on, anytime you get a craving for real New Orleans liver, remember where you stashed this copy!

1 large onion, thinly sliced
1 pt. whole milk
2 lb. calf liver, thinly sliced (about 8 slices)
2 cups + 4 tbsp. all-purpose flour
2 tsp. Frank Davis Beef Seasoning
2 tsp. salt
1 tsp. black pepper
1 cup + 4 tbsp. vegetable oil
3 medium onions, sliced in half-rings
4 cloves garlic, thinly slivered

1 tsp. Kitchen Bouquet
⅓ cup burgundy wine or cocktail sherry
2-4 cups concentrated chicken broth
1 cup Quaker Quick Grits
4 cups water
Salt and black pepper to taste
¼ stick butter
⅛ tsp. Louisiana Hot Sauce
½ cup shredded Velveeta Cheese
½ cup minced parsley

First, find a plastic, glass, or crockery-type container large enough to hold all the liver slices. Then drop into that container about a third of the large sliced onion and half of the milk. Now get ready to make layers—set a single layer of liver (4 slices) on top of the milk and onions; then sprinkle on another layer of onions; then add the second layer of liver on top of the onions. Finally, top off the container with the remaining onions and pour on the remaining milk. Then cover the container tightly and allow the liver to marinate in the refrigerator for at least 4 hours (or preferably overnight).

When you're ready to cook, begin the following steps.

Mix the 2 cups flour with the beef seasoning, 2 tsp. salt, and 1 tsp. black pepper and place the mixture into a shaker can.

Heat the 1 cup oil in a heavy 12-in. skillet over medium-high fire. You're going to use this to fry the liver slices.

Heat the 4 tbsp. oil in a second heavy 12-in. skillet over medium-high fire. Drop the sliced medium onions and the garlic into this skillet and begin caramelizing them (cooking them until they turn a golden brown).

At this point, remove the marinating liver from the refrigerator, discard the milk and onions, and pat the slices dry with a paper towel. Then lay out the slices on a sheet of waxed paper (or freezer wrap) and liberally coat them on both sides with the seasoned flour from the shaker can. *Be generous here—it's the flour that will seal the pores in the liver and keep it crisp on the outside and juicy on the inside as it cooks.* Then as each slice is dusted, shake off the excess flour and place the slice into the skillet containing the 1 cup oil. In the end you want to fry the liver on both sides, trying to turn it only once, until toasty brown and tender. For best results, I suggest you fry only a few slices at a time so that they're not crowded together in the pan. As you remove the fried liver from the skillet, place it on several thicknesses of paper towels on a platter to drain.

While the slices are being fried, keep a close eye on the onion rings—you want them to come out fully browned, but not burned! When they begin to turn a rich dark color, immediately sprinkle over them the 4 tbsp. flour, toss everything together briskly, and cook the combination for approximately 5 minutes (this will actually form the roux that will become your brown gravy).

Next, pour into the onions and roux the Kitchen Bouquet and the burgundy wine, stirring continuously. Follow this by adding to the pan just enough of the chicken broth to give the gravy the consistency you desire—the more you add the thinner the gravy; the less you add the thicker the gravy. When you have it the way you want it, lower the flame, cover the pan, and slowly simmer the gravy and onions until the onions soften and the gravy becomes silky smooth.

While the gravy is mellowing, it's a perfect time to whip up your grits. Cook it according to the package directions, using 4 cups water. When it's cooked, season it with salt, pepper, butter, and cheese.

When you're ready to eat, you can do one of two things:

1. Serve the sliced liver on a dinner plate, liberally covered with gravy and smothered onions, next to a big scoop of grits garnished with parsley; or

2. Take the slices of liver, submerge them in the skillet of smothered onions and brown gravy, put a lid on the skillet, simmer the liver and onions together on low for about 20 minutes, *then serve it all together* next to a big scoop of grits garnished with fresh parsley.

Of course, whichever way you decide to go, a stack of homemade biscuits and a plate of piping-hot, steamed, buttered broccoli will complement the meal.

Chef's Note:

1—Many restaurants (and probably many of your friends) serve beef or pork liver. Usually they are very strong-tasting. Without a doubt, nothing beats "calf" or "veal" for delicateness, so to create the best dishes made with liver, I suggest you purchase these.

2—The flour in the shaker can be covered with plastic wrap, kept in the refrigerator for later use, and used on veal cutlets, chicken, shrimp, and a variety of other foods to be pan-fried.

3—If you'd rather have your liver prepared with an Italian bread-crumb coating as opposed to a flour coating, see the recipe on page 91 of my Frank Davis Cooks Cajun, Creole, and Crescent City *cookbook.*

4—If you can't find my beef seasoning where you shop, you can order it from my Web site (www.frankdavis.com) or by calling 985-643-0027.

5—When frying the liver slices, avoid overcooking them or they will dry out and become tough and chewy.

6—Liver prepared using this method is at its best when served immediately.

Fourth of July Wild Game on the Grill

With all the terrific hunting seasons Louisiana has to offer and with all the harvest from the fields stashed in your deep freezer year 'round, there is really no better time to have a good old-fashioned wild-game feast than on the Fourth of July. Since everything is cooked over an open grill on "the Fourth," it's really easy to marinate a mess of duck breasts, quail, squirrel, rabbit, venison, and whatever else you targeted during the winter hunts and give them their rightful (and tasty) place next to the traditional hot dogs and hamburgers. Here are the tips and tricks you'll need to know.

You'll need to have the following on hand:

1 bottle red wine (I prefer Merlot). This is a mainstay ingredient in marinating heavy-bodied wild game, such as venison, moose, elk, bear, goose, duck, adult rabbit, and adult squirrel. Blended with extra-virgin olive oil, Italian salad dressing, my wild game seasoning, and your favorite herbs and spices, this ingredient tends to bring together all the essential flavors of the marinade while serving to tenderize the meat and keep it moist while cooking.

1 bottle white wine. This is a mainstay ingredient in marinating lighter forms of wild game, such as teal, rail, gallinule, snipe, dove, quail, pheasant, nutria, young squirrels, and yearling rabbits. Blended with extra-virgin olive oil, Italian salad dressing, my wild game seasoning, and your favorite herbs and spices, this ingredient tends to bring together all the essential flavors of the marinade while serving to tenderize the meat and keep it moist while cooking.

1 bottle bourbon. This ingredient makes a suitable and rather earthy substitute for wine in many marinades. Blend it with extra-virgin olive oil, Italian dressing, and your favorite herbs and spices to create a whole new flavor in your grilled meats (and it's excellent as a marinade for steaks).

2 tbsp. minced garlic. This should be incorporated into every marinade formula you put together.

1 bottle Italian salad dressing (I like the Greek vinaigrette). This is the principal mainstay ingredient in most oil-based marinades. Use it alone as a quick flavoring agent or actually "steep" the game in the dressing overnight to give the flavor intensity.

2 tsp. coarse-ground black pepper. This should be in every marinade you make for wild game, regardless of the species.

1 lb. bacon, slab or strips. This is essential for wrapping around dove, quail, pheasant, and squirrel to give an ordinarily dry piece of meat extra flavor and moisture as it grills. Pieces of bacon can be inserted into venison, moose, elk, and bear steaks and chops to keep them juicy as they grill.

1 qt. whole milk. This is the one ingredient you use as a pre-marinade all by itself to (1) remove the unwanted "gamy" taste of wild game and (2) tenderize the game meat to a delicate texture. The lactic acid does the trick. After wild game is marinated in milk, the game should be patted dry with paper towels then placed into a "flavor marinade" to ready the meat for cooking.

1 bottle Frank Davis Garlic Cayenne Hot Sauce. This adds a little extra "kick" to whichever flavor marinade you concoct. It's best if added "to taste."

1 bottle Frank Davis Wild Game Seasoning. This is the only pre-blended mix that is especially formulated just for seasoning wild game, from ducks to deer and everything in between. If you can't find it where you shop, you can order it online from www.frank-davis.com or by calling 985-643-0027.

2 cups chopped seasoning vegetables. Essentially, these are onions, celery, green bell pepper, parsley, green onions, and garlic already chopped and packaged. You need this mirepoix in some of your marinades and its use is mandatory in special sauces.

1 bottle Masterpiece BBQ sauce. This is the barbecue sauce I prefer for final bastings on all my wild game creations on the grill. Of course, if you prefer another brand, knock yourself out!

1 bottle olive oil. Of course, "extra-virgin olive oil" is the assumed standard. In my opinion, it is impossible to make a flavor marinade for any kind of wild game without the infusion of extra-virgin olive oil, even when Italian salad dressing is used as the base. A little "extra" extra-virgin always makes it better. The olive oil also serves to provide the "good fat" that sweetens up wild game and helps the meat retain moisture as it cooks over dry heat.

1 bottle light soy sauce. Soy is one of many extra flavors that can be added to a marinade to pique the taste of wild game. Because of the high salt content of soy sauce, however, you should be discriminating in how much is used.

1 bottle balsamic vinegar. Balsamic vinegar is another flavoring that can be added to your marinade to give it depth and intensity. Actually, balsamic vinegar should be the only vinegar you ever use to make a game marinade. Grandpaw would probably disagree, but all the other vinegars you find in the grocery stores might best be reserved only for window washing.

1 pastry brush. This is used at the end of the grilling process to spread on any prepared barbecue sauce you may want to use as a final dressing, or for dabbing on a small amount of marinade that you may have reserved for the final presentation.

1 bag alderwood or oak shavings. These are outstanding woods for lending a smoky taste to grilled wild game. The shavings can be placed in an aluminum pie pan over hot coals, burned inside a smoke-box on a barbecue pit, or placed on the bottom of the drip pan that goes into a stovetop smoker. The general consensus is that hickory and mesquite are a tad harsh for grilled wild game.

2 aluminum pie plates. These can be used for (1) holding the wood shavings for smoking and (2) catching whatever drips from the wild game as it cooks on the grate (which keeps the flames from flaring up and burning the game).

6 aluminum pans. These are what you place the cooked game in after they come off the grill. Because this is "outdoor cooking," disposable products rank highly amongst those who would ordinarily have to do the dishes after the barbecue.

1 box toothpicks. These are ideal for pinning strips of bacon around rabbit, squirrel, quail, doves, duck breasts, and venison back strap.

1 injector needle. This is a really good way to infuse a piece of wild game with marinade or flavoring. It can also be used to inject olive oil into wild game to keep it moist and juicy while cooking.

1 stovetop smoker. This is a good method of smoking wild game if you don't have a barbecue grill. Smokers are sprinkled with moist wood shavings,

1 box gal.-size Ziploc bags. This is the only container you should use for marinating wild game (or anything else for that matter). Instead of mixing your marinade and pouring it over the wild game pieces in a glass pan, a Corningware dish, or the inside crockery from your Crockpot, simply place the game into a Ziploc bag, pour the marinade down inside the bag, seal the zipper lock, and flip the bag over and over to evenly distribute the marinade. Then stash the whole works in the fridge for several hours or overnight. When you're ready to grill, remove the meat from the bag and discard both the old marinade and the bag. Voila!

Basic Flavor Marinade for Most Wild Game:

1 small bottle Italian salad dressing	1 tbsp. Frank Davis Wild Game Seasoning
1 cup red or white wine	2 tbsp. coarse-ground black pepper
2 tbsp. minced fresh garlic	⅓ cup extra-virgin olive oil
1 tsp. Worcestershire sauce	

Place all the ingredients except the oil into a blender and turn the controls to mid-range. Then, when the mixture is well incorporated, begin adding the oil in a thin stream until an emulsion forms. Pour only as much marinade as you need over the game in a Ziploc bag and save the remainder in a Mason jar—*uncontaminated!*—in your refrigerator for later use. It will keep for about 2 weeks.

Roasted Venison Back Strap in a Black Pot

So home-style it could almost be called "camp cooking," this is one venison recipe you're gonna want to make whether you're at home or at the camp. It tastes downright delectable, even if you've convinced yourself you'll never eat venison!

2 venison back straps	6 cloves garlic, minced
1 qt. whole milk	¾ cup bottled water
4 tbsp. Frank Davis Wild Game Seasoning	¾ cup hearty burgundy wine
⅓ cup peanut oil	4 tbsp. Worcestershire sauce
1 heaping cup diced yellow onions	½ cup prepared barbecue sauce
	1 cup chicken stock
	4 cups cooked brown rice

First, trim away every bit of visible fat and sinew from the back straps, place them into a glass or plastic container, and cover them with the milk. Ideally, you should soak them in the milk overnight in the refrigerator (covered tightly); but if you're rushed, you can shorten the marinating time to a minimum of 3 hours.

After they've been marinated, remove the back straps from the milk (you throw the milk away!), pat them dry with several paper towels, and sprinkle them thoroughly with the wild game seasoning.

Meanwhile, in a heavy cast-iron (or heavy club aluminum) Dutch oven that has a lid, heat the oil to high and toss in the onions. Then, stirring constantly, cook them until they turn a rich brown color. Just before they're ready, drop in the garlic and cook it into the onions *(but don't let it burn!)*.

Now you're ready to begin what the Cajuns call "pot-frying."

With the heat still on high, drop in the back straps and stir them around in the onion-flavored oil until they begin to brown. Almost immediately, mix together the water, wine, and Worcestershire, and a little at a time begin adding it to the pot-frying venison. Note: you don't want to make gravy here! You just want to add enough water/wine to create a steaming effect—you just want the back straps to "fry." And by the way, this part of the procedure is done with the pot *uncovered.*

When all the water/wine has been added, stir the barbecue sauce into the chicken stock and slowly begin adding that mixture to the venison in the pot. The correct procedure for getting the flavor to intensify is to add a little stock, stir everything together, and cook it for about 1 minute. Then cover the pot and cook everything again for another 1-2 minutes. Keep repeating this process until all the stock is used. This entire cooking process—and you will have to stand at the stove to actively cook this dish—takes 1-1¹/₂ hours.

When the venison is tender (and it should begin to fall apart if you've done it right), transfer the meat to a serving platter and place it into a warming oven. At this point you can do one of two things— you can either serve the resultant gravy that forms in the bottom of the pot as is over brown rice, or you can make even more gravy by thinning it out slightly with some canned chicken broth. Either way, it's wonderful!

Chef's Note:
1—The marinating process both tenderizes the meat and helps remove any unwanted "gamy" flavor.
2—Frank Davis Wild Game Seasoning may be obtained by calling 985-643-0027 or by going to the Web site www.frankdavis.com.
3—I like to serve this dish with brown rice because it imparts a nutty flavor to the pan gravy. But if you prefer to use white rice, there's certainly no reason why you can't. Oh—and a cold crisp salad is the only other thing you'll need to round out the meal.

Deep-Fried Country Wabbit

Marinate a couple of young wild rabbits in milk and onions, dust them with a spicy flour coating, and deep-fry them until they're golden brown and crunchy-crispy. What you end up with is a savory delicacy that you'll be able to smell all over the neighborhood!

2-3 wild marsh rabbits, skinned, dressed, and cut into pieces	2 tsp. Frank Davis Wild Game Seasoning
2 cups coarsely chopped onions	2 tbsp. kosher salt
2 cups skim or evaporated milk	2 tsp. cayenne pepper
2 tsp. Frank Davis Garlic Cayenne Hot Sauce	2 tsp. coarse-ground black pepper
1 qt. peanut oil for deep-frying	1 egg, slightly beaten
3 cups all-purpose flour	1 cup half-and-half
	1 cup water

First, take the rabbits and wash them thoroughly under cold running water, making sure you remove all the globular fat, mucus, and other residuals that may not have been removed during processing. Then, after they've been cleaned, set them into a glass, Corningware, or stainless-steel bowl.

At this point sprinkle the onions over the pieces and immediately mix them in with your hands so that each piece picks up the flavor of the onions. Then blend together the skim milk and the hot sauce and pour it over the rabbits and onions to form a marinade. If you can allow the pieces to marinate overnight, that's ideal. If not, be sure to let them soak in the marinade for at least 3 hours.

When you're ready to fry, heat the peanut oil to 400 degrees in an electric skillet or to 350 degrees in a Dutch oven. Then pour the flour into a gal.-size zipper bag and sprinkle in the game seasoning, salt, cayenne, and black pepper (it's important to take a moment to blend everything uniformly to disperse the seasonings throughout the coating). Then whisk together the egg, cream, and water.

All that's left is to lift each rabbit piece from the marinade, pat it dry with paper towels, dip it into the egg wash, liberally dust it in the coating mix, shake off the excess flour, and drop it into the hot oil. You'll find that the pieces will come out just perfect if you allow them to fry for 12-16 minutes. The outside should be crispy and golden brown, the inside should be light and delicately tender from the onion marinade, and each bite should be rich with natural juices!

Chef's Note:

1—Electric deep-fryers are good, but for best results I recommend a black cast-iron Dutch oven. It distributes the heat evenly, cooks the rabbit uniformly, and doesn't give you "hot spots" that will burn the batter. Of course, if you don't have cast iron, club aluminum or Magnalite is a good second choice.

2—The only way to get perfectly fried rabbit (or quail, or chicken, or shrimp, or anything for that matter!) is to be sure the temperature of the oil is perfect. And to do that you got to use a thermometer—you can't guess at it. Clip it to the side of the Dutch oven so that the tip doesn't rest on the bottom, and be sure it reaches the recommended temperature before you drop in the first piece. Do it this way and you'll be guaranteed that your rabbit won't be greasy!

3—I suggest you serve the rabbit piping hot right from the deep-fryer after draining it for a moment or two on several layers of paper towels.

Down da Bayou Cajun Primavera

The Italians do it in New Orleans with pasta and a myriad of cut vegetables sautéed in olive oil! But when the Cajuns do it down on the bayou they substitute rice for the pasta, throw in a little sausage so their taste buds will pass a good time, and cover it all with a gravy made from the pot drippings! Tell you what—Cajun or Italian, you just gotta try this one, *mes amis!*

2 cups raw long-grain rice
1 qt. lightly salted water
2 lb. smoked sausage links, cut in 3-in. pieces
1 qt. unsalted water
4 tbsp. extra-virgin olive oil
4 tbsp. margarine
2 cups diced smoked sausage
1 cup diced onions
1 cup diced portabello mushrooms
⅓ cup julienned sundried tomatoes
⅓ cup chopped zucchini
⅔ cup diced bell pepper, red, green, and yellow mixed

⅓ cup quartered artichoke hearts
⅓ cup broccoli florets
⅓ cup cauliflower florets
⅓ cup snow peas
⅓ cup julienned carrots
⅓ cup diced eggplant
½ tsp. crushed red pepper flakes
2 tsp. Frank Davis Vegetable Seasoning
½ cup chicken stock (optional)
3 tbsp. cornstarch
1 tsp. Kitchen Bouquet
½ cup sliced green onions for garnish

First, boil the rice in the salted water until it becomes tender and separates grain for grain (which should take about 14 minutes). Then strain it in a colander and set it aside. In the meantime, drop the sausage links into the unsalted water in a second pot, bring the pot to a boil, then turn down the heat immediately and let the links simmer for about 30 minutes.

Next, take a heavy 12-in. skillet that has a lid, heat the oil and margarine, and sauté the diced sausage, onions, and mushrooms until they totally wilt. Then immediately begin adding the remaining vegetables, one at a time. As you drop them into the skillet, toss and stir them briskly to make sure they are thoroughly blended with the onions and mushrooms. When all the produce is in the pan, sprinkle in the red pepper flakes and vegetable seasoning, cover the pan with a lid, and cook everything together over a low fire for 4-5 minutes (tossing the mix every now and then) until the vegetables are hot and tender crisp. If you find that you need a little extra steam to get the veggies going, go ahead and add some chicken stock as needed. *Note: just don't overcook the vegetables or they'll turn to mush!*

At this point, remove the sausage links from the poaching liquid and set them aside on a platter. Then turn the fire under the liquid up to high and reduce the stock to about half of its original volume (about a pint). When the stock has become concentrated, mix the cornstarch with a little cold water and gradually stir it into the stock. As it comes back to a boil, it will thicken and transform itself into a gravy. To finish it off, simply stir in the Kitchen Bouquet.

When you're ready to eat, turn up the fire under the veggies once more, spoon in the rice, and mix everything together well (it will look almost like a vegetable casserole). All that's left is to spoon out the hot rice and veggies onto dinner plates, ladle on some of the sausage gravy, and top each dish with a link or two of poached sausage.

Garnish the primavera with green onions. A dish of beet salad dressed with onions, extra-virgin olive oil, and balsamic vinegar makes a nice side accompaniment.

Oh—and a CD playing the strains of "Jolie Blonde" in the background wouldn't hurt!

Chef's Note:

1—If you prefer to cook in smaller servings, it's perfectly okay to prepare this dish in two batches. Just separate all the ingredients in half and make the recipe twice.

2—To tenderize the sundried tomatoes, you can soak them for a few minutes in about $1/2$ cup warm water. But if you prefer them somewhat chewy, all that's really necessary is to sauté them in the hot olive oil.

3—The skin should be left on the eggplant when you dice it. But to remove some of the "bite" on older specimens, you should remove the majority of the seeds, sprinkle the diced pieces lightly with salt, and allow them to rest for about 15 minutes in a bowl before you cook them (the salt sweats out much of the oxalic acid in the eggplant, which is responsible for the so-called "bite").

4—If you like your veggies tender crisp, you can sauté them in the skillet fully raw and unprocessed. If, on the other hand, you prefer them slightly softer, I suggest you quickly blanch the broccoli, cauliflower, snow peas, carrots, and eggplant before adding them to the sautéing skillet.

5—You can get more information about my preblended seasonings by checking out www.frankdavis.com.

Frank's Sausage, Peppers, Onions, and Buns

A great, light, easy-to-fix summertime meal (as well as a hearty, down-to-earth, stick-to-your-ribs wintertime supper), this is one of those N'Awlins neighborhood concoctions you can make anytime. It is also one that is sure to be appreciated by each and every member of the family, regardless of how simple or sophisticated their tastes. I recommend whipping this up at your very first opportunity!

2 lb. smoked sausage (Cajun, pork, beef, or kielbasa)	¼ tsp. salt
4 tbsp. butter or margarine	¼ tsp. black pepper
2 medium white or Vidalia onions, sliced into rings	¼ tsp. Frank Davis Sprinkling Spice
2 medium green bell peppers, sliced into rings	Pinch red pepper flakes
	Hotdog buns
	Mayonnaise
	Brown and yellow mustard

First, cut the sausage into 5-in. pieces. Actually, since they will be served on hotdog buns, if you can find "bun-size sausages," use them instead of full links or rope. I know that Bryan, Ball Park, and Oscar Mayer all produce several kinds of bun-size links, so you might want to look for those brands in your grocery store.

When you're ready to cook, take a large stockpot or Dutch oven that has a lid and bring to a boil enough water to cover the sausages. Then drop in the sausages, cover the pot tightly, and let them poach for approximately 30 minutes or until they become skin-popping tender. When they're ready, remove them from the water, let them drain, and allow them to cool to room temperature.

In the meantime, take a heavy 12-in. skillet that has a lid, melt the butter or margarine on medium-low heat, and drop in the onions and bell peppers. Toss the veggies together well; then cover the skillet. Stir the mixture occasionally until both the peppers and the onions become tender and begin to brown ever so slightly. Once they soften, sprinkle in the salt, pepper, sprinkling spice, and red pepper flakes.

At this point, remove the veggies from the skillet and set them aside on a warming platter. Then add the sausages to the skillet and fry them (agitating the pan constantly) until they turn a golden brown.

Finally, nestle the sausages into hotdog buns that have been slathered with mayonnaise and mustard. Top each off with a heaping helping of onions and bell peppers.

Chef's Note:

1—Regardless of what kind of sausage you decide to use, be sure you allow enough time to adequately boil them prior to browning them in the skillet. The boiling will serve to "temper" the sausages and make them extra tender. Just remember that you need to use smoked sausage in this recipe, not a raw product.

2—If you have trouble finding Vidalia onions, you can substitute Texas Sweets or even regular ol' white onions in their place.

3—A saucer of super-crispy French fries best accompanies these sausages and buns. The best way to prepare them is to heat enough peanut oil in a large heavy skillet to "deep-fry" them. Then drop in either fresh-cut or frozen shoestring-style potatoes and cook them at 400 degrees until they turn extra crispy and crunchy. When you remove them from the skillet, drain them on several layers of paper towels and serve them immediately.

N'Awlins Salsiccia Medley
(A Tasty Sausage Medley)

Imagine a stack of *salsiccia* (that's "sausages," for all you non-Italians), smothered down in a pile of sautéed yellow, red, and green bell peppers and sliced onion rings until the entire panful is richly caramelized and golden brown, then stuffed inside yet another stack of French pistolette-style breads. Mmm! Now you're not gonna tell me that even just the description doesn't make you hungry!

⅓ cup extra-virgin olive oil
½ stick unsalted butter
3 jumbo onions, sliced into half-rings
3 large green bell peppers, sliced
3 large red bell peppers, sliced
3 large yellow bell peppers, sliced
2 tsp. Frank Davis Sicilian Seasoning
1 tsp. kosher or sea salt
½ tsp. coarse-ground black pepper

2 tbsp. minced garlic
3 lb. Italian sausage links (10-12 links average)
½ cup Swanson's or Campbell's chicken broth
¼ cup white wine
12 French pistolettes, oven browned
¼ cup chopped parsley for garnish
1 cup grated Parmesan cheese

First, take a heavy 12-in. aluminum skillet that has a lid and heat the oil and butter together until the butter sizzles. Then, after turning the heat up to high, cook the onions and bell peppers together—a few at a time!—until the mixture wilts slightly and the onions begin to caramelize (they'll turn a rich golden brown). Note that if you over-load the skillet, the veggies will "sweat" instead of "caramelizing." *You don't want that to happen!*

At this point, remove the peppers and onions from the skillet and set them aside for a while. But first, sprinkle them with the Sicilian seasoning, salt, and pepper and fold in garlic.

Next, put the same skillet back on the fire and once again turn up the flame to high. Then, in order, drop in the sausage links, pour in the broth, and pour in the wine.

When the liquids come to a slow bubble, reduce the heat to medium and simmer the sausages—turning them frequently—until no more (or at least very little) liquid remains in the pan. Rolling them over and over at this point will cause them to brown nicely.

When they're the right color, all nice and toasty looking, all you do then is top them with the onions and peppers—just put everything together in the skillet. Then, either by flipping the pan or by using a spatula and folding the ingredients over each other a few times, nestle the sausages, onions, and peppers together, put the lid on the skillet, turn down the heat to low, and simmer the dish until it's piping hot and the flavors marry (or place the pan of sausages and veggies—*uncovered*—into a 350-degree oven and bake them until the flavors marry).

When you're ready to eat, stuff each pistolette with a sausage link and dress it out with a generous scoop of onions and peppers. All that's left then is to garnish the filling with a little parsley and douse it with Parmesan and you got yourself one of those meals that are almost impossible to equal!

Chef's Note:

1—Be sure to use both the oil and the butter—do not eliminate either one to save on fat or calories. Flavor is critical in this recipe and you need the combination of olive oil and butter to produce that flavor.

2—Let me emphasize that the onions and peppers, as well as the sausages, initially are cooked uncovered in this recipe. If you cover either of them you "sweat" them; that means you lose the beautiful rich color as well as the crispiness of the vegetables, and you drive all the moisture out of the sausages. Of course, towards the end of the cooking process, it is okay to cover the skillet when you're "marrying" all the ingredients together.

3—Don't foul up and add the garlic to the onions while the onions are cooking. The garlic needs to go in after the onions and peppers come off the fire, to keep the caramelization sweet. Garlic fried down with the onions and peppers could cause the mixture to become bitter should the garlic scorch!

4—For detailed information on sausages and sausage making, you can always talk with master butcher Pete Giovenco at 504-469-4369. And if you can't find Sicilian seasoning where you shop, simply visit my Web site at www.frankdavis.com or call 985-643-0027.

5—It's a good idea to prick the sausages with the tip of a knife or a sharp fork before you cook them. This procedure keeps the casings from popping and splattering drippings all over as they simmer. And yes—if you don't have time to actually stand there at the stove and cook the sausages in a skillet, you can always cook them in the oven. Simply place them into a baking pan, pour in enough water to cover the sausages about halfway up, and bake them uncovered at 375 degrees for about 1 hour (or until the links are a beautiful golden brown).

6—There are a number of white wines that will work with this dish, but I like the results I get with cocktail sherry or Chablis. Both of these produce the subtle flavor you want.

7—This is another one of those dishes that is no less than wonderful the next day! Oh, it's good right when it comes from the pan; but allow it to marinate in the fridge overnight and whoa . . . !

Pan-Smothered Creole Hot Sausage

This is an exercise in culinary simplicity!

3 tbsp. water	Mayonnaise
3 lb. Creole hot sausage links	Yellow mustard
12 French pistolettes	

Take a large 12- or 14-in. cast-iron skillet with a tight-fitting lid (you can use heavy club aluminum if you absolutely must!), place it on the stovetop over a medium-high heat, and sprinkle the inside of the pan with the water. Now take the sausage links and, starting in the center of the pan, begin laying them down in concentric circles, filling up the skillet to its outer rim. At this point, place the lid on the skillet and let the sausages begin to smother.

When a red-colored spicy liquid begins to accumulate in the skillet (that's actually fat and cayenne pepper!), reduce the fire to medium low, take a basting bulb, and begin removing the drippings. *You don't want to leave any of it in the skillet with the links; otherwise the links won't smother or brown—they'll just boil in the juices.*

Oh—and to render out the maximum amount of excess fat, it is also a good idea to prick the links with an ice pick in several places.

When the sausages are done, which should take about 20 minutes of slow simmering with the pan covered, uncover the pan, completely remove the last of the drippings, brown the links uniformly all over, and serve them piping hot inside freshly baked pistolettes, dressed with mayonnaise and mustard. (Hint: if you want to add the coup de grace, you should also dress each hot sausage sandwich with a half-handful of minced lettuce and tomatoes.)

Bratwursts Poached in Beer

Here's the newest N'Awlins sausage that's really catching on!

4 cans regular beer
3 medium onions, coarsely chopped
3 lb. fresh bratwursts (Johnsonville recommended)
¼ cup melted butter or extra-virgin olive oil

12 French pistolettes
German-style or garlic mustard
Yellow mustard
Mayonnaise
1 large Spanish onion, coarsely chopped
1 cup thinly sliced green onions

First, pour the beer into a heavy, high-sided skillet or fry pan that has a lid, drop in the 3 chopped onions, and bring everything to a gentle boil. Then pierce the brats just once with a fork and drop them into the beer stock (overpiercing will cause the casings to split wide open). Now simmer the sausages, partially covered, for 15 minutes or until they start to swell.

Then, using a pair of tongs, remove the brats from the poaching liquid, place them on a hot grill (or into a hot "grill pan"), and turn them over and over until they become a toasty brown. While they're cooking, liberally butter the pistolettes and place them buttered side down on the grill as well (to toast).

When you're ready to eat, serve each brat on a hot pistolette right off the grate, slathering the link generously with German mustard, yellow mustard, a splash of mayonnaise, a fistful of chopped Spanish onions, and a sprinkling of green onions.

Chef's Note:

1—Bratwursts are fresh pork sausages whose origins date back to Old Germany. They should always be cooked slowly so that the casings do not burst.

2—To get a nice toasty glaze on the brats as they grill, you might want to brush them down with a little extra melted butter or extra-virgin olive oil.

3—Use only regular beer (not dark brew or light beer) when poaching brats or any other sausage. And as soon as the poaching process is done, discard the beer.

Frank's Italian Sausage Rounds
(With Roman Roasted Eggplant)

Actually, we're talking about nothing more than a bunch of pan-roasted meatballs that Pete Giovenco makes out of his Italian sausage mix, served with a casserole of oven-roasted eggplants, fresh tomatoes, and Italian cheeses toasted under the broiler! Mama mia!

7 tbsp. extra-virgin olive oil
1 tbsp. salt and black pepper
3 large eggplants
1 large tomato, minced
⅓ cup sliced green onions
⅓ cup minced parsley
Frank Davis Sicilian Seasoning
   to taste

Frank Davis Sprinkling Spice
   to taste
¾ cup grated Parmesan cheese
¾ cup shredded Romano cheese
1 tbsp. butter or margarine
1 dozen Pete's Italian Sausage
   Rounds
Saltine crackers

First, preheat the oven to 400 degrees.

Then take a heavy, shallow, aluminum sheet pan and brush it liberally with 2 tbsp. oil. When the oil is spread evenly over the bottom of the pan, generously sprinkle the salt and pepper atop the oil and set the pan aside momentarily.

Now take the eggplants, trim away the stems, and halve them lengthwise. Then place them cut side down on the sheet pan and slide the pan into the oven. At this point, you want to bake the eggplant halves—uncovered—for 45 minutes or until an ice pick easily pierces the vegetable through and through.

When the eggplants are tender, remove them from the oven, allow them to cool just enough to handle, and then scrape all the pulp away from the skin. Now coarsely chop the pulp and transfer it to a large mixing bowl, along with 3 tbsp. oil, the tomato, half the green onions, half the parsley, Sicilian seasoning, and sprinkling spice.

At this stage, fold in the Parmesan so that it mixes uniformly and binds with the eggplant. Then transfer the mix to a lightly buttered 10x12 glass baking dish. All that's left, then, is to sprinkle Romano evenly over the casserole, slide the dish into the oven once again (but this time under the 500-degree broiler), and flash cook the top until the cheese is beautifully browned and crusted.

While the eggplant is finishing up, it's time to cook the sausage rounds. Place a heavy 12-in. nonstick skillet on the stovetop over a medium-high flame and add to it 1 tbsp. oil. When the oil gets hot, drop in half of the meatballs and roll them around and around by agitating the pan, searing and pan-roasting them as they cook. When they're done, remove them from the skillet, add in the last tbsp. oil, along with the last 6 meatballs, and repeat the procedure.

When it's time to eat, serve 2 "rounds" per person on a warmed dinner plate, alongside a heaping portion of the eggplant casserole. Garnish with the remaining green onions and parsley. A stack of buttered crackers makes a nice accompaniment.

Chef's Note:

1—Pete's Italian Sausage Rounds are really meatballs made from his special Italian sausage blend. It consists of pork, a textured vegetable protein binder, a proportioned amount of dried Italian seasonings, salt and pepper for spice, and just enough water to create a stiff meat paste sufficient to roll the blend into small "meatballs." If you'd prefer not to make them yourself from scratch, you can order them already vacuum packed directly from Pete by calling 504-469-4369.

2—You can feel free to reduce the quantities of a number of the spices and seasonings (or even add more if you care to) in order to suit your taste.

3—If you want to intensify the tomato's flavor, premix it with half the green onions and parsley and allow the combination to rest in the refrigerator for about 3 hours prior to using it.

4—The eggplant dish may be prepared in advance, kept in the refrigerator for 1-2 days, then put into the oven and "baked" uncovered instead of cooking it under the broiler.

5—Instead of pan-broiling the meatballs on top of the stove, you can opt to set them on an oiled sheet pan into which you add about ¼ cup water, and oven roast them for about 45 minutes until tender. This eliminates having to stand at the stove to carefully watch the meatball browning process.

Glenn and Leah's Authentic Homemade Cajun Boudin

When it comes to Cajun boudin, there's no middle of the road—it's either great or it's bad! Well, the recipe sitting before you is one of those great ones. The flavorings, the texture of the rice, the lack of any liver taste, the finest pork available . . . it all results in a really great boudin. And here's how you make it!

¾ gal. water
2 lb. boneless pork
2 lb. pork bones
1 lb. pork liver
2 onions, minced
½ green bell pepper, minced
¾ tbsp. salt
¾ tbsp. cayenne pepper

¾ tbsp. black pepper
½ tbsp. garlic powder
2 tbsp. cornstarch
1 cup cold water
1 bunch green onion tops, thinly sliced
6 cups cooked rice
25 feet sausage casing

First, take a 16-qt. stockpot that has a lid and pour in the water. Then bring the water to a rapid boil and drop in the pork, bones, liver, onions, bell pepper, salt, cayenne pepper, black pepper, and garlic powder. When the water comes back to a full boil, reduce the heat to a "slow bubble," put the lid on the pot, and cook everything together for at least 2 hours (adding more water as it evaporates) or until the meats are extremely tender.

When the meats are done, strain out all the ingredients from the stock and set them aside to cool; *but bring the water back to a boil.* Then take the cornstarch and dissolve it in the cold water. When the stock is once again at a rolling boil, stir in the cornstarch/water mixture to thicken the stock.

Meanwhile, remove all the meat from the bones and combine it with the boneless pork and the seasoning vegetables used to make the stock. Then, with a large chef's knife, mince the meats and vegetables together. When they're uniform, spoon everything back into the cooking stock—*but immediately take the pot off the fire!*

Now stir in the green onions and fold in the rice. What you end up with resembles a moist "dirty rice" and is technically ready to be eaten as it is. But for it to become a traditional Cajun boudin, it has got to be stuffed into a casing. A sausage stuffer works best, but a sausage funnel will also get the job done. Ideally you want to end up with links 6-8 in. long.

This recipe will yield about 8 lb. boudin. It can be refrigerated or frozen for future use or it can be served immediately.

Most Cajuns simply simmer the links in hot water for 5 minutes or so before they eat it. But I think it's best when it's either grilled or baked in a 350-degree oven until the casing become slightly crisp.

Chef's Note: This boudin is a signature dish of Glenn and Leah Mistich. Hundreds of pounds of it is prepared and sold every day at their Gourmet Butcher Block meat market in Terrytown.

Ish's Fourth of July Barbecued Ribs

These lean pork spareribs are parboiled to ensure tenderness, then coated with a rich barbecue sauce and baked slowly in the oven until they reach fall-off-the-bone delicateness. Serve them with tiny creamer potatoes that are topped with clarified butter, spiced with vegetable seasoning, then oven roasted until crusty brown. And add a totally refreshing cucumber, bell pepper, tomato, and onion salad covered with a balsamic vinaigrette. Now you got what my ol' buddy Ish Taylor says is one of those all-American menus that's guaranteed to bring home the taste of "The Fourth."

5 lb. lean pork spareribs	1 cup vegetable mirepoix
5 tbsp. Frank Davis Pork Seasoning	10 cloves garlic, peeled
2 gal. water	4 cups Hunt's Original Recipe Barbecue Sauce

First, place the slab of ribs on a cutting board on the countertop, remove the silverskin from the back side, and with a sharp knife split the slab into individual ribs. When they've all been sliced, put them into the sink, sprinkle the pork seasoning evenly over them, and toss them thoroughly, making sure that each and every rib is completely and uniformly coated.

In the meantime, bring the water to a rapid boil and add to it the mirepoix. Then drop in the seasoned ribs and the cloves of garlic, bring the water back to a gentle roll, and parboil the meat and garlic for about 30 minutes (almost to the point of the pork starting to fall off the bones). *Oh, yeah—I also recommend you parboil with the pot lid barely in place so that excess steam can escape.*

When the ribs are done, remove them from the pot with a pair of tongs and place them on a platter to cool. Then pour the barbecue sauce into a large bowl and, one by one, with the tongs, *dip* each rib into the sauce to coat it completely. Quickly, without letting the excess sauce drip off, transfer the ribs to a large baking pan. (*Hint: the dish gets even richer if you also pour a little extra sauce over the ribs once they're in the pan!*)

Ideally, you want to cover the pan tightly with heavy-duty aluminum foil and stash it in the refrigerator for the meat to marinate (preferably overnight). Then when you're ready to eat, put the pan—*still tightly covered*—into a 350-degree oven and bake the ribs for 30 minutes or until they turn all hot and bubbly.

When they're ready, serve them piping hot alongside a dish of roasted potatoes. A chilled cucumber, tomato, onion, and bell pepper salad, dressed with an olive oil and balsamic vinegar vinaigrette, rounds everything out into a true, finger-lickin' holiday favorite.

Chef's Note:

1—If you prefer to substitute pork finger ribs, baby backs, or even beef ribs for the spareribs, go right ahead and do so. And there are no changes to be made in the recipe if you decide to make the switch.

2—Depending upon the size and shape of the boiling pot, it may take a little more or a little less than 2 gal. water to cover the ribs. Just make the adjustment accordingly.

3—If you're a garlic lover, don't forget you can retrieve the softened garlic pods from the boiling stock and serve them as an accompaniment to the ribs.

4—It is essential that the ribs reach room temperature before dipping them into the barbecue sauce. If they're dunked while the meat is still hot, the sauce won't adhere to flavor the pork as it bakes.

5—Ish says no barbecue sauce other than Hunt's Original will produce the desired flavor and effect. I didn't believe him and once substituted another brand I happened to have on hand. He was right—I got an entirely different flavor that was no comparison to his recipe. So don't substitute, okay?

6—If you can't allow the ribs to marinate overnight, at least give them about 3 hours of marinating time. It does make a big difference in the final dish.

7—To do the roasted potatoes, boil them until they're done. Then cool them to room temperature, cut them into several small wedges, and place them into a shallow baking pan. Then drizzle on some clarified butter, sprinkle on some Frank Davis Vegetable Seasoning, pop them (uncovered) into a 450-degree oven, and roast them for 20-30 minutes or until crusty brown. Garnish with minced parsley, thinly sliced green onions, and a dollop of sour cream.

8—To make the "Cuke Salad," remove the cucumber skin with a potato peeler and thinly slice the cucumber. Then cut onions and bell peppers (green, yellow, and red make a nice presentation) into rings, and slice tomatoes into small portions. All that's left is to place all the ingredients into a large mixing bowl, drizzle on a balsamic vinaigrette, and season with a generous sprinkling of Frank Davis Vegetable Seasoning. Oh, yeah—make sure all the ingredients are ice cold!

Perfect Pork Tenderloin with Apricot Sauce

It's way too tender and delicate a piece of meat to be treated harshly, so to cook the perfect pork tenderloin, you need to apply the double-whammy technique—first you sear it all over to seal in the juices, then you roast it tightly covered to keep it juicy. In other words, all you have to do is follow this recipe.

Cooking spray
¼ cup vegetable oil
1 pork tenderloin, 2½ lb. average
2 tsp. salt and black pepper
2 tsp. Frank Davis Pork Seasoning
1 cup minced yellow onions

2 tsp. minced fresh garlic
2 tsp. grated ginger
2 tsp. thyme leaves
¼ cup cocktail sherry
2 cups apple juice
1 cup chicken stock
⅓ cup apricot preserves
1 tsp. lemon zest

First take an oval roaster large enough to handle the tenderloin and spray it down liberally with cooking spray. Then preheat the oven to 400 degrees. Place the roaster on the stovetop over medium-high heat and add to it the oil.

In the meantime, while the pan is coming up to heat, generously and briskly rub down the tenderloin with the salt and pepper mixture and the pork seasoning. Take time here to completely rub the seasonings into the meat with your hands—this is really all the seasoning the meat will get, so be sure you do it with special care.

At this point, it is time to sear the tenderloin so that it retains all its juices. The way you do that is by gently lowering it into the hot oil in the oval roaster. But do not keep moving it around. Gradually roll it over and over in the oil—this takes a few minutes to do right. But attempt to turn the pork only when the seared meat that's touching the bottom of the pan releases itself from the metal—that's how you know it's sealed. Each time the release happens, roll the pork a little to sear yet another portion of its surface.

When the entire tenderloin has been seared and beautifully browned, cover the roaster tightly with the lid and slide the whole thing into the oven. Then roast the pork for 30 minutes-1 hour (depending upon its weight) or until its internal temperature reaches 150 degrees on an instant-read meat thermometer.

When the pork is done, immediately remove it from the roaster pan and place it on a warming platter for the time being. Then put the roaster pan back on the stovetop, turn up the burner to high, and immediately stir in the onions and garlic. As soon as they begin to soften and clear, one at a time stir in the rest of the ingredients. Then turn down the fire to medium-low and reduce the sauce to about a half of its original volume (and until it begins to slightly thicken and form a glaze). Expect this process to take about 15 minutes.

When the sauce is ready, thinly slice the pork tenderloin on a slight bias so that you end up with oval-shaped slices. Then dish up 2-3 pieces on a warm dinner plate, drizzle on a liberal serving of the apricot sauce, and serve it alongside a creamy smooth baked sweet potato and a helping of roasted mixed veggies.

This, y'all, is some good!

Chef's Note:
1—To do the Pan-Baked Sweet Potatoes, first rub them down liberally with vegetable oil. Then nestle them—unwrapped—into a Dutch oven, cover tightly with the lid, slide the Dutch oven into a 400-degree oven, and bake them for about 1½ hours until they are tender and creamy. When you're ready to eat, serve them up alongside several slices of the pork and drizzle both the pork and the potatoes with a generous helping of the apricot sauce. A pat of sweet butter, a scant sprinkling of brown sugar, and a dash of cinnamon as garnish tops off the potato presentation.
2—To do the Oven-Roasted Mixed Veggies, first butter a 10x10-in. glass baking dish and preheat the oven to 400 degrees. Then take a

package of frozen mixed vegetables, toss them liberally in a large bowl with about 1 cup vegetable mirepoix, generously sprinkle on some Frank Davis Vegetable Seasoning, and drizzle on about ¹/₂ stick butter, melted. Then give the mixture one more quick toss, transfer it to the glass dish, slide the dish uncovered into the oven, and roast the veggies (stirring occasionally) until they begin to caramelize around the edges (12-15 minutes). Serve piping hot.

Skillet-Paneed Pork Tenderloin Medallions

If you like breaded pork chops, breaded chicken breasts, breaded schnitzels, and breaded eggplant or green tomatoes, then you're gonna absolutely love what I do with these medallions of pork tenderloin. Served up with a nice pilaf and a fresh vegetable, it's a Southern meal even a heart-hardened Yankee would fall in love with, I garontee!

2 vacuum-packed pork tenderloins (they come 2 to the pack)
1 cup coarse French-bread crumbs
¼ cup kosher or sea salt
1 tsp. coarse-ground black pepper
2 tbsp. Frank Davis Sprinkling Spice

1 tsp. garlic powder
2 cups old-fashioned oatmeal
1 cup grated Romano cheese
2 tbsp. dried basil leaves
2 cups extra-virgin olive oil, as needed
1 pkg. EggBeaters
2 tbsp. water
1 cup grated Parmesan cheese

First off, place the pork tenderloins on a cutting board on the countertop and carefully trim away all the excess fat, sinew, and silver skin. Then with an extra-sharp slicing knife, cut the tenderloins crosswise on a bias (45-degree angle) so that you produce a bunch of medallions, each about 1 in. thick.

Next, in a shallow baking pan, mix together the breadcrumbs, salt, pepper, sprinkling spice, and garlic powder. To have the oatmeal at the right texture to produce a crunchy coating, pulse it in a food processor for 45-60 seconds. Then to the breadcrumbs add the oatmeal, Romano cheese, and basil and toss everything thoroughly until uniformly blended.

At this point, pour about half the oil into a heavy 12-in. skillet and set the flame to medium high. Then while the oil is coming up to ideal temperature, whip the EggBeaters and water together in a medium-sized bowl. Then dip the pork medallions a few at a time into the egg mixture and dredge them in the breadcrumb mixture.

All that's left to do now is fry the individual pork slices (on both sides) in the hot oil until they turn golden brown all over. As they finish frying, drain them briefly on several layers of paper towels, sprinkle them liberally with the Parmesan, and serve them piping hot and crispy.

A Great Big Ol' Giant Cajun Kitchen Sink Casserole

Guess what goes into this casserole? Everything but the kitchen sink, as Grandma usta put it! You got every vegetable known to man, shrimp from the Louisiana coastline, prime diced pork fillet, succulently tender chicken breasts, a bowlful of chopped andouille sausage—I mean, there's just no end to it! And to top it off it's crowned with a sheet of flaky crust and it's baked to perfection! Fix this soon, y'all, and especially for big family get-togethers.

The Vegetables:

Cooking spray
4 tbsp. butter
2 cups vegetable mirepoix
4 medium tomatoes, seeded and diced
2 cups canned butter beans, washed and drained
4 tbsp. extra-virgin olive oil
½ cup halved baby carrots
2 cans whole new potatoes, drained and halved, 16-oz. size

½ cup frozen green peas
½ cup coarsely diced celery
1 large onion, coarsely diced
½ lb. fresh mushrooms, halves and quarters
1 small zucchini, coarsely diced
1 small yellow squash, coarsely diced
1 small green bell pepper, chopped
1 small bunch fresh asparagus, cut into thirds

The first part of this four-part recipe is "The Quick Sauté Stage." First, place a large roasting pan on your countertop, coat it thoroughly with cooking spray, and set it aside momentarily. Then preheat your oven to 450 degrees.

Now, in a 12-in. anodized or Teflon-coated skillet, melt the butter over a medium-high heat. Then drop in the veggie mirepoix and stir it around briskly to coat everything liberally.

When the veggies begin to show signs of "clearing and wilting," drop in the tomatoes and sauté them as well, right to the point where they soften and give up most of their juices. Now quickly stir in the butter beans until the entire mixture is fully blended; then transfer the contents of the skillet to the waiting roasting pan on the countertop.

Immediately thereafter, place the skillet back on the stovetop over a medium-high heat, add the oil, and begin quickly stir-frying all the remaining vegetables—one vegetable at a time. As each becomes done (and "done" is defined as lightly tender crisp), take a slotted spoon and transfer it to the roasting pan. Continue the process until all of the vegetables are in the roasting pan.

The Meats:

4 tbsp. rendered bacon fat or margarine

2 links andouille sausage, sliced and quartered

1 lb. Louisiana shrimp, peeled and butterflied

3 boneless center-cut pork chops, diced

6 chicken tender strips, cut into 1-in. pieces

Heat the fat in the heavy 12-in. anodized skillet you've been using and begin the cooking process by dropping in the andouille and sautéing it until it becomes seared and crusty. Then one ingredient at a time, a few pieces at a time, start adding the shrimp, then the pork, and then the chicken. As they become ready, simply remove them from the skillet with a slotted spoon and place them into the roasting pan.

The Gravy:

¼ cup vegetable or Canola oil
⅓ cup all-purpose flour
1-2 cups whole milk
1-2 tsp. chicken bouillon granules
1 can Campbell's Cream of
  Chicken Soup

1 tsp. Frank Davis Vegetable
  Seasoning
1 tsp. Frank Davis Bronzing Mix
Kosher salt to taste
Black pepper to taste

While it may appear complicated, the procedure is very simple. Once again take the heavy 12-in. skillet, pour in the oil, and heat it to the point of it "just beginning to smoke." Then begin sprinkling in the flour a little bit at a time, whisking it all the while with a wire whip until the roux turns smooth and creamy looking. Continue to add flour and whisk it until the texture of the roux resembles a heavy (but smooth) pancake batter. Then when you reach that point, quickly remove the skillet from the fire and allow it to cool. Now you can start pouring in the milk a little at a time and stirring it until you create a nice thick gravy.

It is also at this time that you stir in the remaining ingredients, taking extra care to fully combine each ingredient into the others.

Then when the gravy is ready, spoon it over everything in the roasting pan. Now gently toss everything until the ingredients are thoroughly and uniformly coated.

And now it's time to finish this recipe!

The Crust:

1 double roll Pillsbury Pie Crust
1 small carton EggBeaters or 1
  egg white

You first reset your oven temperature to 425 degrees. Then on a lightly floured surface, take a rolling pin and roll out the pie crust into a rectangle large enough to completely cover the roasting pan. I recommend that you try to seal the edges over the pan as best you can, but be sure to cut a number of slits in the crust to allow for steam to escape while the casserole is baking. Finish up by brushing the crust with the EggBeaters (or egg white).

Finally, place the pan onto the center rack of the oven. All in all, it should take 15 or so minutes for the crust to turn a rich golden brown. When it reaches that point, remove the casserole from the oven, immediately spoon it out on heated plates, and serve it to your guests piping hot alongside a cold, crispy Caesar salad.

Now that's what I'm talking about!

Chef's Note:

1—For best flavor, take time to thoroughly wash the canned butter beans before using them.

2—Avoid overloading the frying skillet! If you sauté a few pieces at a time, they will sear and retain their natural juices; if you overcrowd them, they will sweat out their juices and also lose a considerable amount of flavor.

3—If you don't have any of my blended seasonings on hand, simple salt and black pepper will do nicely.

4—Whatever you do, don't make the gravy too watery. Additional liquids will leach from the ingredients as the casserole bakes. If the consistency is too watery to start with, the crust won't ever get crisp and you'll end up with a soupy casserole.

Pork Chop and Mushroom Jambalaya

You've no doubt had Cajun chicken and sausage jambalaya, huh? And you've probably also had ham and shrimp jambalaya, haven't you? But what about pork chop and mushroom jambalaya? Whip up a batch according to this recipe and you might very well end up with a whole new favorite version! Oh, yeah—if you think it's good today, wait until it sits overnight in the fridge and you dig into it tomorrow!

½ lb. bacon
2 medium yellow onions, coarsely diced
5 ribs celery, coarsely diced
1 large green bell pepper, coarsely chopped
1 cup quartered mushroom buttons
8 cloves garlic, crushed and minced
¼ cup all-purpose flour
5 cups julienned pork chops, boneless or bone-in
2 tbsp. vegetable oil (optional)

2 cans Rotel tomatoes, 8-oz. size
3 cups Swanson's Chicken Broth
2 tsp. Kitchen Bouquet
3 cups long-grain rice
1½ tsp. salt
½ tsp. black pepper
1 tsp. cayenne pepper
1 tsp. basil
½ tsp. thyme
12 green onion tops, thinly sliced
½ cup minced parsley

First, in a large 6-qt. cast-iron Dutch oven that has a lid, render down the bacon until it turns toasty and crispy. Remove the bacon, crumble it, and return it to the drippings. Then, after adding them to the Dutch oven one ingredient at a time, sauté the onions, celery, bell pepper, mushrooms, and garlic in the drippings until all the veggies are fully wilted. You can expect this to take 8-10 minutes. Then sprinkle on the flour and mix it into the seasoning vegetables well.

Next, drop the pork pieces into the pan a few at a time so that they don't dry up and toughen. Stir constantly until the pieces become thoroughly browned. Oh, you can add a little oil if necessary.

When the pork is beautifully browned, stir in the Rotel tomatoes (plus the liquid they came packed in), the chicken broth, and the Kitchen Bouquet. Then stir in the remaining ingredients.

At this point, combine everything thoroughly to ensure a uniform blend of textures and tastes. Then lower the fire to "simmer" and put the lid tightly on the Dutch oven. From this stage forward, allow the rice to cook gently until it completely cooks the pork, absorbs all of the liquid in the pot, and each grain fluffs to spicy tenderness. Total cooking time from the moment the lid goes on the pot to "ready to eat" is somewhere in the neighborhood of 50-60 minutes to, but I suggest you start checking it for doneness at around 40 minutes.

Chef's Note:
1—You can use boneless pork loin or country pork ribs to make this jambalaya; but the most concentrated flavor is produced when you use cut-up pieces of bone-in pork chops. For some reason or another, the presence of the pork bone intensifies the taste.

2—In spite of what you may have heard growing up, it is definitely okay for you to lift the lid and stir the rice occasionally. Contrary to wives' tales, this does not allow all the steam to escape; but it does keep the grains of rice from sticking to the bottom of the pot. I recommend you stir 3-4 times, starting after about 15 minutes of cooking time.

Frank's Famous Piggy Steaks—Pot Roasted

After asking your butcher to take his band saw and slice through the bones in the roast (but only the bones—not the roast!), you rub the pork down liberally with all of the seasonings and place it into a heavy Dutch oven atop a trivet. Then top with the carrots and onions, put on the lid, and slide the pot into the oven. When it comes out, you slice the roast into piggy "steaks" and you eat like royalty!

1 Boston blade shoulder roast
  (5 lb. average)
4 tbsp. Frank Davis Pork
  Seasoning
1 tsp. garlic powder
1 tsp. onion powder
2 tsps. coarse-ground black
  pepper
6 medium carrots, peeled and
  rough cut

2 medium onions, thickly sliced
3 cups low-sodium canned
  chicken broth
3 bay leaves
½ cup all-purpose flour
½ cup minced green onions
¼ cup minced parsley

First, preheat the oven to 350 degrees.

Then take the roast, set it on the countertop, sprinkle one side with half the pork seasoning, half the garlic powder, half the onion powder, and half the pepper. Now make it a point to rub all of the seasonings in well.

Then flip the roast over and rub the remaining pork seasoning, garlic powder, onion powder, and pepper into the opposite side. At this point, allow the seasoned roast to rest on the countertop while you prepare to cook.

For this recipe you will need either a large cast-iron Dutch oven or a heavy aluminum oval roaster (make sure that whichever you use has a tight-fitting lid). Then place a trivet into the pot, set the roast on top of it (fat side up), and cover it completely with the carrots, onions, 1 cup chicken broth, and bay leaves. Then cover the pot, slide it into the oven, and cook the roast for 2½-3 hours or until a meat thermometer reads 170 degrees without touching bone.

When the pork is done, remove it from the pot, along with all the seasoning veggies. But immediately put the pot back on the fire and bring the "pot liquor" up to medium-high heat. You should have about 2 cups at this point. *Note: if you find that you don't have enough pot liquor to make enough gravy for your guests, go ahead and add in as much extra chicken broth as needed.* Then, a little at a time, begin whisking in the flour to create a gravy. When the consistency is to your liking, finish off the gravy by stirring in the green onions and parsley.

When the gravy is done and you're ready to eat, ladle it over a hearty helping of steamed rice and serve it with a cold, crisp tomato and cucumber salad topped with Italian olive salad, a couple of spoonfuls of bottled caponata, and a sprinkling of Parmesan cheese. All that's left is to slice the piggy steaks right off the roast and serve them as the star attraction of the meal! Mmm!

Chef's Note:

1—Be sure to buy the right piece of pork for this recipe. You don't want the Boston butt! You want the Boston blade shoulder roast. And before you leave the meat department, ask the butcher to "cut through the bones with his band saw while leaving the meat in one piece," so that you can slice the roast into "steaks" after it's done.

2—The "trivet" could be a standard stainless-steel trivet you purchase from a kitchen supply store, or a china saucer that you invert in the bottom of the pot, or something as simple as a number of ribs of celery placed crosswise under the roast (just as long as you keep the pork from resting in the fat that accumulates in the bottom of the roasting pan).

3—"Pot liquor" is the juicy renderings that exude from the pork and all the seasonings as the ingredients roast inside of the pot. It is bursting with concentrated flavor and can be transformed into an excellent sauce or gravy.

4—The ideal side dish to serve with this pork recipe is a rice-cooker casserole made with rice, frozen green peas, thinly sliced green onions, minced celery, canned sliced mushrooms, minced carrots, and a sprinkling of minced parsley. Of course, all of the ingredients are tossed with a generous dab of butter and a touch of salt and freshly ground black pepper just prior to service. Hint: you can substitute Frank Davis Vegetable Seasoning for the salt and pepper if you so desire.

5—Caponata is eggplant and sundried tomatoes marinated in extra-virgin olive oil and flavored with Italian seasonings. You can make your own, but for the salad served with this recipe, I recommend you buy a jar of it at the grocery store and drizzle it over the sliced tomatoes and cukes along with the olive salad mix.

CHAPTER 5

Poultry

Redneck Chicken and Rice

Dis is one of dem Sat'day-go-a-callin'-Sundy-come-t'-dinner kinda dinners! Whether you gotta fix vittles for a baby shower, a church potluck, a farmhouse picnic, or jus' Uncle Percy's 90th birthday pawty, dis here's the dish you wanna be fixin'. And whilst it might ruffle the ol' Colonel's feathers a skosh, dere's nuttin' mo' finger-lickin' nowhere!

¼ cup extra-virgin olive oil
1 cup vegetable mirepoix
10-12 chicken drumsticks, skinned
2 tsp. Frank Davis Poultry Seasoning
2 tsp. Frank Davis Pepper-Free Seasoning or Bronzing Mix

2 pkg. McCormick's chicken gravy mix
2 cups bottled water
1 tbsp. Kitchen Bouquet
6 cups steamed buttered rice
1 dozen hot pistolette rolls

First, in a heavy 5-qt. Dutch oven that has a tight-fitting lid, heat the oil until it sizzles. Then stir in the veggies and, over medium-high heat, cook them until they wilt and turn clear. *Note: it is not necessary to caramelize the vegetables for this dish—you just want them softened.*

In the meantime, wash the drumsticks thoroughly, pat them dry with a handful of absorbent paper towels, and season them liberally with both the poultry seasoning and the pepper-free or bronzing mix. You don't want to skimp on this step—this is the only direct seasoning the dish will get. Now, add the chicken to the Dutch oven and sauté the drumsticks until they are nicely browned and seared all over.

Then in a separate saucepan make your gravy—simply prepare the gravy mix according to the package instructions (boil 2 cups water, stir in the packets, and simmer until the gravy turns smooth and thickens). When it's ready, color it up a tad by whisking in the Kitchen Bouquet.

Finally, when the gravy is ready, pour it evenly over the chicken in the Dutch oven, cover the pot tightly, and bake the drumsticks in the oven at 350 for about 1 hour and 15 minutes or until the chicken begins to show signs of falling off the bones.

Then when you're ready to eat, simply skim off whatever excess fat has floated to the surface during oven-simmering and serve the sauce and the chicken with a generous helping of steamed rice and a salad. Oh, yeah—ya gotta have those pistolettes for soppin'!

Variation: You can use skinned chicken thighs for this recipe if you choose, but do not use white-meat pieces. The white meat is way too lean to oven-simmer and it takes the bulk of the flavor away from the dish.

Instead of serving this with rice, you can serve it over your favorite form of pasta or a big pile of fluffy mashed potatoes. And if you keep it a secret, I'll tell you that out in the country they love to dish this up over hot grits!

Baked Parmesan-Paneed Chicken
(With Pan-Grilled Eggplant and Parslied Potatoes)

Crispy oven-baked chicken thighs, coated with Italian seasoned breadcrumbs and loads of grated Parmesan cheese, tender succulent grilled eggplant slices, and a pan of buttered baby potatoes smothered in onions and celery—what better gourmet meal could anyone ask for? And you can fix it right at home in a snap!

The Chicken:

10 chicken thighs, skinned and washed
¾ cup extra-virgin olive oil
2 tsp. Frank Davis Poultry Seasoning
2 tsp. salt and black pepper mixture
2 tsp. Frank Davis Sicilian Seasoning
4 cups Italian seasoned breadcrumbs
1 cup grated Parmesan cheese
1 bottle spray margarine

First thing you want to do is lay out the chicken thighs on a large sheet of either waxed paper or freezer wrap. Then, using a pastry brush, coat the thighs liberally on both sides with the oil. Follow that by generously sprinkling each thigh with the poultry seasoning, salt and pepper mixture, and Sicilian seasoning.

At this point, preheat the oven to 350 degrees and combine the breadcrumbs and the Parmesan cheese. Then take the oil-coated, seasoned chicken and dredge each piece in the breadcrumbs, patting them forcefully to ensure that the crumbs attach to the meat. Now lightly shake off the excess crumbs and place the chicken onto a large, shallow sheet pan (if you place a piece of parchment paper on the bottom of the pan, the pan will be easy to clean later).

Finally, slide the chicken into the oven on the center rack and bake uncovered for 50-60 minutes (or until the crumbs turn a toasty brown and clean juices run from the thighs when pierced with an ice pick). Oh—one more thing: about halfway through the baking process, slide the pan out of the oven briefly and spray each chicken piece with the margarine. This will crisp up the chicken thighs and allow them to brown more evenly (to say nothing of enhancing the flavor).

The Eggplant:

2 medium-size eggplants, thinly
  sliced crosswise
⅔ cup extra-virgin olive oil
2 tsp. salt and black pepper
  mixture

2 tsp. Frank Davis Sicilian
  Seasoning
2 cups Italian seasoned breadcrumbs
⅓ cup grated Parmesan cheese

While the chicken is baking, lay out on the countertop another sheet of waxed paper or freezer wrap and place the eggplant slices on it. Then, again with a pastry brush (but not the same one you used for the chicken!), liberally coat the slices—front and back—with the oil. Follow that up by seasoning each slice (again front and back) with the salt and pepper mixture and the Sicilian seasoning.

At this point, place a grill pan on top of the stove on a medium-high flame and rub it lightly with a little more olive oil. Then uniformly combine the breadcrumbs and cheese. Now dredge each eggplant slice in the crumbs, shake off the excess, and place the slices into the grill pan, trying not to let them touch.

It isn't necessary, but a bacon press or steak press placed on top of the eggplants will allow them to pan-grill quickly and evenly. If one is not available, however, use an egg turner to press them down once or twice to allow for even browning. Cook the eggplant on both sides until they soften (it should take 3-4 minutes on each side).

When they're done, set them aside on a warming platter until the chicken thighs are ready.

The Potatoes:

4 tbsp. margarine, softened
4 tbsp. extra-virgin olive oil
1½ cups vegetable mirepoix
3 cloves garlic, minced
2 cups chicken stock
2 cups minced parsley

3 lb. tiny red new potatoes, washed and stripped around the middle
1 tbsp. Frank Davis Vegetable Seasoning
Salt and black pepper to taste

This side dish will have to begin cooking at about the same time the chicken thighs go into the oven. And to do it right, you will need a large fry pan with a tight-fitting lid, one that will allow you to cook all the potatoes in a single layer.

Start off by heating the pan over a medium-high flame. Then drop in the margarine and oil and bring the combination up to sizzling. Now stir in the mirepoix (if you want to create your own mix, I recommend you use equal parts onions and celery), along with the garlic (but stir the mixture continually and watch it closely so that it doesn't burn).

When the vegetables are soft and tender, stir in the chicken stock along with 1½ parsley. Then bring the stock to a full boil, immediately drop in the potatoes, and toss them in the mixture to fully coat each one. At this point, sprinkle on the vegetable seasoning, salt, and pepper, toss the pan again, and bring the stock back up to a full boil.

Now place the lid on the pan, lower the flame to "simmer," and cook the potatoes for 15-20 minutes or until fork tender.

When you're ready to eat, serve the chicken right from the oven, place 3-4 eggplant slices alongside it, and scoop out a heaping helping of the pan-smothered potatoes. And for a little extra flavor, spoon the pan sauces from the potatoes over both the potatoes and the chicken and garnish them both with the remaining parsley.

Chef's Note:

1—You can do this recipe with other chicken parts if you'd prefer, but the others do not have as much flavor as does the thigh meat.

2—It is not necessary to peel the eggplants to do this recipe, but it's perfectly okay if you prefer. I also recommend that you buy only tender young eggplants, to reduce the "bite" in the final dish.

3—The potato dish cooks best (and creamiest!) if you use the smallest new potatoes you can buy. You can use a potato peeler to cut the strip around the center (which not only gives the dish eye appeal but hastens the cooking time of the potatoes as well).

4—If you can't find Frank Davis Seasonings where you shop, you can click on the Frank Davis icon at www.frankdavis.com to see the entire line or call 985-643-0027.

Deep-in-Dixie Drunk Chicken

A whole chicken, spiced up with salt, pepper, fresh rosemary, olive oil, and poultry seasoning, is then squatted atop a beer can—with the beer still in it!—and slow roasted either in the oven or on the BBQ pit at a tailgate party. It's a special taste treat you only get down South! "Drunk Chicken" (also referred to sometimes as "tipsy chicken") probably yields some of the most intense flavor the slow-cooking process can produce. The inside comes out unbelievably juicy because of the steaming effect of the beer (which also adds rich, but subtle, flavors because of the barley, malt, and hops), and the outside comes out super crunchy-crispy because of the dry heat that surrounds the bird as it cooks.

1 whole chicken
4 tbsp. extra-virgin olive oil
2 sprigs rosemary
2 tbsp. Frank Davis Poultry
   Seasoning

2 tsp. salt and black pepper
   mixture
1 beer, 12-oz. can
1 upright chicken holder
1 very small red potato

First fire up either the barbecue grill (heat source on one side, no heat on the side the chicken will cook on) or the kitchen oven (the proper temperature setting is 350 degrees). Then after cleaning the chicken extremely well, taking care to remove all the debris left inside the cavity and washing the bird inside and out, pat it dry with paper towels.

At this point, rub down the chicken—again, inside and out—with the oil. Then, after gently loosening the skin on the breast with your fingers, slide 2 sprigs rosemary between the skin and the breast meat, 1 on either side. Then liberally sprinkle on the poultry seasoning and the salt and pepper mixture and briskly rub it into the chicken with your hands.

Next, open the can of beer and either drink or pour out about a third of it. Then place the chicken on top of the beer can so that it "squats" in place. In the old days, even back in the days of the depression, aficionados who cooked drunk chicken regularly would have to proceed with caution, since oftentimes the chicken would topple over, the beer would all spill out, the flames would be doused, and the chicken sometimes never cooked. These days, though, there are special "holders" you can get that are designed to support the can as well as the chicken and keep it from toppling.

When the chicken rests atop the can of beer the way you want it, plug the neck hole of the chicken with the potato to keep steam from escaping. Then set the chicken, the can, and the holder into a baking pan (which will catch the drippings) and slide the pan into the oven, or set the chicken, can, and holder directly onto the barbecue grate (no pan). From this moment on, do not open the oven, lift the BBQ cover, or peek at the chicken in any way whatsoever.

The next thing you'll do is remove the chicken from the oven or barbecue pit in $1^1/_2$-2 hours (depending upon the size of the chicken), take it off the beer can and the holder, and cut it into serving pieces. You're going to find that it's magnificently flavored, virtually main-tenance free, and very low in cholesterol and fat (unless you fold a batch of poached veggies into the drippings!).

Just one little note—if you have always made do with 1 chicken for your meals, you might want to cook 2 whenever you fix "Drunk Chicken"!

Chef's Note:

1—To prepare this recipe properly, only regular beer should be used. Do not use "light" beer as a substitute. Of course, you can add whatever special flavors you like to the beer—soy sauce, Worcestershire, liquid crab boil, you name it. And, of course, if you'd prefer to go with alcohol-free alternatives, you can substitute your favorite cola, ginger ale, lemonade, apple juice, etc., in place of the "brew."

2—If you're really, really careful, you might be able to "balance" your chicken just on top of the beer can. But several principal sources supply holders and racks for cooking drunk chicken. If you'd like to order 1 (or preferably 2, if you cook for a family of 4 or more), go to www.frankdavis.com and order online, or call 985-643-0027.

3—If you plan to do the recipe on the barbecue grill, light one side of the grill but not the other, and cook the chicken on the unlighted side to utilize "incidental heat" and to minimize flare-ups. This is not a problem when doing the recipe in the oven. But do not wrap the chicken in foil!

4—To make certain the chicken is cooked to perfection, use a meat thermometer and roast the bird until the internal temperature reaches 180 degrees.

5—Oh, yeah—and be very careful how you handle the can after the cooking time has elapsed. The beer (and the can) could still be extremely hot! Don't get burned!

6—A great accompanying vegetable side dish—and one that is also hassle free—could be concocted with a combination of A-size creamer potatoes, fresh green beans, bias-cut peeled carrots, and quartered baby portabello mushrooms. The mixture can either be steamed in a deep-sided, covered skillet in chicken stock until just tender, or poached in light seafood-boil seasoning until tender crisp, or smothered down until done in a Crockpot. Whichever way you decide to prep them, when they are almost done transfer them to the baking pan holding the chicken so that as the chicken roasts its juices drip into the veggies to flavor them. Add a little butter to finish off the vegetables just before serving and sprinkle lightly with extra salt and pepper if necessary.

Frank's Carnival Chicken Chippewa

A really great home-style recipe that's perfect for every night of the parade season, Chicken Chippewa could best be described as a cross between chicken sausage gumbo and a rich chicken and sausage soup . . . but with a whole lot more soul and spice. To make this dish, you're gonna need a big family-size package of cut-up chicken and 3 lb. of a quality andouille sausage. Combine everything with a bayou-style roux and a stock base that you can simmer until the flavor rattles the cover on the pot, and you got a meal fit for the most notable of Carnival royalty!

⅓ cup vegetable or corn oil
1 family-style pkg. cut-up
  chicken pieces, skinned
4 tsp. Frank Davis Pepper-Free
  Seasoning
3 lb. real Cajun andouille
  sausage, cut into chunks
10 cups canned chicken broth
1½ cups diced yellow onions
1 cup minced celery
¾ small bell pepper, minced
2 cups quartered button
  mushrooms
8 cloves garlic, chopped
¼ cup minced parsley
1 small can Rotel diced
  tomatoes with chilies

2 cans whole kernel corn,
  drained
3 bay leaves
1 tsp. basil
1 tsp. ground thyme
½ cup basic roux
½ tsp. black pepper
½ tsp. crushed red pepper
  flakes
2 tsp. Kitchen Bouquet
  (optional)
8 cups cooked long-grain rice
Filé powder and thinly sliced
  green onions for garnish

First, in a heavy oval roaster or gumbo pot large enough to hold all the ingredients without overflowing, heat half the oil until hot. While that's happening, thoroughly season the chicken pieces with the pepper-free mixture. Then a few pieces at a time, brown them all over in the oil, along with the andouille, and set them aside on a platter.

When everything is nice and golden, place all the chicken and sausage back into the pot and pour on the chicken broth. Bring the broth to a rolling boil, but immediately reduce it to a gentle bubble. Then cover the pot and let the chicken and andouille simmer for a while.

In the meantime, in a heavy 12-in. nonstick skillet, heat the remaining oil until hot, drop in the onions, celery, bell pepper, mushrooms, garlic, and parsley, and fry them—all the while over high heat—until all the ingredients are uniformly combined. This process should take about 5 minutes. Then, while stirring constantly, add the Rotels, corn, bay leaves, basil, and thyme, and stir until the soupy mixture completely melds together.

At this point, transfer the contents of the skillet to the oval roaster and fold everything together. Then ladle a goodly amount of chicken broth into the skillet, bring it to a gentle boil, and whisk in the basic prepared roux to thicken the finished dish ever so slightly—the final product is supposed to have texture, but it is not supposed to be "pasty thick."

When the contents of the skillet become "saucy," pour it back into the oval roaster with the chicken and sausage, tweak the flavor with the black pepper and the red pepper flakes, and color the stock if desired with the Kitchen Bouquet (make it a pretty dark brown for authenticity).

All that's left now is to cover the pot, reduce the fire to "low," and slowly simmer everything for about 1 hour or so until the chicken shows signs of wanting to fall off the bone.

Then, when you're ready to eat, ladle up some of the rich broth, a big chunk of chicken, and 1-2 andouille pieces, pour it all over a mound of steamed rice in a deep bowl, and garnish with a generous sprinkling of filé and green onions.

So is it gumbo? Or is it soup? Actually, it's better than gumbo or soup. It's Chicken Chippewa!

Chef's Note:

1—This recipe is so versatile, should you get the inclination you can even toss in about 1 cup of either fresh, frozen, or canned okra. *Of course, if you select the fresh or frozen variety, you might want to "fry it down" a few minutes after you finish browning the chicken and sausage pieces, to help cut the slime.*

2—If you want to reduce the amount of fat that goes into the dish, quickly sear the seasoned chicken pieces on a sheet pan under the oven's broiler element in a 500-degree oven. You should plan on turning the pieces once or twice during the broiling process to keep them from scorching.

3—Even with skinned chicken and lean andouille, the ready-to-eat dish will probably have a certain amount of fat that will accumulate on the surface. You can easily skim off most of it with a ladle if you want to serve the dish as soon as it is prepared. But to eradicate all of the fat, cook the dish one day, refrigerate it overnight, lift off the congealed fat that rises to the top, and serve it the next day.

4—You might also want to reduce the black and red pepper flakes a tad if you are pepper sensitive. Remember, there is a significant amount of heat in the chilies in the Rotel tomatoes.

5—The Kitchen Bouquet can be added towards the end of the cooking process to deepen the color of the dish if your basic roux didn't turn out dark enough to suit your taste.

Frank's Family-Style Stacked Chicken

Most recipes you run across are designed to feed 4-6 people. But every now and then you need a recipe that will feed a big family or a large neighborhood get-together. Well, this is one of those recipes—three chickens flattened out, stacked one on top of the other, and roasted until toasty and tender. And while it all sounds unbelievably complicated, it's really very simple to do.

12 oz. lean bacon, minced
3 whole chickens, split and
  cleaned
1 tbsp. Frank Davis Poultry
  Seasoning
1 tbsp. Frank Davis Bronzing Mix
  or Sprinkling Spice
1 tbsp. coarse-ground black
  pepper
2 cans Campbell's Cream of
  Chicken Soup
1 lb. button mushrooms
½ bunch celery, separated into
  ribs

4 medium onions, thickly sliced
8-10 cloves garlic, minced
1 lb. fresh carrots, peeled and
  cut into chunks
8 medium red potatoes, peeled
  and halved
2 tsp. Frank Davis Vegetable
  Seasoning
½ cup dry cocktail sherry
1 bunch parsley, minced
1 bunch green onions, thinly
  sliced

First place a large oval roaster that has a tight-fitting lid on the stovetop. Then with the heat set to medium high, sauté down the bacon pieces until they turn crispy and begin to render out their drippings.

While the bacon is rendering, wash the chickens thoroughly under cold running water and then pat them dry with super-absorbent paper towels. While the skin is to be left on the birds, the backbone sections need to be completely cut away using a pair of sharp kitchen shears. Then, with the breast side facing up, push down on the breastbone while pulling the back apart—continue to press until the chicken flattens out. When all of them are done, liberally sprinkle them with the poultry seasoning, bronzing mix, and pepper.

Now take a slotted spoon and remove the bacon bits from the oval roaster (but leave the drippings in the pot) and set them aside momentarily. Then one at a time, place the split chickens into the roaster and brown them on both sides to sear them and seal in the natural juices. As they become browned, remove them with a meat fork and set them on a large platter.

At this point, pour off all but a trace of the remaining bacon fat and set the empty roaster on the countertop. Then, alternating ingredients as you go, nestle 1 chicken into the pot and slather it heavily with half of the soup. Then distribute evenly over the chicken half of the mushrooms, half of the celery ribs, half of the onions, half of the garlic, half of the carrots, half of the bacon bits, and half of the potatoes. Then season the veggie layer with 1 tsp. vegetable seasoning and repeat the entire process after laying on the second chicken.

Finally put the third chicken atop the second layer of veggies. Then gently pour the sherry over the top of the "stack" so that you don't wash away the seasonings. When everything is in the pot, cover the oval roaster with a tight-fitting lid and slide it into a pre-heated 325-degree oven for about 3 hours or until the chicken is "fall-off-the-bone tender."

All that's left to do at this stage is to set the roaster on the table and—with a pair of tongs—begin serving the succulent chicken along with the vegetables. Garnish with a scattering of parsley and green onions. Oh—and a little hot bread on the side might just be the crowning glory.

Chef's Note:

1—The drippings from the chickens and the natural moisture from the mushrooms and the onions, along with the splash of sherry, should give you an adequate amount of jus (natural gravy). But if you find that you need extra, simply add a can or so of chicken broth.

2—If you want to keep the first chicken from resting in the rendered fat, you can first place a trivet in the bottom of the oval roaster and set everything else on top of it. Of course, one of the best ways to defat the jus is to remove the chickens and veggies when they're done, then pour off the jus, refrigerate it for an hour or so, and skim off the fat as it rises to the top in a caked form.

3—Some oval roasters are large enough to allow you to place 2 chickens on the bottom with the third centered on top. If you have that arrangement, simply scatter the other ingredients over the bottom chickens and on both sides of the top chicken so that everything is nestled together.

Frank's Chicken-Sausage Fricassee

Go anywhere into the famed Acadian Triangle in the south-central portion of the state and you'll find that almost every family serves up this dish. That's because Cajuns dearly love their fricassee, whether it's made with duck, rabbit, squirrel, venison, or practically any other main ingredient. Of course, Cajun or not, you're gonna love this chicken version that's been served in New Orleans for as long as I can remember!

⅓ cup vegetable oil
½ cup all-purpose flour
6 strips bacon, cut into small pieces
1 lb. country smoked sausage, medium sliced
8 chicken thighs, skinned and halved
2 cups diced baby portobello mushrooms
1½ cups chopped onions
½ cup chopped celery
¾ cup chopped green bell pepper
1 can Rotel tomatoes with chilies, drained
4 tbsp. Minor's Chicken Base + 1 cup water
4 tbsp. Frank Davis Bronzing Mix
1 tbsp. Worcestershire sauce
1 tsp. chopped basil
¼ cup minced parsley
6 cups cooked white rice

First of all you gotta make a roux, and you do this by combining the oil and the flour in a heavy skillet over low heat and whisking it a lot. Then, once a smooth paste forms, you simmer the mixture slowly, stirring constantly, until the flour and oil concoction becomes dark brown. Of course, you should be careful not to *overbrown* the mixture, or the roux will turn bitter (which means you will have to throw it out, clean the skillet, and start all over again).

In the meantime, in another heavy high-sided skillet, fry down the bacon pieces, sausage, and chicken until the bacon becomes crispy, the sausage rounds show signs of toasting, and the chicken thighs are no longer transparent. When that happens, go ahead and drop in the mushrooms and toss them with the meat until they meld into the mix.

At this stage of the recipe, add to the skillet the onions, celery, bell pepper, and tomatoes and thoroughly work them into the mix, cooking everything over medium heat until the vegetables turn limp. Complete this procedure and there's nothing left to do but to turn the heat down to medium low, stir in the chicken base, sprinkle in the bronzing mix, stir in the Worcestershire sauce, sprinkle on the basil, and fold in the parsley.

With all the ingredients now in the skillet, the final step is to raise the heat to medium and cook the fricassee for about 20 minutes until succulently tender. Then when you're ready to eat, all you have to do is spoon it over a generous helping of hot, steamed, white rice.

Chef's Note:

1—The Minor's Chicken Base that is referenced in the recipe is available at Dorignac's Food Center in Metairie. If you opt to use another brand of chicken flavoring, such as bouillon cubes, you must ensure that the base is not overly salty or it will completely ruin the finished dish.

2—If you don't have any chicken base on hand, you can simply add 1 can Swanson's Chicken Broth to the fricassee.

Poppa Frank's Homemade Fried Chicken

We've been doing homemade fried chicken down South ever since the days of Huck Finn and Tom Sawyer. And everybody but everybody has his or her own secret recipe! Well, I'm no different. After having been coached by and schooled in the talents of the late great soul chef Austin Leslie, I think this recipe will stack up against any of the others out there. Of course, there's really only one way to find out, huh? Go dig out the skillet!

3-6 cups vegetable shortening for frying	3 cups all-purpose flour
2 whole chickens, each cut into 8 fryer pieces	3 tbsp. kosher or sea salt
	1 tbsp. black pepper
2 eggs	1 tbsp. cayenne pepper
2 cups half and half	1 tbsp. Frank Davis Poultry Seasoning
2 cups water	¼ cup minced parsley for garnish

First, preheat the shortening in either a 12-in. cast-iron frying pan or an electric skillet until it is completely melted and up to frying temperature (*but not smoking!*). If you're using a black iron skillet, the correct temperature is 350 degrees; if you're using an electric fry pan, heat it to 400 degrees. *Note: be certain the shortening has reached the proper temperature before even attempting to fry the first piece of chicken.*

Next, wash the chicken pieces under cold running water until thoroughly cleaned; then pat each piece dry with absorbent paper towels. Immediately thereafter, in a medium mixing bowl, beat together the eggs, half-and-half, and water.

Now, in a 2-gal.-size Ziploc bag, uniformly combine the flour, salt, pepper, cayenne, and poultry seasoning. Then precisely in order, first dip a chicken piece into the egg wash to coat it. Then secondly dredge it in the seasoned flour in the Ziploc bag (ideally you want to shake the bag briskly to coat every inch of every piece of chicken). Once coated, allow all the pieces to either remain in the plastic bag or rest on a piece of waxed paper on the countertop for 4-5 minutes. *This step "sets the batter" and keeps the flour from falling off in the shortening as the chicken fries.*

Finally, when you're ready to cook, add 4-6 pieces of chicken at a time to the skillet or fryer (meatiest parts first, which means thighs, breasts, and legs—wings should always go in last). The one thing you don't want to do is crowd them together. Cook until the chicken is tender and the skin is crisp, which adds up to a total of 12-18 minutes (usually 10 minutes on one side and 8 minutes on the other).

Homemade fried chicken should always be drained on several layers of paper towels and then served piping hot. In fact, it's best when it's almost too hot to eat! A good way to complete the meal is with a generous helping of oven-baked new potatoes and an ice-cold tomato/cucumber salad. Garnish everything with a sprinkling of parsley.

Chef's Note:

1—For best results, the perfect-size chicken for frying will weigh 2¹/₂-3 lb. Larger pieces take too long to fry all the way through without becoming dried out and chewy.

2—One of the secrets to good homemade fried chicken is to keep the shortening clean and at a constant temperature. And always, always bring your chicken to room temperature before you fry it. Cold chicken will chill your shortening too much and it will turn out greasy.

3—For exceptionally seasoned chicken, sprinkle each piece independently with extra salt and pepper prior to dredging it in the seasoned flour in the Ziploc bag. A sprinkling of cayenne directly on the chicken before dredging will also intensify the "spiciness" of the finished dish.

4—If you'd prefer not to mix your own dredging coating, you can substitute Frank Davis Chicken Fried Mix. If it isn't available where you shop, you can order it online at www.frankdavis.com.

5—As my old friend Austin once told me, "Don't ever give the milk time to soak into the skin, or the sugar in the milk will cause your chicken to turn black."

6—The chicken pieces will fry much crispier and turn out much more flavorful if after about 8 minutes of cooking you pierce each piece at its thickest part with a large 2-pronged meat fork. This will guarantee that the chicken will cook all the way to the bone. And don't worry—chicken prepared this way will not dry out, nor will it be greasy.

7—To reheat cold chicken properly, first bring the pieces to room temperature. Then heat them in the oven, uncovered on a shallow cooking sheet, at about 300 degrees until hot and crispy.

Frank's Deep-Fried Turkey

It seems everybody's doing it these days. But the original recipe was conceived and perfected by my old friend the late Justin Wilson in his backyard in Crowley in the 1930s. It's been a novel Louisiana taste treat that has endured all this time. Over the decades, many cooks have duplicated Justin's creation, but still no one does it quite like the old master. Here's his time-tested recipe, along with a few added innovations he passed along to me.

1 turkey (12-15 lb. average)	2 tbsp. Frank Davis Poultry
30-qt. aluminum turkey	Seasoning
fryer/stockpot	2 lb. hickory-smoked bacon
3-5 gal. peanut oil	1 bottle Frank Davis Sprinkling
6-gal. propane tank	Spice

First, place the raw turkey (it can even still be in its wrapper) into your turkey fryer. Then begin adding tap water to the pot in measured amounts—*quarts, half-gallons, gallons, whatever, but keep track.* Then when you have the turkey completely covered with water (about 3 in. over the top of the bird is perfect), note how much water it took, remove the turkey, pour out the water, completely dry the pot, and refill the pot with the same premeasured amount of peanut oil. At this point place the pot of oil over your propane burner outside (do not ever deep-fry a turkey inside or on a wooden deck unless you want to chance burning your house to the ground!) and heat it to 350 degrees.

While the oil is heating, remove the entrail debris as well as the giblets from inside the turkey and wash it thoroughly inside and out. Then, with a handful of paper towels, pat the bird dry (you want to put as little moisture into the oil as possible to reduce the amount of steam that escapes when the turkey cooks). Next, liberally sprinkle the turkey with the poultry seasoning and rub it in briskly with your hands, actually forcing it into the pores of the bird. Now set the turkey aside to allow the seasoning to "seep" in.

Let's have a conference here! I don't believe in injecting "stuff" into the turkey to season it. I don't think it's necessary because I don't think it works! Follow me on this—you make a bunch of holes with a hypodermic needle, shoot about 55 gallons of "stuff" into the turkey, and drop the critter into hot oil. Know what happens next? The hot oil causes the cold turkey to expand, the holes get bigger, the pressure builds inside the turkey, and all the "stuff" comes squirting out of the holes! So what was that all about? Why not flavor the oil and let the oil flavor the turkey? Makes sense, doesn't it? And the best way to flavor the oil is . . .

Begin frying down all the strips of bacon you bought, right in the peanut oil. As the bacon cooks, the oil takes on a great, subtle hickory flavor, a flavor that penetrates the turkey during the 50 minutes or so it's frying. A hot turkey in hot flavored oil? Hey, that's seasoning! What's more, you remove the strips from the oil with a pair of tongs as they crisp up, drain them on several layers of paper towels, and either snack on them as the turkey fries or set them aside for BLT sandwiches later.

But let's talk technique for a minute. When your oil is right at 350 and you've played with the propane regulator to stabilize it there, get ready to lower the turkey down. This is the most dangerous part of the entire recipe—*third-degree burns have occurred here . . . houses have burned to the ground here!* Either completely truss the turkey with heavy cord and lower him in that way (it's a two-man operation, anyway you look at it!) or place him into a basket or onto a frying trivet and lower him down that way. Either way, be sure you're wearing heavy gloves or barbecue mitts. Once the steam hits your wrists, you'll turn the bird loose unless your skin is protected. Can't help it! And that's what causes the problem. So lower him down slowly!

Procedurally . . .

1—You want to fry the turkey 3-5 minutes to the pound at somewhere between 325 and 350 degrees. Keep a watchful eye, though, because smaller turkeys cook faster than larger turkeys (larger turkeys could take the full 5 minutes to the pound to cook). Just in case you need a benchmark, a 15-lb. bird will be done to perfection in 1 hour, provided the temperature is constant.

2—Be just as cautious taking the turkey out of the oil as you were putting it in. Be careful not to lift it and then accidentally drop it back into the oil and create a splash! This is how third-degree burns are made! A large, extra-heavy meat fork is a perfect aid in turkey deep-frying. And whatever you do, keep children far away from the pot the entire time the turkey is cooking, *but especially while it is being lowered into and taken out of the oil!*

3—When the bird is done (and it's done when the internal temperature reaches 180 degrees), remove it from the oil and set it butt side down on several layers of highly absorbent paper towels to let it drain. It's at this stage that you liberally season the hot turkey all over—inside and out—with the sprinkling spice. Done properly at the right temperature, the turkey should turn out anything but greasy.

While lots of folks eat deep-fried turkey cold from the fridge the next day, it's flat unbeatable when it's carved hot from the oil and transformed into N'Awlins-dressed fried-turkey po'-boy sandwiches loaded with crispy lettuce, Creole tomatoes, spicy brown mustard, dill pickles, and a double layer of mynaze!

Chef's Note:

1—Just so you'll know, Justin intended deep-frying a turkey to be a novelty, not an economically sound method of culinary artistry. First, even on sale, 5 gal. peanut oil are going to cost you in the neighborhood of $28-$32 (that's without ever seeing a turkey). Then add the gobbler to that, say, another $20 on sale, and you're approaching $50, a pricey dinner by anybody's standard. So lemme suggest that if you wanna do this, do it as a "Deep-Fried Turkey Party." You get the turkey and have each couple you invite bring along 1 gal. peanut oil as contribution. Now we're into something that's affordable! In fact, now we're "Naturally N'Awlins cheap!"

2—You lower and deep-fry a turkey "breast down, legs up." That means the front end of the bird goes into the fryer first. But I wouldn't suggest you lift the turkey out of the oil by its drumsticks! If they break off and the bird drops back into the oil, you're headed for the emergency room!

3—One of the most important things you can remember is never allow the turkey to rest directly on the bottom of the fryer. If you're not going to cook it in a basket, take a steamer trivet (one of those little grate-like things that hold your vegetables off the bottom) and put in down in the hot oil. Unless you do this, the breast portion of the turkey will probably burn.

4—You can use a sharp serrated knife to do the carving, but to slice into a hot turkey it's best to use an electric knife.

5—The turkey oil can be used 2-3 times, provided the temperature stabilizes at 350 degrees and you don't let it burn. Of course, it should be stored in the refrigerator between uses.

Frank's Pot-Smothered Turkey Shanks

They're nothing more than turkey drumsticks, trimmed and skinned and cut into 3 pieces crosswise to form bone-in shanks. So if you're an osso-bucco kinda person and you like veal shanks, German pork shanks, and beef shanks, wait until you try these, especially slow cooked in a spicy, white-wine-flavored brown gravy over brown rice with green peas.

¼ cup vegetable oil
12 pieces skinned turkey shanks
1 tbsp. Frank Davis Poultry
  Seasoning
Kosher salt and coarse-ground
  black pepper as needed
1 cup diced onion
¾ cup diced celery
½ cup diced green bell pepper
1 cup sliced mushrooms
2 tbsp. minced garlic

2 tbsp. minced parsley
2 bay leaves
¼ cup all-purpose flour
⅔ cup chicken stock
½ cup white wine
½ cup heavy cream (optional)
1 tsp. red pepper flakes
1 tsp. Kitchen Bouquet
Sliced green onions for garnish
1 tbsp. butter to smooth

First, in a heavy 6-qt. cast-iron Dutch oven that has a lid, heat the oil over a medium-high flame. Then while the oil is coming up to temperature, lay out the turkey shanks in a single layer on several sheets of freezer wrap and liberally season them with the poultry seasoning, salt, and pepper, coating all sides to ensure a uniform flavor.

Next, drop the shanks into the Dutch oven and brown them all over to seal in their natural juices. When they're ready, remove them from the pot and set them aside momentarily. You'll notice some bits sticking to the bottom of the pot—that's mostly seasoning coming off the shanks, so don't be concerned. This will form the base for a rich brown gravy later in the recipe.

Once all the shanks are out of the pot, drop into the pot the onions, celery, bell pepper, mushrooms, garlic, parsley, and bay leaves. At this point, immediately reduce the heat to low and vigorously stir the seasoning vegetables—this is where the temperature falls and the pot becomes "deglazed" (which means the crust that is stuck on the bottom loosens up and becomes part of the flavoring). *Note: this won't happen while the heat is turned up—the temperature will have to drop to "loosen" the debris.*

It's right about this time that you also stir in the flour. To keep it from "lumping," I suggest you sprinkle it in a little at a time and thoroughly mix it into the vegetables with a wire whisk as you go. Then add the chicken stock, wine, cream, red pepper flakes, and Kitchen Bouquet and combine everything into the base gravy.

All that's left now is to put the shanks back into the pot, submerging and basting each one with the brown gravy as they're dropped in. Then when all the turkey is in the Dutch oven, either (1) cover the pot and simmer it on low heat on the stovetop for about 1½ hours, or (2) cover the pot and slide it into a 350-degree oven for about 2 hours.

Finally, about 10 minutes before you're ready to eat, stir in a handful of green onions as well as the butter. The onions will top off the flavors and the butter will "smooth" the gravy. Gotta tell ya, this recipe is best served ladled over buttered brown rice (gravy and all), alongside green peas and diced purple onions, and accompanied by a stack of hot biscuits right from the oven.

Chef's Note:
1—To convert turkey drumsticks into "turkey shanks," ask your butcher to skin 4 legs then run each crosswise through the band saw to cut it into 3 pieces.

2—If your local supermarket doesn't stock turkey legs outside of the holiday season, you can call Glenn or Leah Mistich at the Gourmet Butcher Block in Terrytown at 504-392-5700. They keep them in the coolers most of the year.

3—This same recipe can be used to fix pork cubes, beef round steak, venison backstrap, or anything else your imagination conjures up.

4—Be sure to use a good table wine—piesporter, Chablis, chardonnay, chenin blanc, etc.—in this dish. How much to use? As much as you need to your taste—you can use the ½ cup that the recipe calls for, or add another ½ cup, or use most of the bottle! It will depend upon how "soupy" you want the final gravy to be. Just cook the wine so that the harshness and the alcohol is eliminated. Oh, and do not use what is commonly referred to as "cooking wine"! It's horrible!

5—Take care not to make the original gravy base too watery at the outset. You have to remember that renderings will come from the turkey to liquefy the gravy as the recipe cooks.

6—Turkey shanks are good the day they're cooked; but like red beans, jambalaya, and gumbo, they're always much better the next day after all the flavors have married!

Frank's Slow-Poached Hen Turkey
in a Creamed Poulet Sauce

New Orleanians have always wanted turkey for Thanksgiving: maybe not fixed any particular way, but turkey nonetheless. And this is how New Orleanians have always wanted their classic poulet sauce, whether it's been served with roasted turkey, baked turkey, fried turkey, or turkey erky lerky! This is how I suggest you make your turkey and sauce this year for *your* Thanksgiving—a slow-poached presentation!

The Turkey:

2 gal. water to cover turkey
1 large onion, diced
3 ribs celery, diced
1 small green bell pepper, diced
1 head garlic, cloved out
3 large carrots, peeled and chunked
1 bouquet garni (thyme, bay leaf, basil, rosemary)

3 lemon slices
1 cup Chablis wine
1 tbsp. red pepper flakes
3 tbsp. salt
1 young, plump hen turkey (10-12 lb. average)
4 tbsp. Frank Davis Poultry Seasoning

In a tall cylindrical stockpot that has a lid, bring the water to a rapid boil and drop in all the ingredients except the turkey and the poultry seasoning. Then, when the water comes back to a boil, lower the fire, cover the pot, and simmer the "broth" for at least 30 minutes to create an intense poaching stock. *Note: at this point you don't want the water to boil, otherwise the stock will turn cloudy; just a gentle bubble will render out and mellow all the flavors of the seasoning vegetables.*

While the stock making is going on, clean the turkey inside and out of all giblets, fat, and debris and wash it thoroughly under cold running water. After patting it dry with paper towels, sprinkle the bird generously with poultry seasoning and set it to the side to wait for the stock.

Then when you're ready to begin poaching, place the turkey (skin attached) in the stockpot and be certain that it is completely submerged in the poaching liquid. Then cook it gently—just below the boiling point—without turning it. *Note: after you've wedged the turkey into the pot, make sure that the stock covers the bird by at least 6 in.*

You want to poach the turkey, covered, until it becomes *"fall-off-the-bone tender."* (Actually, you don't want it to fall off the bone or you'll end up with the makings of turkey fricassee—you just want it cooked all the way through so that the turkey can be removed from the stockpot whole, cooled, and then sliced.) As a general rule of thumb, figure about 15 minutes to the pound; but to guarantee cooking perfection you should insert a thermometer in the breast of the bird as it poaches and continue to cook it to an internal temperature of 180 degrees.

When it's done, gently remove it from the stockpot (and I emphasize the word *gently,* because it's going to want to fall apart), place it on a large platter, and allow it to cool and drain. You have 2 options here: (1) you can either wrap the poached bird in a ribbon of cheesecloth—*kinda like a mummy*—to keep it together and formed for formal carving later at the table, or (2) you can allow it to cool enough to handle so that you can slice it in the kitchen and stash it on a platter. Whichever you select, remember that the turkey will need to be reheated (preferably tightly wrapped in foil in the oven) prior to serving at the main meal.

The Poulet Sauce:

4 cups reduced poaching stock
2 cups heavy cream
½ stick salted butter
4 tbsp. freshly squeezed lemon juice
4 tsp. Dijon mustard
Dash Worcestershire sauce
Dash Frank Davis Garlic Cayenne Hot Sauce
4 drops yellow food coloring
6 tbsp. butter roux
½ cup finely grated Romano cheese
¾ cup julienned green onions
¾ cup minced parsley

Now, after the turkey has poached, it's time to put together the poulet sauce. In a deep saucepan, combine the turkey stock and cream and bring the mixture to a slow boil. Then stir in the butter, lemon juice, mustard, Worcestershire, hot sauce, and food coloring. I suggest you use a wire whisk to get all the ingredients uniformly blended.

Then when everything is mixed thoroughly, add the roux and whip it into the sauce until it becomes velvety smooth. The amount specified in the recipe should give you the amount you need to thicken the sauce, but if you'd prefer to use a little more or a little less to change the consistency, go ahead.

At this point, reduce the heat to low and let the sauce simmer for about 10 minutes. Then just moments before you're ready to eat, gently stir in the Romano cheese, ladle the sauce liberally over slices of the turkey, and garnish with the green onions and parsley.

Personally, I recommend that when you're ready to gather the family at the Thanksgiving table you have a large skillet of the poulet sauce bubbling on the stovetop and a platter full of sliced hot poached turkey directly from the oven. Then the turkey goes into the sauce, everything gets simmered together, and it's all ladled hot and succulent into a deep-fried French-bread boat, garnished with green onions and parsley, and served along with, maybe, some potato stew, some buttered mustard greens, and a complement of glazed yams.

Sounds almost as good as being a Pilgrim, huh?

Chef's Note:
1—The turkey can be poached ahead of time and kept in the refrigerator for 1-2 days before serving with the poulet sauce. Of course, as the recipe mandates, it must be reheated prior to service (unless you're serving leftovers as po' boys, which happen to taste pretty good ice cold).

2—If you're going to remove the skin, it's best to wait until the turkey has thoroughly cooled. It's also a good idea to allow the stock you poached the turkey in to chill in the refrigerator before you use it (that way you can remove all the excess fat from the stock before you convert it to your poulet sauce).

3—The poaching liquid you end up with after the turkey is poached should be reduced to one-half of its original volume before you use it to make the poulet sauce. To get the richness you expect from this dish, it's most important to do the reduction!

4—To thin out the poulet sauce as you use it to heat up the sliced turkey, simply add a little milk to the mixture as it thickens in the skillet.

5—To make the Thanksgiving menu heart healthy, remember a few basic rules—eliminate or reduce as much added fat as possible, cut way back on the salt you put into the dishes, substitute 1 percent milk for heavy cream and thicken it with gravy flour (or cornstarch), and utilize as many of the fat-free products on the market as possible.

6—To create French-bread boats, simply take a number of New Orleans-style heat-and-serve pistolettes, cut off the tops lengthwise with a paring knife much as you would hollow out a pirogue, and deep-fry them in a skillet full of hot peanut oil until they turn a crispy crunchy golden brown.

Frank's Country-Style Fried Turkey Necks

It's a pure finger-lickin' goodness that can be described only as down-home and full of soul! Served up alongside a plate of smothered green beans, a dish of spicy boiled baby potatoes, and a big pan of black-pot cornbread, these fried turkey necks are Southern cookin', yeah!

6-8 qt. water, as needed	6 cloves garlic, smashed
2 tbsp. salt	¼ cup minced parsley
1 tbsp. coarse-ground black pepper	3 bay leaves
1 tsp. red pepper flakes	2 tsp. Frank Davis Poultry Seasoning
1 cup coarsely chopped onion	2 tbsp. Worcestershire sauce
¾ cup coarsely chopped celery	3-4 lb. turkey necks
½ cup coarsely chopped green bell pepper	6 cups peanut oil for deep-frying

First, take a heavy 10-qt. stockpot that has a lid, pour in about 6 qt. water, and bring it to a rapid boil. Then stir in the salt, pepper, red pepper flakes, onions, celery, bell peppers, garlic, parsley, bay leaves, poultry seasoning, and Worcestershire sauce. The water will stop boiling; when it comes back to a boil, lower the fire and simmer the seasoning ingredients, slightly covered, for about 15 minutes.

Meanwhile, with a sharp paring knife, remove the silverskin from the turkey necks and wash the necks under cool running water. When they're all done, drop them into the simmering stock and stir them around once or twice. Again the water will stop simmering; but when a gentle simmer returns, cover the pot and allow the necks to "poach" in the flavored broth for $1\frac{1}{2}$ hours or until the meat turns delicately tender.

This is a good time in the recipe to fix the side dishes—perhaps a pot of green beans smothered in bacon drippings with a little rice to go with them, maybe a couple of pounds of baby Irish potatoes that you can boil to tender in the same stock in which you poached the turkey necks, and for certain a big skillet of homemade cornbread.

When the necks are tender, take a strainer spoon, remove them from the poaching stock, and allow them to drain momentarily. While this is happening, take a heavy, high-sided fry pan, fill it with the peanut oil, and a few at a time drop the necks into the fryer and let them cook until they are richly browned. It should take the necks no more than a few minutes to fry and "crisp up." When they turn a deep golden color all over, remove them from the fry pan and set them to drain on several layers of paper towels. Note: you're frying the necks totally uncoated—no cornmeal, no flour, no breadcrumbs, no nothing.

Serve the necks piping hot with the side dishes. Oh, yeah—and forget the knives and forks! This is finger food!

Chef's Note:

1—For a little more versatility, you can add drumsticks and wings, and boil then fry them together with the necks.

2— Since this recipe uses a significant amount of open oil, it requires constant attention. Just take your time and keep a close eye on the hot grease.

3—These necks are best eaten hot right out of the fryer, but I don't know many who wouldn't palm a whole passel of them and snack on 'em even ice cold.

Spicy Black-Pot Turkey Necks

I gotta tell you, very few dishes I've ever cooked taste this good. This is succulent! This is the ultimate in finger-licking goodness! You'll want to make this for your family and friends every chance you get!

½ cup peanut oil, as needed
3-4 lb. turkey necks, silverskin
   removed
1 tbsp. salt
1 tbsp. coarse-ground black
   pepper
1 tsp. cayenne pepper
2 tsp. onion powder
2 tsp. garlic powder
2 tsp. Frank Davis Poultry
   Seasoning
1 tsp. basil
2 cups thinly sliced mushrooms
2 cups minced onions

¾ cup minced green bell
   peppers
6 cloves garlic, mashed
¼ cup minced parsley
½ cup thinly sliced green onions
2 tbsp. Worcestershire sauce
½ tsp. Kitchen Bouquet
¼ cup all-purpose flour
⅓ cup cocktail sherry
½ cup chicken stock, as needed
2 bay leaves
1 tsp. paprika
6 cups cooked rice

First, take a heavy cast-iron Dutch oven that has a tight-fitting lid (about 4-qt. size will do) and set it on the stovetop over medium-high heat. Then drop in the peanut oil and bring it to "almost smoking"—this is what the temperature must be in order to sear the necks and seal in the juices.

While the oil is heating, generously sprinkle the turkey necks with the salt, black pepper, cayenne pepper, onion powder, garlic powder, poultry seasoning, and basil. Then a few at a time, drop them into the hot oil and fry them down until they are richly browned. When they're just right, remove them from the pot and allow them to drain on several layers of paper towels.

Immediately upon removing the necks, drop in the mushrooms and fry them down until they too reach a golden-brown color. Then immediately thereafter toss in the onions, bell pepper, and garlic and fry down these seasonings as well until they wilt, soften, and pick up the rich brown color of the mushrooms.

At this point, while continually stirring the pot, drop in the parsley, green onions, Worcestershire, Kitchen Bouquet, and flour. Then place the necks back into the pot and *stir, stir, stir* everything together until the necks are evenly coated with the flour and seasonings.

At this stage of the recipe you start the natural gravy going. To do that, just blend in the sherry and the chicken broth (and I'd use the entire amount), drop in the bay leaves, and sprinkle on the paprika. Then mix everything together one more time, tightly cover the pot, and slide it into a preheated 350-degree oven. What you want to do is roast the necks inside the cast iron until they are succulently tender and bubbling in their own juices.

It should take about 1½ hours (adding a little extra sherry or chicken broth as it is needed) to finish the necks to "fall-off-the-bone" tenderness. But as soon as they're done, be sure to serve them piping hot over a mound of steaming rice to savor the full flavor of the gravy. Of course, a little bowl of smothered green beans and a pan of cornbread wouldn't hurt none!

Chef's Note:

1—This recipe can be done entirely on top of the stove, but it requires constant attention so that the turkey necks don't stick to the pot and burn on the bottom. Personally, I think you get the best results in the oven and it's the easy way to go.

2—Like red beans, jambalaya, and gumbo, this recipe is good when it's first cooked, better the next day, and best 2 days down the line.

MawMaw's Deep-Fried Country Quail

Marinate a batch of young, tender quail in milk and onions, dust them with a spicy flour coating, and deep-fry them until they're golden brown and crunchy crispy! Now you got ya some finger-lickin' vittles here, son!

8-12 young wild or farm-raised
    quail
2 cups coarsely chopped
    onions
2 cups skim or evaporated milk
2 tbsp. Frank Davis Garlic
    Cayenne Hot Sauce

1 qt. peanut oil
4 cups all-purpose flour
2 tbsp. Frank Davis Wild Game
    Seasoning
2 tsp. cayenne pepper
2 tsp. coarse-ground black
    pepper

First, take the quail and wash them thoroughly under cold running water, making sure you remove all the globular fat, mucus, and other residuals that may not have been removed during field dressing. Then, after they've been cleaned, set them into a glass, Corning ware, or stainless-steel bowl.

At this point sprinkle the onions over the birds and immediately mix them in with your hands so that each quail picks up the flavor of the onions. Then blend together the milk and hot sauce and pour it over the quail and onions to form a marinade. If you can allow the birds to marinate overnight, *that'll make 'em perfect.* If not, be sure to let them soak in the marinade for at least 3 hours.

Now, when you're ready to fry, heat the oil in either an electric or stovetop fryer to 350 degrees (use an instant-read thermometer if you have to). Then pour the flour into a large baking pan and sprinkle in the game seasoning, cayenne, and black pepper (it's important to take a moment to blend everything uniformly to disperse the seasonings throughout the coating).

All that's left is to lift each quail from the marinade, liberally dust it in the coating mix, shake off the excess flour, and drop it into the hot oil. Be sure not to overcrowd the fryer! They'll come out absolutely perfect if you allow them to fry for 10-12 minutes, turning them gently with tongs during the cooking process. Incidentally, the outside should be crispy and golden brown, the inside should be light and delicately tender from the onion marinade, and each bite should be rich with natural juices!

Chef's Note:

1—Electric fryers are good, but for best results I recommend a black cast-iron Dutch oven. It distributes the heat evenly, cooks the quail uniformly, and doesn't give you "hot spots" that will burn the coating. Of course, if you don't have cast iron, club aluminum is a good second choice.

2—The only way to get perfectly fried quail (or rabbit, or chicken, or shrimp, or anything for that matter!) is to be sure the temperature of the oil is perfect. And to do that you got to use a thermometer— you can't guess at it. Clip it to the side of the Dutch oven so that the tip doesn't rest on the bottom, and be sure it reaches 350 degrees before you drop in the first quail. Do it this way and you'll be guaranteed your quail won't be greasy!

3—I suggest you serve the quail piping hot right from the deep-fryer after draining them for a moment on several layers of paper towels.

4—Remember where this recipe is located in the cookbook. It works beautifully for any kind of wild game that you want to fry—doves, squirrel, snipe, pheasant, chukkas, rails, etc.

Dixie Roasted Goose with Molasses Glaze

Charles Dickens could not have described it better: a freshly hunted wild goose basted and brushed with the darkest and sweetest molasses ever to come from the cane. It would make any Cajun/Creole table exceptionally special, especially if it were served with a little wild rice or oven-baked sweet potatoes and maybe a dish of smothered collard greens.

1 tender young wild goose (8-11 lb.), dressed	4 tsp. Frank Davis Poultry Seasoning
4 tsp. Frank Davis Wild Game Seasoning	2 tsp. coarse-ground black pepper

Start off by preheating the oven to 425 degrees. Then rinse the goose in cold water, removing as much fat as possible from the body cavity and the neck skin. Then pat the bird dry with multiple layers of paper towels and immediately pierce the skin all over with the tines of a large fork.

At this point, liberally sprinkle the goose inside and out with the remaining ingredients. Then arrange it breast side up on a rack in a large oval roasting pan. Cover the bottom of the pan with enough water to come up about $1/2$ in. Then tightly cover the pan with a sheet of heavy-duty aluminum foil and roast the goose at 425 for about 20 minutes to render out some of the excess fat and to begin the browning process.

After the allotted "rendering time," reduce the oven to 350, loosen the foil so that it just "tents" the goose, and continue roasting for 20 minutes per pound or until a thermometer inserted between the drumstick and the thickest part of the thigh registers 180 degrees (make sure the thermometer does not touch bone). When the proper temperature is reached, drain off all the fat from the pan.

The Molasses Glaze:

1 cup blackstrap molasses
2 tsp. Frank Davis Garlic
   Cayenne Hot Sauce

1 tsp. ground ginger
½ tsp. coarse-ground black
   pepper

Very simply, in a medium-size bowl combine all the ingredients. Then take a wire whip and mix them together well.

Liberally brush about half of the mixture completely over the goose, to create a glaze. Continue to roast the goose another 20 minutes, this time uncovered, and brush on the remaining glaze after 10 minutes.

That's all there is to it! All that's left is to remove the goose from the oven and let it stand for about 15 minutes before carving it.

Granny's Double-Baked Mallards
(With Honey-Amaretto Glaze)

If this year you'd like to put a special treat on the table during the peak of hunting season, try fixing this recipe. It's exceedingly simple and it's unlike any other baked duck dish you ever had—the inside is tender and juicy and the outside is crunchy crisp! It's the nicest thing you can do for your taste buds!

3-4 mallards (2-4 lb. each)
4 tsp. Frank Davis Wild Game
   Seasoning
2 tsp. Frank Davis Poultry
   Seasoning
1 cup chicken stock

2 cups clover honey
½ tsp. lemon zest
1 cup amaretto liqueur
4 tbsp. unsalted butter

I told you this was a simple recipe! Watch this!

Take the ducks, wash them thoroughly inside and out, pick through them to make certain they are "shot free," and pat them dry with paper towels.

Next, liberally sprinkle them inside and out with the wild game seasoning and poultry seasoning and, with your hands, rub them down briskly and thoroughly, making sure the seasonings are forced into the duck skin. I also suggest that you wrap the ends of the wings and drumsticks with pieces of aluminum foil to keep them from burning as they bake.

At this point, preheat your oven to 450 degrees. When the thermostat indicates the right temperature, place the ducks in a large baking pan, breast side up (but don't let them touch!), and cook them—*uncovered*—on the middle rack of the oven for 30 minutes. Then turn them over in the pan (breast side down) and bake them for 20 minutes more. Finally, turn them back right side up and bake them for another 10 minutes.

Now, take them out of the oven and let them cool to room temperature (you can even stash them in the refrigerator for finishing later). Of course, while you're waiting, make your honey-amaretto glaze. Here's how you do it.

In a saucepan, bring the chicken stock to a gentle boil. Then stir in the honey, lemon zest, and liqueur and cook it over medium-high heat until the sauce begins to thicken (figure it's going to take you about 20 minutes). At that point, drop in the butter and stir it gently into the sauce until the glaze turns shiny. Then remove the pan from the heat, swirl the pan around a few times, and allow the ingredients to blend thoroughly.

When you're ready to eat, preheat the oven again to 400 degrees and slide the pan of cooled ducks back into the oven.

Expect to bake them for 25-30 minutes, because what you want is for the inside of the ducks to get piping hot and juicy and the outside skin to get crispy and crunchy! Believe me . . . they will!

About 10 minutes before it's time to serve them, open the oven, slide the ducks out, and liberally brush on some of the glaze. Then place the ducks back into the oven and continue to bake them until the glaze sets. You should repeat the glazing procedure until a pretty crust forms on the ducks; just watch that it doesn't burn.

All that's left is to cut the birds into serving-size pieces. And for a little touch of elegance, I suggest you cut them in front of your guests at the table!

Chef's Note:

1—If you don't have any mallards, any other "good ducks" will do—French hens, canvasbacks, wood ducks, teal, etc. Just try to avoid doing this recipe with poule d'eau or dosgris.

2—It isn't necessary to pour off the duck fat as the ducks bake the first time—I promise, the birds won't be greasy. Of course, go ahead and remove the drippings from the pan before the second baking;

otherwise they will splatter wildly. Remember, these ducks are cooked unstuffed.

3—When ready to serve, cut the breasts into slices, cut the drumsticks and thighs off the carcasses, and top each piece with a little extra honey-amaretto glaze. By the way, at my camp, 1 duck will serve 2 persons! I recommend you take the remaining duck bones, brown them in the oven, and turn them into duck stock for future dishes.

CHAPTER 6

Seafood

Mardi Gras Mustard-Dredged Fried Fish
(With Oven-Crusted Grits)

When we get a hankerin' for good ol' Southern-fried fish, most of us just pour a little Aunt Jemima's Corn Meal (*or better yet a little Frank Davis Gourmet Fish Fry*) into a shallow-sided pan and season it up with salt and black pepper. But look what my ol' fishing buddy taught me. Mardi Gras Mustard-Dredged Fried Fish—sounds good, huh? Well, it tastes even better than that!

6-8 fresh fish fillets (4-6 oz. average)
64 oz. vegetable or Canola oil for frying
1 large bottle French's Yellow Mustard

½ bottle Frank Davis Garlic Cayenne Hot Sauce
4 cups Frank Davis Gourmet Fish Fry
1 lb. green onions, sliced

First, you start off by preparing the fish for cooking—wash each fillet, cut it into chunks, and dry the chunks off.

Now take a deep-sided, heavy fry pan, place it on the stovetop, and fill it about a third of the way up with the oil. Then turn on the fire and heat the oil to about 375 degrees (I really like cast iron for this since it distributes heat evenly).

Next mix the mustard and hot sauce. I suggest you place them in a disposable aluminum pan.

When the 2 ingredients are totally combined, place the fish fry in a second aluminum pan and set the 2 pans right next to each other. Then take a third aluminum pan and position it next to the one containing the fish fry. Line it with absorbent paper towels—this will be the pan you use to drain the fish and serve the pieces from.

When you're ready to cook, take the fish chunks, dredge them a few pieces at a time in the mustard/hot sauce mixture, then coat them thoroughly in the fish fry, and then drop the pieces into the hot oil. It will quickly become apparent that the mustard "dredge" will create a heavy coating on the fish, which will serve to keep it from falling off during frying.

At this point, fry the pieces for a couple of minutes—flipping them over once—until they turn a rich golden brown and super crispy. If you're concerned that the mustard will yield a taste you won't like, dismiss that thought: you hardly taste the mustard when you fry fish this way, especially if you do the procedure properly. And the half-bottle of hot sauce isn't detected much either.

When the fish pieces are done, remove them from the hot oil with a slotted spoon and place them in the paper-towel-lined pan to drain away any excess oil. I recommend that you eat the fish pieces while they are super hot! It's the only way to get the full effect of the flavor that the mustard plus hot sauce creates.

Serve the pieces right out of the fryer, covered with handfuls of sliced green onions, accompanied by 1-2 squares of oven-crusted grits.

The Oven-Crusted Grits:

8 cups bottled water
¾ tsp. sea or kosher salt
2 cups Quaker Old Fashioned
  Grits
1 stick sweet cream butter

1 bunch green onions, thinly
  sliced, as desired
1 cup shredded Velveeta cheese
1 cup shredded Pepper Jack
  cheese for topping

First, bring the water to a rapid boil in a 5-qt. heavy Dutch oven. Go ahead and add the salt.

Then, in a rapidly swirling motion, gently add in the grits (but stir briskly enough to keep them from clumping in the pot). This is also the time to stir in the butter. At this point, prepare the grits according to package directions, simmering them over low heat for 5-7 minutes (still stirring occasionally) until cooked.

When they're done, add in the green onions and Velveeta cheese, and fold the mixture until the cheese fully melts and is incorporated into the grits. Now pour the hot grits out into a well-greased disposable aluminum baking pan (or as many pans as it takes, depending upon the size of the pans you have). Then sprinkle the Pepper Jack cheese evenly over the top of the hot grits to form a heavy cap.

When the Jack cheese fully melts, allow the grits to cool to room temperature and firm up. In fact, once cooled to room temperature, you can place them into the refrigerator or cooler until the fried fish are ready.

Then, just before it's time to eat, place the pan of grits under a 550-degree broiler element until a lightly browned crust forms. All that's left is to cut 1-2 squares from the pan, place them on a heated dinner plate, and serve hot fried fish alongside as a truly Southern home-cooked favorite.

Chef's Note:
1—Just for the record, almost any "friable" fish will work for this

recipe—catfish, speckled trout, redfish, flounder, drum, sheepshead, and so forth. Just be certain the fillets are washed well to remove excess fish oils and patted dry with paper towels before beginning the preparation process.

2—The fish can be fried at home and brought to the parades to be eaten "warm." Or they can be fried at the parades, using one of those portable emergency propane cooktops. Or they can be fried back at home after the parades to provide a "hot" evening meal following a full day of "junk food."

3—Oh—and my mom and her friends say they even like fried fish ice cold the next day, right from the fridge! I gotta try dat!

4—The pan of grits can be cooked in advance and kept covered in the refrigerator until ready to serve as a side dish. Which reminds me . . . no "instant grits," y'all! This recipe requires and mandates real, old-fashioned, pot-cooking grits.

5—If you'd prefer to "toast" the grits prior to service, instead of broiling them in the oven, place the squares into a hot, Teflon-coated skillet and brown on both sides (flipping just once) until they're ready to eat.

Baked Trout Napoleon
(With Schirling Sauce and Steamed Rice)

Top fresh speckled trout fillets with a tomato and brandy sauce concocted by my culinary friend Larry Schirling, and you've got one fantastic mouth-watering gourmet treat that'll get rave reviews wherever food connoisseurs congregate. Try serving this one to your discriminating guests!

6 fresh speckled trout fillets
Kosher salt and freshly ground
    black pepper to taste
12 oz. Hellman's Dijonnaise
6 large, vine-ripened tomatoes
6 tbsp. extra-virgin olive oil
2 tsp. Durkee's Garlic Bread
    Sprinkles (or garlic powder)
1 tbsp. Frank Davis Seafood
    Seasoning
2 heads garlic, roasted

½ cup warm brandy
1 tbsp. Worcestershire sauce
1 tbsp. balsamic vinegar
3 tbsp. chopped basil
2 tbsp. chopped fresh rosemary
1 tbsp. Frank Davis Garlic
    Cayenne Hot Sauce
2 tbsp. tomato paste (optional,
    but recommended)
6 cups steamed jasmine rice

First, thoroughly wash and pat dry the speckled trout fillets. Then, after laying them out on the countertop on a sheet of freezer wrap, lightly sprinkle them on both sides with the salt and pepper. Then immediately brush each fillet, again on both sides, liberally with the Dijonnaise (a pastry brush does this most effectively).

Now gently cover the fillets with a sheet of plastic wrap and allow them to "rest" in the refrigerator for $1^1/_2$ hours (which just so happens to be the same amount of time it is going to take you to roast the tomatoes).

And speaking of the tomatoes . . .

First, preheat the oven to 325 degrees. Then cut the thoroughly washed tomatoes vertically into halves and remove their cores. When they're all done, place them cut side up onto a cookie pan and brush each one liberally with olive oil. Then season each half first with the garlic bread sprinkles and then with the seafood seasoning (plain salt and pepper will suffice if you have no seafood seasoning on hand). Now slide the tomato halves into the oven and let them bake—uncovered—for $1^1/_2$ hours.

In the meantime, when it's almost time for the tomatoes to come out of the oven, take the trout fillets from the refrigerator, drop them into a hot skillet, and bronze them on both sides over a high fire until flaky and tender. But try not to break up the fillets too much as they cook. When they reach just the right color, place them side by side in a large, buttered, glass baking pan. Momentarily set them aside.

At this point, remove the tomatoes from the oven and set the cookie pan on the counter on top of a couple of hot pads (*careful—the pan will be really hot!*). Next take the roasted garlic, remove all the little pods from the main heads, and drop them into the pan *in other words, distribute them evenly throughout the tomatoes.* Add a bit of water to the cookie pan and incorporate the caramelized tomato juices into the dish. Now return the pan to the oven for 1 hour more.

At this stage of the recipe, it is time to remove the pan from the oven and mash the tomatoes with a potato masher, scraping the bottom and sides of the dish to get all the brown bits into the mix. Then transfer the tomatoes to a bowl and stir in the brandy, Worcestershire sauce, vinegar, basil, rosemary, and hot sauce. If, after everything is thoroughly mixed together, the tomato sauce appears too thin, or it seems as if it will separate too easily, then whisk in the tomato paste to thicken it slightly.

Finally, gently ladle the tomato reduction over the pan of trout and place the pan in the oven (for 15 minutes at 350 or so) to rewarm and finish. Then when you're ready to eat, spoon the sauce, along with a generous serving of trout, over freshly steamed jasmine rice. A frosty glass of richly brewed iced tea and a chilled Romaine and radicchio salad covered with balsamic vinaigrette will complete the meal!

Chef's Note:

1—If you don't have trout on hand, this recipe works just as well with sheepshead, redfish, tilapia, snapper, catfish, or whatever else you have in the fridge, including chicken breasts or pork fillets. And it is even super-fantabulous served simply over pasta and crowned with either Romano or Parmesan cheese.

2—This sauce not only serves as an appropriate cover for speckled trout and other tender-fleshed fish, it also works very well with zucchini, eggplant, or veal Parmesan. But since it has a tendency to separate easily when used with these liquid-producing mainstays, I recommend that you heat the sauce separately, add it to the specific dish as a topper, then run it under a broiler to reheat as quickly as possible.

3—To keep the sauce from "breaking" or to thicken it slightly for various applications, you can also whisk in a couple of tablespoons of prepared butter roux. The best way to make your own is to gently cook equal amounts of unsalted butter and all-purpose flour over low heat until totally combined into a smooth paste. A butter roux will keep in a Mason jar in the refrigerator for several weeks.

Stuffed Speckled Trout Fillets

Figured at 2 fillets per person, served alongside a dish of oven-roasted, sour-cream potatoes and a buttered summer squash and zucchini medley, this is one of those recipes you prepare only when the dinner guests deserve the very best (or at least every other day of the week for your family!). Try this the next time you think "fish."

8 strips thinly sliced center-cut bacon (plus drippings)	2 tsp. Frank Davis Seafood Seasoning
1 cup vegetable mirepoix	8 speckled trout fillets (6-8 oz. average)
2 cups diced mushrooms	
2 tbsp. heavy cream	2 tsp. Frank Davis Grill-N-Broil
⅔ cup breadcrumbs, as needed	¼ cup extra-virgin olive oil
	1 bunch green onions, poached
1 tbsp. minced garlic	½ cup dry white wine
3 tbsp. minced parsley	⅓ cup shredded Parmesan cheese

First, fry down the bacon under a bacon press so that the strips cook up flat. Then remove them from the pan and set them aside on 1-2 sheets of paper towels to cool and drain.

In the meantime, using the bacon drippings, sauté the mirepoix, mushrooms, and cream until the veggies wilt and the mushrooms begin to soften (which should take you 5-6 minutes over a medium-high heat). By this time there will be an appreciable amount of liquid from the onions and mushrooms in the pan, so begin stirring in just enough breadcrumbs to absorb the liquid and form a stuffing (not wet and pasty, but not dry and crumbly either). When it's just the right consistency, stir in the garlic, parsley, and seafood seasoning and set the mixture aside to cool.

At this point, preheat the oven to 400 degrees and begin preparing the fish fillets. To do this, place the fillets on a cutting board, parallel to your body. Then, using a very sharp knife, slice the fillets horizontally in equal parts so that you create an upper and a lower half. *But do not slice all the way through!* Leave a small section of the top half still attached to the bottom half at the back of the cut, giving you 2 "flaps." Between the 2 flaps is where the stuffing goes.

When you're ready to put the dish together, lay the flaps on each fillet open, sprinkle on a little Grill-N-Broil (or seasoned salt and pepper mix), drizzle on some oil, and spoon between the split fillets 2 tbsp. mushroom stuffing. Then top the stuffing with the strips of bacon and close the fillets.

Finally, tie each fillet shut with strips of the green onions. Then place them into a shallow baking pan, splash on the wine, top with Parmesan cheese, and slide them into the oven. It should take 12-15 minutes for the trout to cook to perfection.

This trout dish is best when served alongside a stack of oven-baked B-size creamer potatoes dotted with butter and sour cream. A bowl of poached zucchini and yellow squash on the side completes the meal.

Chef's Note:

1—This recipe can be prepared with almost any species of fish you prefer—trout, redfish, sheepshead, drum, bass, catfish, tilapia, cobia, wahoo, and even tuna. All you have to do is slice the fillets length-wise to form a place for the stuffing to go.

2—Plain French-bread crumbs make the best bread mix for this stuffing, but the finer crumbs can also be used. Just keep in mind that with finer crumbs the stuffing will be heavier and denser.

3—This mushroom stuffing is good not only for fishbut also chicken, ducks, veal rolls, and pork chops.

4—Essentially every step in the preparation process can be done in advance. Simply put the ingredients (or even the finished stuffed fillets) in the refrigerator until you are ready to bake them. Uncooked stuffed fillets may be kept at the ready under refrigeration for up to 3 days.

Frank's Trout Ranchero

One day while I was fishing, Lake Pontchartrain veteran Terry Googins pulled his boat up alongside mine and said he had a recipe for me! He took a moment to explain how it involved speckled trout fillets, a little butter, a splash of lemon juice, some spicy seasonings, and a big ol' dollop of ranch dressing, all rolled up in aluminum foil. Then he cranked the outboard and took off! Well, I've cooked it enough times now that I figured it's time I shared it with others. So here's tonight's supper!

8 speckled trout	1 cup ranch dressing
4 tsp. Frank Davis Seafood Seasoning	4 cups mashed potatoes or steamed rice
1 stick butter, melted	8 tbsp. imitation bacon bits
4 lemons	4 servings cucumber, carrot, and cherry tomato salad
Zest of 4 lemons	
2 tsp. red pepper flakes	

First, fillet the fish and wash them thoroughly under cool running water. Then, using several layers of absorbent paper towels, pat each fillet "bone dry" and set it aside on a platter.

Next, tear off 8 sheets aluminum foil to accommodate the size of the trout fillets (individual baking-potato sheets work well if you can find them at your neighborhood supermarket). Then, after placing 1 fillet on each sheet, prep the fish—*in steps*—as follows.

1—Sprinkle evenly with the seafood seasoning (you should use approximately $1/2$ tsp. on each fillet and rub it in well with your hands);

2—Evenly pour about 2 tbsp. warm butter over each fillet;

3—Drizzle the juice of $1/2$ lemon, along with a pinch of the zest, over each fillet;

4—Sprinkle on $1/4$ tsp. red pepper flakes over each fillet;

5—Then top each fillet with a uniform coating of 2 tbsp. ranch dressing.

At this point, agitate each foil sheet gently to level out the seasonings and toppings. Then roll each fillet tightly inside of the foil, seal it up, and set them all in a single layer on a shallow sheet pan. Then slide the pan onto the center rack of a preheated 400-degree oven and bake the fillets for 30 minutes. When they're done, remove them from the oven and let them rest on the countertop for about 5 minutes before serving.

When you're ready to eat, place 2 fillets on each plate, slit the foil open, pipe on a generous portion of mashed potatoes (or spoon on some rice), crown with a scattering of bacon bits, and complete with a cold and crispy cucumber, carrot, and cherry tomato salad. The fish and seasonings will yield a rich, almost creamy sauce that truly complements whatever side dishes it accompanies.

Warning—you're going to make this a lot!

Chef's Note:

1—This recipe can also be done using redfish, sheepshead, or drum fillets. Just make certain that the fish is trimmed meticulously and the bloodlines are completely removed.

2—The fillets may be prepared a day in advance. Simply place the foil-rolled pieces in the bottom of the refrigerator overnight. The marinade will significantly enhance the flavor of the fish when the fish is baked the next day.

3—If you don't have seafood seasoning on hand, you can make your own mixture of salt and black pepper and use it as a substitute.

4—Lemon zest is the outermost skin of the lemon, scraped off in ultra-thin layers with a zesting tool so as not to include the bitter white pith. Only small amounts should be used in recipes because the flavor is intense.

5—This dish can also be done outdoors on a charcoal or gas grill. Fire up the pit with heat on one side only. Then simply place the foil-wrapped fish atop the grate on the side that is away from the flames. What happens is the fish cooks gently—and doesn't burn—by radiated heat instead of direct heat. Depending upon the grill, however, you may have to vary the cooking time somewhat.

6—The salad I recommend you serve with this dish is one made with peeled and seeded sliced cucumbers, slivered carrots, and halved cherry tomatoes, chilled and tossed with a homemade Italian vinaigrette and sprinkled with shredded Parmesan cheese.

Pan-Bronzed Fresh Salmon
(With a Mixed Vegetable Grill)

A beautiful, fresh salmon fillet, brushed with butter, spiced with lemon pepper, and seasoned with a touch of Acadiana, is dropped into a hot skillet and bronzed on both sides until toasty and crusty. Served with grilled marinated vegetables, this recipe quickly transforms into a gourmet meal that's fit for royalty!

1 cup extra-virgin olive oil	4 medium red potatoes, sliced
1 cup Italian salad dressing	1 bunch fresh asparagus spears
1 tbsp. Frank Davis Vegetable	6 ears white corn with husks
Seasoning or Bronzing Mix	Softened butter
1 young tender eggplant, sliced	1 fresh salmon fillet, deboned
in disks	(3 lb. average)
4 young medium yellow squash,	1 stick butter, melted
sliced lengthwise	1 tbsp. Frank Davis Seafood
4 medium zucchini, sliced	Seasoning (or salt and black
lengthwise	pepper)
2 medium Vidalia onions, sliced	1 tbsp. lemon pepper seasoning
into rings	½ cup grated Parmesan cheese

The first thing you want to do, even way before planning to cook, is to make your marinade. To do that, take a large glass, plastic, or crockery container and mix together in it the oil, salad dressing, and either the vegetable seasoning or bronzing mix. Then, begin dunking the eggplant, yellow squash, zucchini, onions, potatoes, and asparagus spears into the marinade mix. (At this point you can also pull the husks back on the corn, brush on the softened butter, sprinkle on some of the spices, and replace the husks.) When the vegetables are fully seasoned, place them into a plastic storage container with a tight-fitting lid, pour the remaining marinade over them, and stash them in the refrigerator for about 3 hours (or preferably overnight).

To bronze the salmon, first set a heavy, 12- or 14-in. nonstick skillet on the stovetop and start heating it over a medium-high flame. At the same time, fire up your grill (either gas or charcoal will do). While things are heating up, place the salmon on the countertop, skin side down, and check to see that all of the pin bones have been removed from the fillet (most often they are, but if they aren't, simply take a pair of pointed-nose pliers and pull them out one at a time).

Now with a sharp fillet knife, remove the skin from the fish and discard it. Then, double-fillet the salmon by evenly slicing through it lengthwise, thereby converting 1 large fillet into 2. When this is done, slice both fillets crosswise to create serving portions roughly 3x3 in. square.

Immediately place them on a sheet of waxed paper or freezer paper. Then liberally brush the pieces all over with the melted butter, sprinkle on the seafood seasoning and lemon pepper, and drop them into the hot skillet a few pieces at a time. *Note: (1) don't overcrowd them in the pan so that they have room to cook; (2) be sure you cook them "hot" so that the fish crust over nicely and turn all toasty on the outside; and (3) cook the pieces only until they "just turn opaque" all the way through—do not overcook them or they will dry out and become tough! The best salmon is salmon that's still somewhat pink in the middle.*

Of course, it goes without saying that since the salmon cooks rather quickly the vegetables can be placed on the grill long before the fish cooking begins. In fact, you can even grill the veggies ahead of time, then heat them up slightly before serving. Serve both fish and vegetables piping hot! Garnish with Parmesan cheese.

Chef's Note:

1—All the veggies should be done over a medium-high heat on an open grill or with a medium-high flame under a grill pan. It's okay to brush on a little extra olive oil or melted butter as they cook, but salt and pepper should be added only moments before they are served, to keep them from drying out.

2—Grill the corn in their own husks (and you don't wrap them in aluminum foil). Just continually turn them over and over as they cook so that they roast evening inside the husks.

3—And whatever you do, do not overgrill the veggies! Cook them until tender crisp. They don't have to be burned to a crisp to be called "grilled."

4—The best way to cook fresh salmon is to cook it as natural as you can—very light seasoning, no sauce that will overpower its delicate flavors, and nothing exotic to "spice it up." Simplicity is the key-word.

5—If you want to squeeze on a splash of fresh lemon juice just before you serve the salmon, that's okay. But again, strive to keep the fish as natural as possible.

6—This recipe works well for Pan-Bronzed Fresh Tuna as well. You don't even need to look for pin bones. You can use whatever species of tuna you have: blackfin, bluefin, yellowfin, etc.

Frank's Classic Catfish Courtbouillon

Oftentimes a whole redfish covered with red gravy and baked is referred to in New Orleans as a redfish "courtbouillon." But that's not courtbouillon—that's baked redfish! Courtbouillon, the classic version, is done just as the following recipe directs, whether it is made with redfish or catfish (even though catfish has always been the most popular). So fix this, kick back, and enjoy!

8 pond-raised catfish fillets, 4-6 oz. each
4 tsp. Frank Davis Seafood Seasoning
½ tsp. cayenne pepper
1 cup vegetable or peanut oil
⅓ cup all-purpose flour
1 medium-large onion, diced
6 cloves garlic, minced
⅔ cup diced celery
⅓ cup diced green bell pepper
½ cup thinly sliced green onion tops

¼ cup minced parsley
2 cans Rotel tomatoes with chilies
Juice and zest of 1 lemon
½ cup white wine
1 cup Swanson's Chicken Broth
2 bay leaves
1 tsp. Worcestershire sauce
2 tsp. basil
6 cups cooked long-grain rice

Ideally, you should allow for the equivalent of about 2 6-oz. fillets of dressed, cut-up catfish for each adult (in the end this will accommodate "seconds" without a problem and will feed a family of 6 very well). If using "wild" catfish in this recipe, be sure to meticulously trim away all of the bloodline before frying the fish—*the bloodline produces a strong fishy taste in the finished dish.*

The next step is to cut each fillet into 3-4 pieces, depending upon how big the fillets are. Then generously sprinkle each piece with the seafood seasoning and cayenne. Heat the oil in a 12-in. nonstick skillet. When the oil is hot, drop the fish pieces in and fry them until crispy and golden brown all over. Then drain all the pieces on several thicknesses of paper towels while you prepare the courtbouillon. Here's how it's done.

As we say in Louisiana, "make a roux" by slowly cooking together about ⅓ cup of the oil you used to fry the catfish and an equivalent amount of all-purpose flour. Keep in mind that you don't want a heavy, dark, Cajun roux, just one that barely turns a beige color (about 5 minutes is all it should take). Set it aside.

Then, in a large shallow-sided brazier that has a lid, reheat the remaining oil and sauté the onion, garlic, celery, bell pepper, green onions, and parsley over medium heat. This should take 6-8 minutes.

Now stir into the vegetable mixture the tomatoes, lemon juice and zest, wine, chicken broth, bay leaves, Worcestershire sauce, and basil and blend everything together well. Then over a low flame, cover the pan and simmer the ingredients for 12-15 minutes or until they create a rich flavorful stock—*the courtbouillon!*

Then, a small amount at a time, spoon in, stir in, and dissolve just enough of the roux to thicken the courtbouillon to the consistency of a very light pancake batter (depending upon your taste, it may take most of the roux you made). Finally, place all of the fried fish pieces into the pan, gently nestling each piece into the sauce so that no piece layers on top of any other piece.

At this point, keeping the flame low, re-cover the pan, and heat the courtbouillon for about 20 minutes to piping hot; *but at all costs, do not stir, because this would break up the fish.* If you must mix the ingredients to blend them, gently agitate the pan with the lid in place from side to side. *But try your best not to break up the fish.*

When you're ready to eat, spoon the chunked Catfish Courtbouillon gently over plates of hot buttered rice and serve with crispy French bread rolls and a chilled tossed green salad.

Chef's Note:

1—A brazier is a squatty Dutch oven that starts at about 15 qt. It's traditionally used to make courtbouillon and many other Louisiana dishes.

2—The courtbouillon can be made a day in advance and stashed in the refrigerator until you're ready to serve it to your family and friends. Simply reheat it in the oven, but, again, do not stir and break up the fish pieces.

MawMaw's Good Ol' Days Codfish Balls

One of the most remembered New Orleans dishes of them all, "codfish balls" at one time could be smelled cooking in virtually every neighborhood every Friday in Lent. But when the Gorton Company quit canning fish flakes, this dish all but disappeared from the Crescent City diet . . . until now! Here's how you can do it again . . . these days!

1 lb. dried salted codfish	4 cups small-diced cooked
1 tbsp. pickling spice	potatoes
2 sticks + 4 tbsp. butter	3 raw eggs, beaten
1 cup minced onions	Frank Davis Seafood Seasoning
1 cup minced green onions	to taste
½ cup minced celery	1 tsp. dill
½ cup minced parsley	2 cups seasoned breadcrumbs
4 cloves garlic, minced	1 cup peanut oil for frying

The first thing you do is take the cod, place it in a nonreactive baking pan, and soak it in cold water for about 4 hours in your refrigerator, changing and discarding the water every 1 hour or so. You'll know the fish is ready for the next step in the recipe when it has softened (actually rehydrated)—continue the soaking process until it has.

Next, wrap the softened, *de-salted* cod in a layer of cheesecloth, place it in a pot of boiling water (to which you've added the pickling spice), and cook it over medium-low heat for 25-30 minutes or until the fish flakes easily. Then pour off the water, remove the cheesecloth, and let the cod drain well.

Now, in a 12-in. nonstick skillet, melt 1 stick and 4 tbsp. butter over medium heat and lightly sauté the vegetable medley—onions, green onions, celery, parsley, and garlic. While the veggies are sautéing, shred the codfish into small flakes with a fork.

Then in a large mixing bowl, blend the seasoning vegetables and the codfish together. When they are mixed well, gradually begin adding the potatoes and "fold" them into the codfish mix (keep in mind that the blending goes better if the potatoes are still hot when they're folded into the fish). At this point, very quickly stir in the eggs until the total consistency is uniform; then season the mixture with the seafood seasoning and dill (*but watch the salt—if you didn't get it all out of the cod during the soaking process, you could end up with a dish that's too salty!*).

Now's the time when you wet your hands and begin forming "codfish balls"—ideally, they should be about the diameter of a drink coaster and a little less than $1/2$ in. thick.

As the patties are shaped, lightly dredge them in the seasoned breadcrumbs and place them on waxed paper to "set" for about $1/2$ hour. (Actually, you can make them as far as a day in advance and keep them in the refrigerator.)

Finally, when you're ready to eat, combine a couple of tablespoons of both peanut oil and butter in a nonstick skillet, bring it up to medium-high heat, and pan-sauté a few codfish patties—on both sides—until they turn a crusty golden brown. Repeat the process with the oil, butter, and patties until all are cooked.

It would be a mortal sin not to serve them piping hot, topped with a sauce made with buttered creamed peas and accompanied by a stack of sautéed onion rings and a plate of cold sliced tomatoes.

Chef's Note:

1—So where do you buy salted cod? You can find it at Central Grocery on Decatur Street in New Orleans, as well as at Nor-Joe Import Company in Metairie. Elsewhere in the country, simply look in the telephone directory for an old-time Italian grocery—they'll have it as bacala.

2—Another little hint—if you'd rather use something other than salted cod, some markets offer fresh cod in their seafood cases. Follow the recipe above, only eliminate the soaking process. Oh— and it's perfectly okay to make this recipe using poached white trout, drum, sheepshead, croakers, flounder, or channel mullet instead of cod.

3—If you want to serve codfish balls traditionally, the old-fashioned way is to take 2 slices white bread, slather them with Blue Plate mayonnaise, slap a codfish ball between the slices, open a Barq's Root Beer, and chow down! Dat's da whole meal!

Everything You Ever Wanted to Know About
Preparing Calamari

Calamari is Italian for *squid.* And the absolute most important step when cooking calamari (unfortunately, it's the one that is most often neglected by cooks) is cleaning them properly. The difference in whether they taste delicately tantalizing or "just like fish bait" depends on that process alone. Here's how to do it right.

1—Pull the tentacled part of the calamari off the body, tearing right behind the eyes. This will usually take with it the very small entrails, which can be pulled of and discarded. A small gray-silver part of this is the ink sac, which can also be tossed out.

2—Turn the tentacle section inside out, which will cause the beak and a small ball of inedible tissue to protrude. Cut off those parts, as well as the eyes, but keep the tentacle section in one piece. Also pull away any loose membranes you see. The tentacles are what you want—not the "stuff" in the middle.

3—Insert your finger into the body of the squid and remove everything you find on the inside. One of these items will be the "pen" or bone, which looks like a thin piece of flexible, clear plastic. It goes!

4—A rather tough exterior skin will cover the body, and that has to be removed as well. Actually, it comes off fairly easily most of the time. Occasionally, to loosen this skin, you will have to plunge the squid into boiling water for a minute (followed by a quick cold-water bath, so it won't keep cooking).

5—Finally, while the tentacle section is kept in one piece, it is best to slice the body into rings about $1/2$ in. wide (and even a little less than that if they are to be deep-fried).

And speaking of frying calamari, here's my recipe for doing just that.

Frank's Fried Calamari

16 fresh small squid
Peanut or corn oil for deep-
    frying
3 egg whites, well beaten
½ cup all-purpose flour

1 tsp. Frank Davis Seafood
    Seasoning
Pinch salt
Dash white pepper

After you have completely cleaned your calamari according to the directions I've given you above, preheat the oil in a fryer to 375 degrees.

Beat the egg whites yet again, then dip the calamari into the eggs.

Next sift the flour, seafood seasoning, salt, and pepper together. Then liberally dredge the egg-dipped calamari pieces in the flour mixture.

Now drop them into the hot oil and cook them until they float high in the oil (*but never more than 3 minutes!*).

Finally, drain the calamari pieces on several layers of absorbent paper towels and serve them piping hot with a side of homemade marinara sauce for dipping. This recipe makes 4 appetizer portions, so adjust your quantity to suit your needs.

The Fine Points of Boiling Seafood

10 lb. crabs, shrimp, or crawfish
2 large onions, quartered
¾ bunch celery
6 lemons, quartered or sliced

3 heads garlic
4 bay leaves
1 cup Frank Davis Complete
    Seafood Boil

For each 10 lb. of seafood, use the ingredients above. Then add enough water to cover the seafood by 4 in. Bring the water to a boil.

Regardless of the amount of water you use to boil seafood, remember that it must actually be "too" salty and "too" peppery! To achieve this, taste the stock periodically as it comes to a boil, and add more seafood boil until you feel the stock is too strong. This will give you seasoned seafood that will turn out "just right."

The Culinary Art of Backtiming:

Potatoes   1—2—3—4—5—6—7—8—9—10—11—12—13—14—15—
                                                  16—17—18
Corn   11—10—9—8—7—6—5—4—3—2—1
Shrimp   3—2—1

   *Explanation: If you're also going to add small potatoes and sec-
tions of corn on the cob, the potatoes need to boil for a total of 18 minutes, but the corn only needs to boil for 11 minutes. So you drop in
the corn after the potatoes have been boiling for 7 minutes. Then if
your seafood is shrimp, for example, the shrimp boil for only 3 minutes, so you drop in the shrimp after the potatoes have been boiling
for 15 minutes. That's backtiming.*
   *Now, things like sausage or weenies can be put into the boil at the
same time that the potatoes go in—they only get more tender with
the added boiling time.*

After the Water Returns to a Boil:

Boil crabs for 8-10 minutes
Boil shrimp for 1-3 minutes
Boil crawfish for 1-2 minutes

   For exceptionally small seafood, boil only until the water comes
back to a boil once you have added the seafood. When the boiling
time has elapsed, remove the pot from the hot burner and drop in a
bag of ice. This causes the shells on the seafood to contract, thereby
drawing the seasoned boiling stock well inside the shells to flavor the
meat. The ice also causes the seafood to sink in the seasoned water,
which results in better seasoning absorption. *Soak all seafood for a
minimum of 20 minutes after icing.* Then you're ready to chow down
on your seafood boil!

Authentic New Orleans Boiled Crabs

In Southeast Louisiana, there must be a gazillion recipes for boiling crabs. But that doesn't mean they're all good! This one, though, is not only good, it's absolutely authentic and the way we've boiled crabs in the Crescent City since the first one crawled up out of Lake Pontchartrain! If you truly love the little critters, this is the way you want to cook 'em!

5 gal. water
1 cup Frank Davis Granular
 Seafood Boil
4 lemons, sliced
6 medium onions, quartered
6 ribs celery
3 heads garlic

4 bay leaves
½ cup salt or to taste
4 tbsp. red pepper flakes
 (optional)
2-4 dozen live crabs
1½ bags ice

In a 48-qt. pot over propane heat, bring the water to a rolling boil. Then toss in the seafood boil, lemons, onions, celery, garlic, bay leaves, salt, and red pepper flakes, and allow the water and seasonings to boil rapidly for about *10 minutes* so that the flavors meld into a rich boiling stock.

Meanwhile, chill the crabs with a bag of ice (this keeps their claws from falling off when they are added to the boiling water!).

Then when you're ready to cook, put the crabs into the pot. The water will stop boiling. When it comes back to a *rolling boil,* time the crabs . . . *8 minutes for small to medium crabs, 10 minutes for medium to large crabs.*

When the boiling time is over, shut off the fire, remove the pot from the burner (because if you don't, the crabs keep cooking from the secondary heat stored in the steel burner grate), drop another half-bag of ice on top of the crabs (which will cause them to sink to the bottom and start absorbing the seasonings), and let them soak for at least 20 minutes (or until they reach the seasoning intensity you desire).

Chef's Note:

1—This recipe can be reduced or increased proportionately without affecting the flavor of the boiled crabs.

2—Large quantities of seafood boil best over propane heat. Natural gas or electricity from kitchen stoves just doesn't provide the

BTUs necessary to boil large volumes of water. What you end up with is incorrect cooking times and mushy crabs.

3—If you plan to cook small potatoes with your crabs, put them into the pot and boil them by themselves for 8 minutes. Then add the crabs, time them out as instructed above, and the potatoes and crabs will be ready at the same time. Always re-season the water every time you cook an additional batch of crabs and potatoes.

4—To boil corn with your crabs, put segments of corn on the cob in the pot and boil them by themselves for 1 minute. Then add the crabs, time them out as instructed above, and the corn and crabs will be ready at the same time.

5—Never, never *put cooked crabs back into the same container you used for the uncooked crabs without first washing that container thoroughly with lots of soap and extremely hot water! That is how you get sick from bacteria!*

6—If you can't find *Frank Davis Granular Seafood Boil where you live, you can order it by calling 985-643-0027 or online from www.frankdavis.com.*

Frank's Southern Crab Claw Quiche

You've probably heard people make lots of snide remarks about "quiche." But I'm here to tell you that for an omelet, quiche is not only very sophisticated but one of the most fantastic-tasting pies you'll ever eat as well. Oh, yeah—and it's not all that difficult to make either!

1 pkg. (24 oz.) frozen shredded hash browns
6 tbsp. butter, melted
½ cup shredded Swiss cheese
½ cup shredded Pepper Jack cheese
1 cup real crab claw meat
2 tbsp. margarine, softened
½ cup chopped raw bacon
¼ cup chopped green onions
¼ cup chopped red bell pepper
¼ cup chopped yellow bell pepper

¼ cup chopped green bell pepper
4 eggs, slightly beaten
1½ cups half-and-half
1 tbsp. butter, melted
½ tsp. Frank Davis Seafood Seasoning
¼ tsp. coarse-ground black pepper
½ cup grated Parmesan cheese

The first thing you do is thaw out the package of hash browns. Then you spread them out in a thin layer on paper towels to remove their excess moisture (I also suggest that you pat them from the top with extra paper towels). When they're just right, press them evenly into 2 well-greased 9-in. pie plates (be sure to bring the potatoes evenly up the sides too). Now liberally brush both crusts with the melted 6 tbsp. butter and bake them at 425 degrees for 20-25 minutes or until richly browned. Then remove the crusts from the oven and reduce the heat to 350.

At this point, uniformly combine the Swiss and the Jack cheeses in a medium-size bowl. Then, while the hash-brown crusts are still piping hot right out of the oven, evenly sprinkle the cheese mixture plus the crabmeat into them.

When that's done, place the margarine in a nonstick skillet and sauté until tender the bacon, green onions, and bell peppers. While this is going on, take a large bowl and whisk together the eggs, cream, butter, seafood seasoning, and pepper. Add the vegetables (slightly cooled) to the egg filling, then *gently* pour it directly into the crusts so that the cheese and crabmeat are not displaced.

Finally, all that's left is to bake the quiches at 350 degrees in the center of the oven for 25-30 minutes or until a knife inserted near the center comes out clean. Then when you're ready to serve, sprinkle the pies with the Parmesan cheese, *but let them stand for about 10 minutes or so before slicing into wedges.*

You'll find this to be the ideal recipe for an early-morning breakfast, a midday special lunch, or even a gourmet dinner after 8:00. Whichever meal you choose to prepare it for, chances are there will be no leftovers!

Chef's Note:

1—Always buy the highest-quality hash browns you can find. The potatoes form the foundation of the entire dish. Remember, the higher the quality, the crunchier the crust. And that's what you want!

2—If you'd prefer to different cheeses in this recipe, that is totally up to you. Pepper Jack and Swiss complement the crab claw meat nicely, but if you'd prefer to substitute cheddar, Colby, provolone, ricotta, or any other cheeses that suit your personal tastes, go right ahead and substitute to your heart's content!

3—I know that because of price it is tempting to buy imitation crabmeat to use in this dish, but don't do it! Get the real McCoy. What you produce as a consequence of originality has no equal. Or to put it another way, that imitation stuff just don't cut it!

4—If you don't have seafood seasoning on hand, you can substitute to your taste a mixture of kosher salt, coarse-ground black pepper, onion powder, garlic powder, and paprika.

Frank's Crabmeat au Gratin Deluxe

Most folks think *au gratin* means cheesy or bubbly or something. Actually, it doesn't! It means "with a crust." So what I do in this recipe is take backfin lump white crabmeat and cover it with an intensely flavored cheese and sherry sauce and bake it until it turns all bubbly and crusty! You really shouldn't let another day go by without trying this one!

1 stick butter
1 cup minced onions
1 rib celery, minced
4 cloves garlic, minced
⅓ cup all-purpose flour
13-oz. can evaporated milk
2 egg yolks, slightly beaten
1 tsp. Frank Davis Seafood
   Seasoning or kosher salt
½ tsp. cayenne pepper
1 tsp. fresh-squeezed lemon
   juice

2 tbsp. cocktail sherry
½ cup thinly sliced green onion
   tops
1 lb. lump crabmeat, picked
   through for shells
1 cup crushed potato chips
1 cup shredded mild cheddar
   cheese
½ cup minced parsley
12 French bread pistolettes

First thing you do is take a heavy, high-sided skillet and melt the butter until very lightly browned (*but not burned!*). Add and auté the onions, celery, and garlic. Then when all the veggies are wilted and soft, immediately whisk in the flour until it is totally combined.

Next, pour in the milk (but do it gradually to create a silky smoothness in the sauce). Then temper the egg yolks gently with some of the warmed milk, so that they do not curdle in the sauce, and stir them into the mixture. At this point, it's time to add in the seafood seasoning, cayenne pepper, lemon juice, and sherry. Thoroughly blend all the ingredients together and cook them into a sauce for 5-7 minutes or until velvety.

All that's left to do now is to fold in both the green onions and the crabmeat, pour the concoction into a lightly greased casserole pan (or individual ramekins), evenly sprinkle on the potato chips, and liberally top with the cheddar cheese. The dish is done and ready to eat after you bake it for 10-15 minutes in a 375-degree oven (or until nicely browned and crusty).

I recommend that you serve the au gratin piping hot with a garnish of parsley, a cold tossed salad, and hot, buttered, crispy pistolettes.

Chef's Note:

1—You can use either lump crabmeat or crab claw meat in your au-gratin dish. But do not use canned crabmeat! And whatever you do, never use imitation crabmeat!

2—You can use either mild or sharp cheddar cheese for making an au gratin. You might even prefer an equal-part mixture of both.

3—Once again, remember that the term au gratin *doesn't mean "cheesy," as many folks believe. Instead, it means "with a crust." In this deluxe recipe, the combination of potato chips and richly baked cheddar cheese provides that crust. So don't take it out of the oven until it gets crusty!*

Variation: Make the sauce portion of the recipe. Then evenly lay out the crabmeat in the greased casserole or in individual ramekins and pour the au-gratin sauce over the top. Complete the recipe by baking it as directed. This is the method I usually use and the one I truly prefer.

Frank's Maryland Crab Cakes
(South Louisiana Version!)

I'll betcha MawMaw usta make codfish balls when you were a kid (actually they were fish cakes made either with Gorton's Fish Flakes or poached white trout or croaker fillets packed tightly into boiled and mashed potatoes). But ever since the dawn of man, everyone everywhere has raved over authentic "Maryland" crab cakes, and folks in the Crescent City have probably raved the loudest. But that's because while the method of making the cakes is *Maryland* style, you just can't get the ultimate in flavor unless you use *Louisiana* crabmeat! Here's the recipe.

2 lb. Louisiana whole lump or
  white select crabmeat
1 cup seasoned breadcrumbs
1 extra-large egg, well beaten
½ cup real mayonnaise
2 tbsp. chopped parsley
2 tbsp. minced celery
4 tbsp. sliced green onions
½ tsp. salt

½ tsp. white pepper
½ tsp. Frank Davis Seafood
  Seasoning
1 tbsp. Worcestershire sauce
½ tbsp. Dijon mustard
½ tsp. dry mustard
Margarine and butter for frying
  (equal amounts)

First, place the crabmeat into a deep glass bowl, pick through it gently, and carefully remove all shell fragments you find.

Then, in a second bowl, uniformly mix together the breadcrumbs, egg, mayonnaise, parsley, celery, green onions, salt, pepper, seafood seasoning, Worcestershire, Dijon, and dry mustard.

At his point, add the crabmeat to the breadcrumb mixture and gently *fold* everything to a "stuffing" consistency. I emphasize the word *fold* because you don't want to break the large lumps of crabmeat into shreds. In other words, mix thoroughly but gently. *Here's a hint: if the texture appears to be too dry, add a little more mayonnaise.* Now the next step, and it's an important one, is to chill the mix for at least 2 hours—if you don't allow the mix to "bind," the cakes will fall apart in the pan.

Finally, when you're ready to eat, take your hands and shape the mix into about a dozen 3-in. crab cakes. Then, using just enough margarine and butter to prevent sticking, cook the cakes in a frying pan until they are toasty brown (it will take about 5 minutes on each side).

Serve them piping hot right from the skillet with tartar sauce and Louisiana Hot Sauce, alongside a small mountain of mashed potatoes and a Romaine and avocado salad.

Chef's Note:

1—I prefer to use white select or jumbo lump crabmeat. But there's not a thing wrong with crab cakes made with claw meat either. You can alter this part of the recipe without seriously affecting the final flavors. However, under no circumstances can you substitute imitation crabmeat! Never!

2—To get the recipe to come out right, the ingredients must *be chilled for 2 hours. But that's the minimum amount of time. It's actually possible to prepare the cakes a day in advance and keep them refrigerated until time to sauté.*

3—Some recipes call for pan sautéing in pure butter. Some suggest straight margarine. For the ultimate in flavor, I recommend that you use equal portions of margarine and butter—butter for the taste and margarine to raise the sautéing temperature.

4—I suggest that you use 2 spatulas to turn the crab cakes, and turn them gingerly. They are so light and delicate that if you treat them too rough they'll literally fall apart.

To Purge or Not to Purge?
That's the Question, Bubba!

At least three or four times a week, I get e-mails, postcards, or phone calls asking "the question." Well, I hereby ask *you* the question. Do you know the correct answer? Have you fallen victim to the rumors? What say we go back to the beginning?

Do you have any idea which three questions are most often asked of outdoors writers and cookbook authors?

The first is, "How do I season a big ol' cast-iron skillet or Dutch oven so that I can fix blackened redfish?"

The second is, "Somebody said there's an easy way to clean sheepshead—can you tell me how to do it?"

And thirdly, "How do you go about purging crawfish before you boil them?"

The answer to the first question, about seasoning a cast-iron skillet, is just instructional—wash the skillet real good, rinse it until there is absolutely no trace of soap left (since this will be the one and only time you use soap on cast iron), dry it over an open flame on the stovetop until all the water is evaporated, cool it down, then rub on a light layer of bacon fat or lard, baking the fat into the skillet in the oven at 300 degrees. Repeat this last procedure over and over again, rubbing on another light layer of fat and baking it. As each new layer of fat is applied and baked into the pan, the "seasoning" gets richer and richer until the pan is "cured." From this point on, you clean it only by rubbing it down with a little salt on a paper towel to remove stubborn burned-on food. Then, after each use and cleaning, wipe it down with a little vegetable oil on a soft rag before you put it away.

The answer to the second question, about cleaning sheepshead, is also instructional—lay the fish on its side, take a very sharp 8-in. filleting knife, insert the tip at the start of the dorsal fin (there's a groove there that the fin nestles into when the fish relaxes it), and with the knife blade separate the fillet from the backbone by cutting along the backbone to the tail fin. Then lift up the fillet with your fingers and continue to remove the side by cutting the meat from around the rib cage. At this point, the whole fillet will be ready to come off—just cut it crosswise from the top of the dorsal to the bottom of the belly and *voila!* Repeat the same procedure on the other side of the fish and it's clean as a whistle!

All that remains is to separate the scales from the two filleted pieces. You'll wind up with two beautiful white slabs of fish and you toss out the carcass without ever breaking open the belly cavity.

But the answer to the third question is simply *"you don't!"* Period! Amen! No discussion necessary!

No one really knows how this wives' tale got started, where it got started, when it got started, or why it got started, but it has probably produced the biggest misconception in seafood cookery since this whole business about eating oysters only in the *r* months.

I guess the practice kinda spread like chickenpox throughout our neighborhoods way back in the days when PawPaw and MawMaw were runts. Somebody on the block, or on the bayou, obviously was spotted dumping a two-pound box of salt over a pile of crawfish in No. 3 washtub. The conversation probably went something like this:

"Hey, whatcha doin'? Why ya puttin' all that salt on your mudbugs?"

"Just because of the fact that they *are* mudbugs, that's why. They're all dirty. Full of swamp grime and grit. Probably covered in nasty muck. And you know good and well that they done ate some of it! It's all up inside of 'em now. So this here salt is gonna clean 'em up and clean 'em out!"

"Say what?"

"Yep—my pappy told me it's called 'purging.' First I cover 'em in a lot of salt—two, three pounds sometimes. Then ya wet 'em good with a whole lot of water from this here hosepipe."

"Then what happens?"

"Well, the salt dissolves and makes the water really really salty. And when the tub fills up with this salty water, the crawfish breathe it in and it purges 'em."

"It what?"

"It purges 'em! When they breathe in enough of the salty water, it goes through 'em like castor oil!"

"What?"

"It cleans 'em out! Goes right into their old poop-chutes. And they, let's see the best way for me to say this, they dispel the mud and grit and grime and their little ol' intestines end up empty as a broken piggy bank! That way you got really clean crawfish!"

"And all this takes place because they breathe in salty water?"

"Sure—didn't you ever study biology in school?"

"Yeah, but I never learned that a bunch of salty water sucked up into your lungs—or in the case of your mudbugs, their gills—would cause you to get the runs!"

"Get the what?"

"The poops! See, I thought the crawfish would have to swallow the salt so that it would go down their gullets, traverse the stomach, enter the intestines, liquefy the matter in the intestinal canal, and cause that to be eliminated!"

"That's what I just tried to explain to you!"

"No—you told me the crawfish would breathe in the salty water. You didn't say anything about the alimentary function, the intestines and all. Cuz last I heard didn't nobody ever got the poops because they breathe in anything. The lungs, er, I mean the gills just aren't connected to the intestines. Not in any species we know of!"

Then there was this long pause, which purportedly resembled something of a thought process. And suddenly there came the revelation.

"Well, if everything I just explained to you ain't so, why does everybody I know purge their crawfish, huh?"

"Because they're mean! They're all crawfish killers!"

"No, wait—I'm not the only one doing this. Neighborhoods all over New Orleans, whole towns up and down the bayous, everywhere you go in Louisiana you're gonna find people purging their crawfish. You mean to tell me you don't purge your crawfish?"

"No, I don't!"

"Why not?"

"Because as I just told you, it isn't necessary and it doesn't do what you claim it does because it's biologically impossible."

"Whoa—that's way too over my head. Explain it simple-like for me."

"Okay, follow this. First of all, those crawfish that you dump all that salt on are not saltwater creatures—they're freshwater creatures. Salt shuts down their gills so that they can't take in oxygen. That means that this sudden surge in salt is gonna kill 'em deader than a doornail in pretty short order!"

"Well, that's kinda true—I notice a lot of 'em kick the bucket while I'm purging 'em!"

"Now you know why. Salt water: freshwater animal. See, you don't need salt any more than you need Ajax Cleanser. You can get all the dirt from the swamp off of them simply by washing them down with plain water from your hosepipe. When the runoff turns clear, the mud is gone from your mudbugs."

"Yeah, but what about all the poop and stuff they got inside of them?"

"Well, your salt bath certainly won't do anything about that! Because it can't!"

"Why not, Mr. Smart Guy?"

"Because there ain't no way on God's green earth that those little crawdads can drink enough of that salty water to have it work like a shot of Milk of Magnesia or Dulcolax or GoLightly before it kills them!"

"Yeah, I'd probably boil 'em before that would work."

"So let me ask you, why do you continue to insist on purging your crawfish?"

"Dang it, I don't know now. Seems like a big ol' waste of time. Just wash 'em off, you say?"

"Yep—a little fresh running water is all it takes!"

Then there was another brief period of silence. Then all of a sudden . . .

"So I guess purging crabs would be out of the question, huh?"

Eastertime Mushrooms and Mudbugs

This recipe is all about puff pastry shells, crawfish, mushrooms, butter, and Lorraine Swiss cheese. You got to make a big platter of these that you can serve to your family on Easter Sunday.

½ stick salted butter, softened
¼ cup extra-virgin olive oil
¾ cup vegetable mirepoix
1 lb. fresh mushrooms, sliced
1 medium tomato, seeded and diced
3 tbsp. minced parsley
¼ cup thinly sliced green onions
1 tbsp. minced garlic
2 lb. Louisiana crawfish tails

⅔ cup Swanson's Chicken Broth, as needed
1 lb. sour cream
¾ cup shredded Parmesan cheese
1½ tsp. Frank Davis Seafood Seasoning
12 puff pastry shells, baked light and crispy
12 half-slices Lorraine Swiss cheese

In a heavy 12-in. skillet or fry pan, melt down the butter and briskly combine it with the oil. Then, over medium-high heat, rapidly whisk in the vegetable mirepoix and sauté the veggies until they wilt and completely soften.

At this point, with a slotted spoon, remove all of the veggies from the pan and set them aside momentarily.

Now, with the heat turned up to high, begin adding the mushrooms to the empty pan a little at a time, and start stir-frying them in the residual oil until they become brown and toasty and nutty flavored. As the individual slices brown, continue adding more slices to the pan (and extra olive oil as needed) until all the mushrooms are done. *Note: Be sure they are "sautéing" and not "sweating out their natural juices." Place too many slices in the pan initially and the 'shrooms won't sauté!*

When the mushrooms are ready, return the sautéed vegetables to the pan, along with the tomato, parsley, green onions, garlic, and crawfish tails. Then reduce the fire to medium and combine all the ingredients thoroughly. By the way, it's okay to splash on a little of the chicken broth right about now to loosen up the stuffin' mix to a workable consistency.

Then when the mixture in the pan takes on the appearance and texture of a creamy stuffing, transfer it from the pan to a large mixing bowl. At this point, immediately stir in the sour cream and Parmesan and sprinkle on the seafood seasoning.

When you're ready to fill the pastry shells, place them side by side on a baking pan that has been lined with a sheet of parchment paper. Then spoon the crawfish and mushroom stuffing into the shells. When they have all been filled (actually they should be "overfilled"), gently lay a half-slice of Lorraine Swiss over the top of each over-stuffed pastry shell.

All that's left to do now is to slide the baking pan into a preheated 450-degree oven just long enough to fully melt the cheese caps (8-10 minutes should do it). Then when you're ready to eat, serve your guests a couple of pastry shells each, directly atop a chilled plate of cold salad, including lettuce, tomatoes, celery, cucumbers, bell peppers, hard-boiled eggs, shredded Parmesan, pesto salad dressing, and a healthy splash of Frank Davis Hot Sauce.

Chef's Note:
1—These pastry shells are at their absolute best when served piping hot right out of the oven. But if they need to be served the next day, they can be reheated in a convection oven preset to 250 degrees. Heat only, though, until they are warm throughout.

2—Finally, even if you're an absolute teetotaler, it's hard to serve this menu without a stout glass of chilled white wine alongside. But, hey, maybe that's just me!

Frank's Jazz Fest Crawfish Bread

Next to crawfish Monica, cochon-de-lait sandwiches, and a half-dozen or so other long-standing popular favorites, crawfish bread is right up there at the top with Jazz Fest goers! Of course, this version might not be an exact replication of the one they serve at the New Orleans Fair Grounds every spring, but I can promise you this much . . . fix it and the last thing you'll want to do is throw it out!

1 stick butter, softened
½ cup chopped onions
½ cup chopped green bell pepper
¼ cup chopped celery
¼ cup dry white wine
1 cup clam juice or chicken stock
⅓ cup prepared roux
⅛ tsp. ground thyme
⅛ tsp. dried basil
2 bay leaves
2 tbsp. minced garlic
2 lb. crawfish tails with fat

½ cup minced ripe tomatoes
1 can cream of shrimp soup
¼ cup chopped parsley
⅓ cup sliced green onions
½ tsp. Frank Davis Seafood Seasoning
1 tsp. salt (optional)
4 loaves French bread "Twin Shorties"
8 oz. shredded Colby cheese
8 oz. shredded Monterey Jack cheese
1 cup grated Parmesan cheese

In a large heavy skillet, melt the butter and heat it until it bubbles. Then lower the heat and add the onions, bell pepper, and celery. Sauté the mixture until the veggies turn limp, but do not let them brown (figure that it should take about 3 minutes).

Next add the wine to the seasoning base and bring it to a boil. Then, after about 1 minute, pour in the clam juice and add to it the roux, thyme, basil, bay leaves, and garlic. At this point, return the mixture to a boil once again but immediately lower the heat and simmer everything together for about 5 minutes more or until thickened.

Now add the crawfish tails, tomatoes, soup, parsley, green onions, seafood seasoning, and salt (if needed). When everything is thoroughly combined, simmer the skillet for 8-10 minutes or until you can pick up the sauce with a fork..

All that's left to do is to slice the loaves of bread lengthwise and sprinkle each half with a thin but complete layer of Colby and Jack cheese. Then place the bread onto a sheet pan and slide it under a hot broiler or toaster oven until the cheese fully melts. Finally, take the bread halves out of the oven, generously spoon the crawfish sauce down the center of each loaf, then top them liberally with Parmesan cheese.

Return the crawfish bread to the oven one more time, but only until the sauce begins to bubble. Then slice the "breads" into appropriate individual portions and serve the pieces piping hot.

This is absolutely outstanding with a "brewski" in a tall frosted glass!

Mudbug Moonpies

If you've always liked those old-timey Natchitoches meat pies, then you're just gonna love these Mudbug Moonpies! Made of well-seasoned crawfish stuffing packed inside crispy, golden-brown pie crusts and served piping hot right out of the oven, these are your "can't-eat-just-one" specialty treats that the whole family will fight over. Make a batch!

6 single premade pie crusts (Pillsbury recommended)	3 tbsp. minced parsley
½ cup chopped crisp-fried bacon (plus drippings)	¼ cup thinly sliced green onions
⅓ stick butter	1 tbsp. minced fresh garlic
1 medium white onion, minced	2 tsp. Frank Davis Seafood Seasoning
½ cup vegetable mirepoix	2 tbsp. white wine
1 lb. Louisiana crawfish tails, coarsely chopped	1 cup chicken broth, as needed
1 can cream of shrimp soup	2 hard-boiled eggs, minced
¼ tsp. ground thyme	1 cup shredded Colby cheese
¼ tsp. ground oregano	2 egg whites, well beaten
	¼ stick butter, melted

When you're ready to start making the moon pies, allow the crusts to come to room temperature for 20-30 minutes before attempting to roll them out.

In the meantime, combine the bacon, drippings, and butter in a heavy anodized or nonstick skillet and sauté the onion and vegetable mirepoix until they are tender and softened. *Note: if you're working at trimming away cholesterol, you can substitute extra-virgin olive oil or pecan oil for the butter and bacon fat.*

At this point, add to the skillet the crawfish tails and quickly sauté

218   FRANK DAVIS MAKES GOOD GROCERIES!

them into the vegetable seasonings (this should take no more than about 3 minutes—you don't want to overcook the tails and reduce them to a rubbery texture).

Next, stir in the soup, thyme, oregano, parsley, green onions, and garlic. I recommend that you take 1-2 extra minutes to uniformly combine all these ingredients. Now gingerly add in the seafood seasoning and wine, drizzle on as much chicken broth as needed to keep the stuffing light and moist, and fold everything together once again. When the crawfish mixture is fully blended, add the chopped eggs and cheese and allow the mixture to cool.

All that's left to do now is to roll out the pie dough into 1, thin, giant circle (placing the dough between 2 sheets of plastic wrap will make this task easier). Then using an inverted soup bowl, cut out about 5 dough circles 6 in. across (you should easily get 5 if you rolled out the dough thinly enough).

Now place about 2 heaping tbsp. mudbug mixture onto 1 side of a circle, fold the pastry over the stuffing, and bring the edges together, forming a half-moon. Before pressing the edges together, however, moisten 1 edge with a little of the egg whites. Then with a dinner fork, crimp them tightly. Repeat the process over and over again on the remaining circles.

To finish up the pies, spray a sheet pan with a coating of cooking spray or line it with a sheet of parchment paper, place the moon pies on the pan, and liberally brush each with both the melted butter and the egg whites (you should also poke 1-2 slits in the top of each pie with a paring knife to allow for the escape of steam).

Finally, slide the pan into a preheated 400-degree oven and bake the pies for 25-30 minutes or until they turn a crispy golden brown.

For the ultimate flavor, I recommend that you serve them piping hot alongside a cold, crisp salad immediately after they're baked.

Chef's Note:

1—The new Pillsbury refrigerator pie crusts come packaged in single units that roll out into 1 crust. These are what I recommend for making "moonpies."

2—If you don't have any Frank Davis Seafood Seasoning on hand, you can use ³/₄ tsp. salt, ¹/₂ tsp. black pepper, and ¹/₄ tsp. garlic powder or order it by visiting my Web site, www.frankdavis.com.

3—If you'd rather not make individual moon pies, you can make 1 or 2 full-size mudbug pies (kinda like pot pies) by baking them until the top crusts turn a golden brown. Then all you do is spoon them out on dinner plates when it's time to serve them. It's your call, but either way they're flavorfully delicious!

Grammy's Louisiana Oyster Rice Pilaf

Add rich Louisiana spices to Louisiana rice—along with a few dozen Louisiana oysters—and the dish you get is 100 percent Louisiana, y'all, and perfect for any time you want to eat!

½ cup chicken livers
½ cup chicken gizzards
1 cup lightly salted water
3 dozen oysters with oyster
    liquor
1 cup minced yellow onions
1 cup thinly sliced green onions
¼ cup minced celery
¼ cup minced green bell
    pepper
3 cloves garlic, minced
2 bay leaves
2 tsp. Frank Davis Poultry
    Seasoning

½ tsp. rosemary
1½ tsp. kosher or sea salt
1 tsp. black pepper
2 cups raw rice
2 cups water
4 tbsp. margarine
1 cup thinly sliced mushrooms
¼ cup minced parsley
Frank Davis Garlic Cayenne Hot
    Sauce to taste
2 tbsp. butter, melted

In a small saucepan, poach the chicken livers and gizzards in the water until they are tender. Then discard the poaching water, mince the livers and gizzards, and set them aside.

Next, drain the oysters in a colander, but save the liquor and add it to a stockpot that has a lid along with the onions, ¹/₂ cup green onions, celery, bell pepper, garlic, bay leaves, poultry seasoning, rosemary, salt, and pepper. Then put the stockpot on the fire, bring the seasoned mixture to a slow boil, and stir in the rice and water. Now cover the pot and simmer the rice over low heat only until it absorbs most of the liquid and is almost done, which should take about 15 minutes. Oh—to keep the grains from sticking together and possibly scorching on the bottom, it is a good idea to stir the mixture every 5 minutes or so.

While the rice is cooking, take a 12-in. skillet, heat the margarine until it sizzles, toss in the mushrooms, and quickly sauté them until they brown. Then add the oysters and fry them with the mushrooms only until their edges curl.

Then when the rice mixture is done, transfer it to a large bowl. And when the oysters are ready, cut them in half and gently fold them (plus all of the mushrooms) into the rice, along with the chicken giblets, the uncooked green onions, and the parsley. At this point you can also mix in the hot sauce and adjust the salt and pepper to taste.

Finally, spoon out the pilaf into a lightly buttered casserole dish, drizzle on the melted butter, cover with aluminum foil, place in a preheated 300-degree oven, and heat—*do not bake*—until piping hot.

Y'all . . . this is good stuff!

New Orleans Spicy Poached Oysters
(a.k.a. Oyster Scoops)

Pour several cans of chicken broth into a large deep-sided fryer, bring it to a boil, and spice it up with seafood seasoning, granular seafood boil, a half-bottle of premium hot sauce, and a few pounds of thinly sliced andouille sausage. Then drop in the oysters, poach 'em till the edges curl, place them into tortilla scoops, cover 'em with cheese, and finish 'em off under the broiler until hot and bubbly.

4 cups Swanson's Chicken Broth
2 tbsp. Frank Davis Seafood Seasoning
1 tbsp. Frank Davis Granular Seafood Boil
½ bottle Frank Davis Garlic Cayenne Hot Sauce
3 lb. andouille sausage, thinly sliced
½ cup extra-virgin olive oil
1 stick sweet cream butter

3 tbsp. minced parsley
3 tbsp. minced fresh garlic
2 qt. Louisiana oysters (preferably unwashed)
1 bag Fritos Scoops
2 cups shredded Parmesan cheese
1 bottle Frank Davis Jalapeño Hot Sauce for garnish

Start off by placing a heavyweight, 12-in., high-sided fry pan that has a tight-fitting lid on the stovetop. Then pour the chicken broth into it and bring it to a rolling boil.

At this point, whisk in the seafood seasoning, seafood boil, and hot sauce until fully incorporated into the chicken broth. Then, when the stock comes back up to a boil, drop in the andouille slices and distribute them evenly in the stock. When the broth returns to a boil, put the lid on the pan, reduce the heat to low, and simmer the sausage until it becomes "fall-apart tender," which should take about 10 minutes.

After the allotted time, take a strainer spoon, remove all the sausage slices from the pan, and set them aside for a while. Reserve the stock.

Meanwhile, as the sausage is cooking, also place a 2$^{1}/_{2}$-qt. saucepan that has a lid on the stovetop and add to it the oil and butter. Over gentle heat, melt them together until slightly sizzling. Then whisk in the parsley and garlic, tightly cover the saucepan, reduce the heat to very low, and simmer what will become the "basting sauce" for about 10 minutes. When it's ready to serve, start poaching the oysters.

To do this, bring the stock in the fry pan back to a gentle boil and begin dropping in the oysters 1 at a time until you have the fry pan about half-filled with the oysters. *Note: Don't overcrowd the pan. And be sure you stand by and watch this operation—the oysters will poach very quickly, so if you don't keep a close eye on them they will overcook and ultimately be reduced to unpalatable rubbery wads. Remove each batch of oysters when their edges curl, before adding the next batch.*

Now, while the oysters are poaching, lay out the Fritos Scoops on a nonstick sheet pan. Then as you remove the oysters from the poaching liquid, drop them into the Scoops (1 oyster in each Scoop—if the oysters are large, simply cut them in half). Then immediately top each with a slice of andouille, drizzle on a generous spoonful of butter/garlic sauce, and crown with a heaping helping of Parmesan cheese. A dash of hot sauce over each Oyster Scoop gives the presentation a final touch.

When you're ready to eat, quickly pop the sheet pan full of Oyster Scoops under the broiler for 1-2 minutes to melt the cheese and form a crust over each. All that's left is to serve them—about a half-dozen per person—with a glass of merlot and a chilled tossed green salad.

Chef's Note:

1—If oysters are not your thing, and you want to try some variations, you can fill the Scoops with chunks of chicken, or shrimp, or spoonfuls of lump crabmeat, or poached veggies, or macerated fresh fruit topped with cream cheese, or even peanut butter, jelly, and mashed bananas. The variety is limited only by your imagination!

2—As the individual batches of oysters poach, it may become necessary to "re-spice" the poaching stock occasionally. Just add 1-2 sprinklings of the seafood seasoning and seafood boil, along with 1-2 dashes of the hot sauce, as needed.

3—The oysters are best removed from the poaching stock with a pair of tongs. A fork or other pointed object will poke holes in the oysters and cause them to deflate.

Broiled Bacon-Wrapped Oysters Decatur
(With Green Onion Butter)

If you like fried oysters, baked oysters, oyster dressing, oyster pudding, and oysters on the half-shell, then you're going to simply rave over this oyster recipe. The name just about says it all—oysters, bacon, and butter. Of course, MawMaw would always caution us that you need to make lots of these, 'cuz you can't eat just one!

½ tsp. salt
¼ tsp. black pepper
½ tsp. paprika
4 tbsp. minced parsley
Juice of 1 lemon
Dash thyme

Dash marjoram
1 tsp. Frank Davis Seafood
    Seasoning
24 large oysters
12 slices lean bacon
Cooking spray

First, thoroughly blend together in a bowl the salt, pepper, paprika, parsley, lemon juice, thyme, marjoram, and seafood seasoning. Then cover the mixture with plastic wrap, set it aside, and let all the ingredients "marry" for about 30 minutes.

Meanwhile, place the oysters in a large colander so that they can drain. For best flavor, I suggest you use unwashed, fresh-shucked oysters; but you can also make the dish using the iced-down oysters you find packed in a tub at the supermarket. After they've drained, drop them into the marinating mixture, toss them around well, and let them sit for about 10 minutes so that they'll absorb the seasonings.

While you're waiting, cut the bacon crosswise into half-slices. Then after the marinating process, wrap each oyster in 1 piece bacon, holding them together with toothpicks. Now place a baking rack on a shallow cooking sheet, spray the rack with cooking spray, put the oysters on the rack, and slide them under the broiler until the bacon *begins* to turn crisp (you don't want to overcook the oysters—5-6 minutes should do it). When they're ready, set them aside to cool momentarily.

At this point you make your green onion butter.

The Green Onion Butter:

½ cup dry burgundy wine
¼ cup minced green onions
3 cloves garlic, minced
4 tbsp. minced parsley
½ tbsp. paprika
1 lb. sweet cream butter, softened

1 tbsp. Frank Davis Garlic Cayenne Hot Sauce
1 tsp. Frank Davis Bronzing Mix or salt and black pepper to taste
1 cup cracker or Panko crumbs

And here's the procedure.

In a small skillet, combine the wine, green onions, garlic, parsley, and paprika and cook the mixture over medium-high heat until just about all of the wine has evaporated. Then, using a rubber spatula, cream the wine-vegetable mix into the softened butter, along with the hot sauce, until everything is thoroughly blended. Then sprinkle in the bronzing mix (or salt and pepper) and cream the mixture again.

Now take 12 small aluminum baking cups or ramekins, set them on a shallow baking sheet, and place 2 bacon-wrapped oysters in each cup (remove the toothpicks). Then top each ramekin with a heaping teaspoon-size dollop of the softened green onion butter, sprinkle on enough cracker crumbs to cover the oysters, and put them into a preheated 450-degree oven.

All that's left is to bake the oysters until the green onion butter is hot and bubbly and the crumbs are toasty brown (about 15 minutes).

I suggest you serve them immediately with a little French bread on the side to sop up the juices! Aw, yeah!

Chef's Note:

1—Don't skimp on the bacon! You want to buy the meatiest, leanest bacon you can find. Fatty bacon won't wrap around the oysters properly (and besides, it will make the finished dish rather greasy).

2—If you want to make extra green onion butter to keep on hand, simply wrap the mixture in plastic wrap in the shape of a sausage-like roll. Then place it into the freezer to harden. When you need some for a recipe, all you do is take the wrap off and slice the roll into as many medallions as you need. Then rewrap what's left and stash it again in the freezer.

3—Panko breadcrumbs are Japanese-style breadcrumbs found in Asian stores. When used as a coating, they toast up beautifully and give the finished product a light, crispy texture.

CHAPTER 7

Pastas

Andrea Apuzzo's Sicilian Recipe for Homemade Pasta

There's really nothing to it! In all actuality, my old friend Chef Andrea says that making pasta is no more difficult than making any other kind of dough, and his recipe (which he told me I could share with you) produces superior results, even for the rank beginner. All you need is to set aside the few minutes it takes to make homemade pasta.

There are many complicated (usually electric) pasta machines on the market, but both Andrea and I highly recommend that you invest in a small, hand-operated pasta machine for your kitchen. It's easy to use and simple to master. A good one will be made of stainless steel and can be ordered from most kitchen-supply houses (even those on the Internet). Now, it probably won't be cheap, but it will last you a lifetime and pay for itself time and time again in the pasta in produces. The better ones consist of a set of gear-driven rollers about 6 in. long. All you have to do is vary the space between the rollers and you control the thickness of the pasta. In fact, with the machine, a wooden cutting board, and a glass bowl, you can become a pasta master.

Now, regardless of what shape you will ultimately make your pasta into, here is the recipe for making the dough.

2 cups semolina flour	1 tbsp. extra-virgin olive oil
2 cups all-purpose flour	½ tsp. salt
2 eggs	1½ cups ice-cold water

Mix the flours together and make a mound on top of a clean surface. (This is where your cutting board comes in handy.) Now make a well in the center of the mound of flour.

In a large glass bowl, beat the eggs well and mix in the oil, salt, and 1 cup cold water. Then pour this into the flour well.

With your hands, mix the flours and liquids together and knead everything together until you have a ball of dough. You can add up to another $^1/_2$ water if you think that the dough requires the moisture (the amount that you add will depend on the temperature and humidity of your kitchen).

Now the proper way to work the dough is to roll it away from you on the countertop while simultaneously tearing it in half. Then pull it back together while rolling it back towards you, always keeping some pressure on the dough with the balls of your hands. Keep rolling and tearing (this is good exercise for your upper arms) for 5 minutes (or until the texture is uniform and smooth). Be sure to dust the counter with flour every now and then to keep the dough from sticking.

Shape the dough like a round bread loaf and dust it with white flour. Then cover it with a dry cloth and allow the "pasta ball" to rest for 15 minutes.

When you're ready to make your pasta, cut off a piece of dough about the size of your fist—*about 6 oz. by weight.* (This is approximately enough for 2 servings of most basic pasta dishes.) To get it ready for the machine, flatten it into a disk and dust it lightly with flour.

All you do now is set the dial on the pasta machine at 1—the thickest setting. Then run the disk of pasta dough through it. When it comes out the other end, dust it with flour, fold it over end to end, and run it through again. Now change the setting to 3 and repeat the above procedure. Then set the machine to 5, and go through the procedure yet again. By now, you'll have a long strip of pasta. Simply catch the end of it with your hand and pull it away as it exits the machine, so it doesn't pile up. Finally, change the setting to 6—the thinnest setting—and run it through just once more (*but don't fold it over this time*).

You now have a basic flat pasta sheet that can be cut into any shape you want.

Authentic Sicilian Marinara Sauce

½ cup extra-virgin olive oil
¼ cup chopped yellow onions
2 cups chopped canned Italian
   plum tomatoes
1 cup juice from tomatoes
4 tsp. minced flat-leaf parsley
1 tbsp. chopped fresh oregano
   leaves

1 tbsp. chopped fresh basil
2 tsp. minced fresh garlic
2 tsp. Frank Davis Sicilian
   Seasoning
4 anchovies, mashed
Salt and black pepper to taste

First, pour the oil into a hot 12-in. skillet. Then toss in the onions and sauté them, stirring constantly, over medium-high heat until they turn a rich golden brown.

When the onions have caramelized, add in—one at a time—the tomatoes, juice, herbs, garlic, and Sicilian seasoning. Then bring the contents of the skillet to a rolling boil, but immediately lower the heat and simmer the mixture for 15-20 minutes (or until the resultant sauce is reduced by about one-third of its original volume).

At this point, whisk in the anchovies, taking special care to fully incorporate them into the sauce. This is also the time to adjust the final taste by adding as much salt and black pepper as desired.

Finally, finish off the recipe by simmering the marinara—*uncovered*—on the stovetop for an additional 5 minutes.

Chef's Note:

1—This recipe makes enough marinara for 4 appetizer portions or 2 full entrées, so you can adjust the quantity according to your needs.

2—The sauce will keep nicely in the refrigerator for about 5 days if packed in an airtight container.

Frank's Classic Pasta Alfredo

There must be several dozen versions of this classic old Italian dish, but this recipe, which I have kept secret until now, is right up there with the very best. You can make purist Alfredo with nothing but pasta, egg yolks, and cream, or you can change the recipe entirely by adding cooked shrimp, crawfish, crabmeat, scallops, anchovies, crumbled bacon, cooked Italian sausage, shredded sautéed chicken, or artichoke hearts or as the main flavoring ingredient. But regardless of what variety you create . . . this is great stuff!

1 lb. fettuccini noodles
⅓ cup + 6 tbsp. extra-virgin olive oil
1 head garlic
½ cup minced onions
2 pt. heavy cream
1 tsp. Frank Davis Sicilian Seasoning

⅛ tsp. white pepper
¼ stick unsalted butter
1 egg yolk
⅛ tsp. freshly grated nutmeg
½ cup grated imported Parmesan cheese
¼ cup chopped parsley for garnish

Boil the fettuccini noodles until they turn al dente. Then rinse them in cold water, drain them well, coat them with 4 tbsp. oil, and set them aside.

Take the head of garlic, cut off the top just enough to expose the pods, drizzle with about 2 tbsp. oil, wrap in aluminum foil, and bake in a 400-degree oven for 45 minutes (or until tender and soft).

Take a 5-qt. Dutch oven (or a high-sided skillet) and place it on medium heat. Add ⅓ cup oil. Then sauté the onions in the oil until they wilt. Then turn the fire up to high and pour in the cream. At this point, bring the cream to a rapid boil, but stir it constantly or it will rise up and spill out of the pot (in other words, it will boil over). Once the cream comes to a boil, whisk in the Sicilian seasoning and white pepper until they are totally incorporated into the sauce.

Next, cook the cream over high heat until it starts to thicken (and I promise you, it will thicken!). Then, *in pats,* gradually stir in the butter, along with at least half of the garlic (which is best if you first cream it with a fork). Continue to stir. You want the sauce nice and thick.

Once the sauce reduces about 75 percent and reaches the consistency you desire (which should be very similar to viscous pancake batter), you can add in whatever main ingredients you prefer—shrimp, crawfish, crabmeat, and so forth. If you want to do pure pasta Alfredo, however, remove the pot from the fire at this point and set it aside.

Here's the secret, though! To a thoroughly beaten egg yolk in a small bowl, slowly add some of the sauce to warm up the yolk (this keeps the yolk from scrambling). Then when the yolk comes up to heat, whisk it into the main sauce until it marries.

Finally, stir into the finished sauce the nutmeg and almost all of the Parmesan cheese. Then reheat the fettuccini to piping hot (you can do this either in a water bath or even in your microwave oven), thoroughly toss it with the hot sauce, and serve it immediately (liberally sprinkled with a little more Parmesan and garnished with parsley).

And that, paisanos, is classic pasta Alfredo!

Chef's Note:
1—If you decide to add some seafood ingredients to the Alfredo (shrimp, crawfish, crabmeat, etc.), simply heat them in the sauce. Overcooking will make them way too mushy. But more importantly, overcooking them will "sweat" out the natural juices and thin out the sauce too much.

2—Personally, I love the flavor of the roasted garlic in this Alfredo, so the whole head of garlic is not too much for my taste. You might want to try it full strength—it's really Sicilian done that way.

3—For the ultimate in flavor, try not to toss and coat the pasta with the sauce until just minutes before you serve it. Blending too far in advance will not only produce a dish less than piping hot, it will give the finished cream sauce a diminished, chalky taste.

Franco's Sicilian Meatballs and Spaghetti

Of all the gourmet dishes we relish here in New Orleans, quite possibly it's the meatballs and spaghetti that ranks right at the top of our Crescent City favorites. If you never really learned to make the authentic version, stash this recipe away in your special files and guard it. It's extremely easy and there's none any better anywhere.

The Meatballs:

2 lb. ground beef, 93 percent lean	1 cup whole milk
1 lb. lean ground pork	2 tsp. salt
1 medium onion, minced	1 tsp. black pepper
4-6 cloves garlic, minced	1 tsp. basil
2 eggs, beaten	2 tsp. Frank Davis Sicilian
1 cup coarse breadcrumbs	Seasoning

First you make your meatballs. Here are the steps.

In a large mixing bowl, combine the beef and pork until uniformly blended. Then drop in the remaining ingredients and, with your hands, work everything together until you end up with a smooth meat mixture—but be careful that you don't overmix or the meatballs will turn out heavy and dense instead of light and fluffy.

Now, keeping your hands wet so that the mixture doesn't stick to your fingers, begin rolling out the meatballs (you want each to be slightly larger than a golf ball). As each one is shaped, place it on a lightly greased shallow baking sheet.

When they're all made, slide them into a 400-degree oven and bake them—*turning them once*—for about 20 minutes or until the meat begins to firm and brown slightly. Baking your meatballs first does 2 things: it helps them hold together later while they're cooking in the gravy, but more importantly it renders out most of the excess fat from the meat and keeps your gravy from being greasy.

The Spaghetti and Tomato Gravy (Sugo):

¼ cup extra-virgin olive oil
1 medium onion, minced
6 cloves garlic, minced
2 small cans tomato paste
6 tomato-paste cans filled with
   chicken stock or water
2 tsp. basil

2 tsp. Frank Davis Sicilian
   Seasoning
2 bay leaves
Salt and black pepper to taste
2 lb. #4 spaghetti, cooked al
   dente
1 cup grated Parmesan cheese

While the meatballs are baking, it's time to make your tomato gravy. If you follow these directions to the letter, it will be some of the best you ever had!

In a heavy 5-qt. Dutch oven that has a lid, heat the oil over medium-high heat. Then drop in the onion and garlic and—*stirring constantly*—lightly sauté them together until they just soften (it is not necessary to brown the onion, and you don't want the garlic to burn). About 2-3 minutes should do it.

When the onion and garlic are ready, add the tomato paste to the pot and rapidly stir it into the mix. You don't have to fry the tomato paste for eternity to make good red gravy. Actually, if you fry the paste for much longer than 2 minutes, you will increase the acidity of the tomatoes and the gravy will be strong, harsh, and bitter. You want it to come out light and sweet, so just cook it for 1-2 minutes until the paste, onion, garlic, and oil are mixed well.

At this point, add the chicken stock or water and stir again until the mixture is silky smooth. Keep in mind that the secret to making a tomato gravy the right consistency is to use *3 cans liquid for every 1 can tomato paste.*

When the sauce is thoroughly mixed, add the basil, Sicilian seasoning, bay leaves, salt, and pepper.

Now you're ready to drop in the meatballs—*but just the meatballs: throw the pan drippings away!* Gently place them into the pot with a spoon or a pair of tongs, being careful not to break them apart and positioning them so that they're completely submerged in the gravy. All that's left now is to cover the pot and cook it at a "simmer" for about 2 hours.

When you're ready to eat, cook the spaghetti in about 1½ gal. rapidly boiling, lightly salted water until al dente. When it's ready, drain it thoroughly (don't rinse it!), toss it with 1-2 cups tomato gravy to keep the strands from sticking together, sprinkle it liberally with Parmesan cheese, and serve it piping hot with the meatballs!

I don't care where you've eaten meatballs and spaghetti before, I promise this is gonna be your all-time favorite!

Chef's Note:

1—Just for the record . . . you don't add sugar to an authentic Italian gravy. Prepare it properly and it will be light and naturally sweet.

2—For perfect spaghetti that doesn't stick together, season the water with about 1 tbsp. salt, add 3-4 tbsp. olive oil to the water while it is boiling, cook the spaghetti uncovered, and stir it almost constantly. Then when the spaghetti is done, drain it thoroughly in a pasta colander, immediately put it back into the pot you boiled it in, coat it lightly with some hot tomato gravy, and serve it piping hot.

3—I suggest that you also serve up a couple of garlic breadsticks with each plate of meatballs and spaghetti you put on the table. A glass of Italian red wine at each place setting will provide the crowning touch.

Cajun Meat Sauce and Mushrooms Over Noodles

You'll never convince your nosey ol' next-door neighbor that it's not Hamburger Helper right out of the box, but who cares? You know it's made from scratch! You know it's an old authentic Cajun mawmaw recipe from down on the bayou! You also know there ain't nothin' in a box that can even come close to it . . . 'cuz it's that good!

3 lb. ultra-lean ground round
¼ cup vegetable oil
2 cups diced onions
1 cup diced celery
½ cup minced green bell pepper
6 cloves garlic, minced
1 lb. mushrooms, sliced
⅓ cup all-purpose flour
4 cups Campbell's Chicken Broth
¼ cup minced parsley
3 bay leaves

1 tsp. basil
1 tsp. cumin
1 tbsp. Worcestershire sauce
1 tsp. red pepper flakes
2 tsp. kosher or sea salt
1 bunch green onions, thinly sliced
2 lb. extra-broad egg noodles, cooked al dente
2 cups finely shredded cheddar for garnish

First, take a large oval roaster that has a lid and drop in the ground round. Then stirring continuously, cook the meat over a medium flame until it becomes beautifully seared. *Hint: the beef will brown more easily if you take a ladle and remove the rendered fat from the pot as it accumulates.*

When the meat is done, remove it from the oval roaster, place it into a colander, place the colander into a large bowl to catch the drippings, and allow the excess fat to drain off the meat (but be sure to keep the drippings—you'll need them).

Next, in the same oval roaster, but this time with the flame set to high, pour in the oil and sauté the onions, celery, bell peppers, garlic, and mushrooms until they begin to caramelize (they will become a rich golden brown *without burning*). Then when the seasoning veggies are ready, remove them from the roaster as well and place them to drain on top of the ground beef in the colander.

At this stage, it's time to make your roux. In the same oval roaster, pour in the drippings from the meat and veggies (they'll give you a concentrated flavor as opposed to oil straight out of a bottle) and, using a wire whisk, work in the flour to make a smooth paste. Keep the flour moving continuously! If you stop whisking, the roux will burn and produce a bitter taste in the final dish. After it goes through all the color stages from beige to a light tan to a light brown to a dark brown, the roux is ready.

Immediately at this point, stir all the ingredients in the colander back into the roaster and pour in the chicken broth. Then with a spoon, mix everything together uniformly, reduce the flame to low, cover the pot with the lid, and simmer the mixture for about 10 minutes. After this short simmering time, stir in the parsley, bay leaves, basil, cumin, Worcestershire sauce, red pepper flakes, and salt; cover the pot once more; and simmer the dish for 1 hour, stirring occasionally. Following the exact measurements listed in this recipe, you should get just the right consistency in the final dish. But if for some reason or another the mixture becomes too thick, simply stir in a little extra chicken broth.

About 1-2 minutes before you're ready to serve, stir in the green onions. Then ladle the meat sauce over soup bowls heaped with the hot egg noodles, and gently fold everything together. A generous sprinkling of cheese over each bowl completes the presentation, and a piece of hot buttered French bread on the side provides the perfect lagniappe.

Chef's Note:

1—Heat the beef drippings for about 10 minutes in the oval roaster to drive off the moisture (thereby leaving only the beef fat) before sprinkling in the flour to make the roux.

2—The proper way to serve this dish is always to ladle the meat sauce over the noodles; never mix the noodles into the pot of meat sauce. To do the latter would cause the noodles to completely absorb the sauce, thus producing a dry final dish.

Daube with Portabellos and Penne

Thin cuts of marinated chuck roast, slowly cooked down until it practically falls apart and served atop a steaming plate of al dente penne pasta covered with Parmesan cheese . . . that's daube the old-fashioned New Orleans way. Put this together sometime this week for your family!

4 lb. boneless chuck roast
2 onions, 1 quartered, 1 minced
3 carrots, peeled and sliced
8 sprigs thyme
1 sprig rosemary
2 bay leaves
2 tsp. salt
2 tsp. black pepper
12 garlic cloves, minced
4 strips orange zest (each ½ in. wide)
1 bottle zinfandel or hearty burgundy
2 tbsp. balsamic vinegar
⅓ cup minced salt pork
2 tbsp. all-purpose flour
1 cup water
14-oz. can Italian tomatoes, sliced
2 cups coarsely chopped portabello mushrooms
1 lb. penne pasta, cooked al dente
1 cup freshly grated Parmesan cheese
Chopped parsley for garnish

First off, cut the chuck roast into 2-in. squares, taking care to trim away any large pieces of fat. Then place the meat into a large glass, plastic, or ceramic bowl (or into a gal.-size zipper bag).

Next, add the quartered to the meat, along with the carrots, thyme, rosemary, bay leaves, 1 tsp. salt, 1 tsp. pepper, half the garlic, and the orange zest. Then pour the wine and vinegar over everything, and toss it thoroughly to mix. At this point, seal off the meat mix and let it marinate in the refrigerator overnight (or at least 4 hours).

Now, when you're ready to cook, drop the pork into a heavy, cast-iron Dutch oven that has a tight-fitting lid and is large enough to hold all of the ingredients, and fry down the pork over medium-low heat until it releases its fat (which should take about 5 minutes). Then discard the pork and immediately drop into the pot the minced onion and remaining garlic. Now sauté the onions until they turn clear (they don't have to brown), and as soon as they do, remove the mixture from the pot with a slotted spoon and set it aside.

Next, drain the meat and pat it as dry as possible with absorbent paper towels (but save the marinade). Then, a few pieces at a time, add the meat to the Dutch oven (but don't crowd them, so that they can sear to seal in their juices). You want to sauté the pieces for about 6 minutes, turning them once or twice. The beef will darken, but it may not truly "brown." That's okay, though—simply remove the meat from the Dutch oven with a slotted spoon and set it aside too, with the seasoning mixture.

At this point, it's time to add the flour to the pot and cook it until it browns (be sure to keep stirring it so that it doesn't lump and burn). Then increase the heat to high, slowly pour in the marinade that you saved, and deglaze the pot, scraping up any bits that cling to the bottom. Now return the onions, garlic, meat, and any meat juices to the pot, add 1 tsp. salt, 1 tsp. pepper, the water, tomatoes, and mushrooms, and bring everything to a near boil. But when it reaches that stage, reduce the heat to very low, cover the pot, and gently simmer the daube for about 3 hours or until it can be cut easily with a spoon and the liquid has thickened.

Finally, when you're ready to eat, place a mound of hot pasta into a serving dish and ladle over it, directly from the pot, the daube and the sauce it cooked in. All that's left is to shake on a little extra salt and pepper or a preblended beef seasoning if you need it and top it all off with a garnish of Parmesan cheese and parsley.

Chef's Note:
1—The orange strips should consist of only the zest part of the orange, not the pith. Either a paring knife or a fillet knife can easily separate the 2.

2—Feel free to use another kind of mushroom in place of the portabellos. Common white buttons, shiitakes, or Italian cremini will substitute nicely.

Frank's N'Awlins Yakamein

Depending upon whom you talk to, yakamein (sometimes spelled ya-ca-mein) is either Chinese or Creole, or possibly a combination of both! The "noodles" (usually thin spaghetti) and the soy sauce exemplify the Chinese influence; the beef, pork, or ham (the traditional meats used in yakamein) and rich broth signify the Creole influence. Apparently the chopped egg and sliced green onions, which adorn the top of every finished dish, have always been nothing more than garnish. Regardless of the origin, however, this is yet another one of those classic recipes that's truly Naturally N'Awlins.

1 gal. bottled water
5 cans Campbell's or Swanson's
  Chicken Broth
1 large onion, diced
6 ribs celery, diced
2 bay leaves
¼ cup minced parsley
8 cloves garlic, peeled
2 tsp. crushed red pepper
  flakes

3-4 lb. boneless beef shoulder
  roast
1 lb. thin spaghetti (white or
  wheat), cooked al dente
1 dozen eggs, hard-cooked and
  chopped
¾ cup thinly sliced green onions
1 small bottle soy sauce

The first thing you do is select a soup pot that has a lid and is large enough to hold all of the ingredients plus a couple of inches of head space to allow for "the boil." Then, very simply, pour in the water and chicken broth, drop in the onions, celery, bay leaves, parsley, garlic, and red pepper flakes, and bring the mixture to a rolling boil. Immediately, though, reduce the fire so as to produce a "gentle bubble" in the pot, and simmer the mix for about 20 minutes or until the vegetables fully wilt.

In the meantime, while the stock is brewing, trim the beef. You want to cut away and discard as much of the tallow and sinew as possible. Then when the broth is just at the right stage, gently lower the trimmed beef down into the pot and adjust the flame so that, again, the broth does nothing more than just gently bubble. *At all costs, avoid a rolling boil—that gives you a cloudy stock and actually toughens the meat!*

Ideally, you want to let the beef cook in the broth—*covered*—for about 4 hours, stirring only occasionally, until the meat begins to fall apart. When that happens, take a strainer spoon, remove the meat from the broth, and set it aside to cool. Meanwhile, return the broth to the fire and continue to simmer it—*this time uncovered*—until it reduces to about one-fourth of its original volume. This step concentrates the flavors and slightly thickens the broth!

When you're ready to eat, chop the beef into small debris pieces (or slice it thinly across the grain) and place a generous portion into the bottom of a soup bowl. Then ladle a hearty helping of the piping hot broth over the beef. Finally, spoon a serving of hot spaghetti (you can reheat it in the microwave) over the broth and the beef, garnish with the chopped eggs, sprinkle on a handful of green onions, and then dress the finished dish with a splash of soy sauce to taste!

Some folks say this goes best on those cold winter nights. Creoles tell you this is great anytime!

Chef's Note:

1—When I checked with some of the old-time Creoles down in "the hood," they told me that in the olden days, folks made 3 kinds of yakamein—beef, pork, or ham. Pork seemed to be the most popular, they recalled; but the beef and ham came in a close second. Today, neighborhood restaurants that still serve the dish usually serve beef.

2—To make pork or ham yakamein, follow the same recipe exactly—just substitute pork shoulder or fresh ham for the beef.

3—Boneless chuck roast can also be used to make yakamein, but if it is, the broth needs to be defatted before serving. This is best accomplished by allowing the cooled broth to rest in the refrigerator overnight. The hardened fat can then be lifted off the surface and discarded.

4—Don't expect the broth to be the consistency of rich brown gravy! It will have some body to it, but it will remain a broth, almost soupy. Some folks admit to thickening their yakamein with a little roux—don't do it! That's not yakamein!

Frank's Pasta Antoinina

This recipe could very well be the epitome of what the Sicilian taste is all about! You got eggplant, Italian sausage, rich red gravy, and al dente pasta combined under a generous showering of both Romano and Parmesan cheeses. My mother-in-law, Nina Scalia Bruscato, taught me how to do this one, and for that—and her daughter—I'll be forever grateful!

¼ cup salt
1 bowl water, about 1 gal.
3 medium purple eggplants, peeled and cottage cut
2 lb. Pete Giovenco Special Blend Italian sausage
¼ cup extra-virgin olive oil
1 cup diced onions
⅔ cup diced celery
6 cloves garlic, minced
½ cup minced green bell pepper
¾ cup seeded and diced fresh tomatoes
2 cups diced portabello mushrooms
1 large can Contadina Tomato Paste

2 tomato-paste cans filled with water
2 tomato-paste cans filled with chicken stock
2 bay leaves
4 tbsp. minced flat-leaf parsley
½ cup chiffonade-cut basil
2 tsp. Frank Davis Vegetable Seasoning
1 tsp. Frank Davis Sicilian Seasoning
Salt and black pepper to taste
1 lb. #4 spaghetti, cooked al dente
1 cup mixed grated Romano and Parmesan cheese

First, stir the salt into the bowl of water until it is completely dissolved. Then drop in the chunks of eggplant ("cottage cut" means cut like really thick French fries) and swoosh them around in the solution several times until they are thoroughly coated. Allow the pieces to float in the brine until you get the sausage prepared and the gravy started (remember that the salt will remove the excess oxalic acid from the eggplants and take away their sometimes characteristic "bite").

Now for the prep.

In a heavy 12-in. anodized skillet, sauté the sausage (which you've removed from its casings) until it begins to brown slightly—but be sure to take the time to drain off whatever excess fat renders out as pan drippings (it keeps the gravy from becoming greasy). And here's another little trick—to keep the sausage from scorching in the pan, I suggest that you constantly agitate or stir the pan as the sausage cooks.

In the meantime, take a 5-qt. heavy aluminum Dutch oven that has a lid and heat the oil over a medium-high heat. Then stir in the onions, celery, garlic, bell pepper, tomatoes, and mushrooms and cook them down—*again stirring continuously*—until they fully soften. When the veggies are ready, whisk in the tomato paste, along with the water and 1 can chicken stock. Now combine all the ingredients thoroughly and continue to stir until the paste disappears and the resultant sauce becomes velvety smooth.

It's at this time that you drop in the bay leaves, parsley, basil, vegetable seasoning, Sicilian seasoning, salt, and pepper. Then stir the pot thoroughly and taste the sauce—this is the time to adjust the seasonings.

Now add both the sausage and the eggplant chunks (which you've drained and patted dry) to the Dutch oven and stir them into the mix. Then lower the flame, put the lid on the pot, and allow the dish to simmer for 20 minutes or until the eggplant pieces turn translucent. *Note: if you find that the gravy thickens a little too much for your liking as it simmers, simply stir in a little of the chicken stock you've held off to the side.* Then once again readjust the seasonings to taste.

One final word of caution—*do not overcook the eggplant!* It will soften yet still be slightly firm when fully cooked. Overcook it, though, and it will turn to mush and practically disintegrate in the gravy. That, you don't want!

Finally, when you're ready to eat, place a generous portion of hot pasta in the center of a plate, ladle on the eggplant, sausage, and gravy, and liberally cover it all with the cheese mix. Serve with a piping hot, buttered slice of Italian bread for sopping and a cold cucumber and carrot salad. *Buon appetito!*

Chef's Note:

1—For a more subtle eggplant flavor, try using green seedless or Jerusalem eggplants. Both are seasonal, so they could be slightly difficult to find at certain times of the year. Of course, the common purple eggplant is usually available.

2—If you can't get hold of Pete Giovenco's Italian sausage, you can substitute your favorite Italian sausage from wherever you buy yours. Of course, if you want to order a supply from Pete, call him at 504-469-4369.

3—This is the undisputed formula for the ultimate tomato gravy— 1 can tomato paste and 3 cans liquid (water, stock, wine, etc.). Use this ratio whenever you need a red sugo for beef, pork, shrimp, redfish, chicken, whatever.

Beanies, Weenies, and Macaroni and Cheese

Ask any kid from toddler to teen what he'd rather eat most of the time, if given a choice, and he'll invariably answer, "Beanies, weenies, and macaroni and cheese." I'm tellin' ya, they're wild about the stuff! So that's the meal I've put together here. This is the only dish that your kids expect you to have "ready to eat" all the time. You don't think so? Ask 'em!

1 qt. water
2 lb. wieners (your kids' favorite kind)
28-oz. can baked beans
15-oz. can chili without beans
⅔ cup hickory-flavored barbecue sauce
2 boxes macaroni and cheese, 7¼-oz. size

12 cups water
2 tsp. salt
½ cup butter, melted
½ cup milk, room temperature
½ cup shredded mild cheddar cheese
2 pkg. hotdog buns

The first thing you want to do is bring the water to a rapid boil in a 4-qt. Dutch oven. Then drop in the wieners and make sure that they're all submerged. The water will immediately stop boiling; but when it comes back to a full boil, reduce the fire to medium low and let the wieners simmer for at least 5 minutes. (Note: after the initial boiling process, you may allow the wieners to remain in the water—over low heat—so that they stay hot while you prepare the beans.)

Speaking of preparing the beans, very simply pour the contents of the can into another 4-qt. Dutch oven or a 4-qt. oval roaster that has a lid. Then set the fire under the pot to medium low and heat the beans until they are hot and bubbly. *Caution: watch the flame and continually stir the beans as they heat to keep them from burning.*

Now when the beans come to serving temperature, stir in the can of chili along with the barbecue sauce and thoroughly combine the ingredients to a smooth consistency. Once complete, reduce the fire to low, drain the wieners and submerge them in the beans, cover the pot, and let everything simmer until you're ready to eat.

In the meantime, whip up the macaroni and cheese. Notice that most children don't insist that you make this from scratch—they seem to love the boxed varieties just fine! So open the boxes of your favorite brand, bring the 12 cups water and the salt to a boil in a large stockpot, drop in the pasta, and cook it at a rapid boil for 10 minutes or until it is tender (but still al dente).

When the pasta is done, drain it thoroughly in a colander. Then transfer it to a large mixing bowl and, while still hot, stir into it the butter, milk, and shredded cheddar (along with the cheese packets that came in the boxes). Take a little extra time to do this step right—you want to stir and stir so that the sauce comes out creamy and smooth.

Finally, all that's left is to spoon out on the kids' plates a helping of beans, 1-2 weenies, and a mound of macaroni and cheese. Believe me, they'll be back for seconds and they'll go off and tell all their friends that you're the greatest cook in the whole wide world!

Oh, yeah—the hotdog buns are there because you can bet they'd want them if you didn't have them! Do I know your kids or what?

Chef's Note:

1—The choice of which "weenies" to buy is up to you—you can get beef, pork, chicken, a combination of all three, or those "el cheapo" red ones in the family packs that most kids think are the gourmet kind. Whichever you decide to use, the trick is to boil them the minute you get them home from the grocery and have them ready to eat (once boiled, they can be kept in the refrigerator and reheated in the microwave for "instant feeding").

2—Even after you combine the weenies and beans, the mixture can be stashed in the fridge and served up a la carte whenever a hungry child beckons. Again, that's why God invented the microwave.

3—Beans can also be served a la microwave directly from the refrigerator, so you're encouraged to keep a good supply on hand at all times. By the way, if your family prefers the old-timey "pork-n-beans" over dem high-fangled baked beans, serve them what they like best. I would, however, doctor up either variety with the barbecue sauce. It makes a significant difference in taste.

4—One more thing: I leave the addition of the shredded cheese to the pasta entirely up to your fancy. I find that it transforms the ordinary into the extraordinary. But that's just me—you need to determine how your eaters want it. If your kids prefer just the powdered cheese packets that come in the boxes, do it that way. If, like my grandkids, they like a "cheesier" flavor, whisk in the shredded cheddar. Tell 'em it's what we call "lagniappe."

Italian Chicken and Spaghetti in Tomato Gravy

Milder and sweeter than cacciatore, this tasty chicken dish is peasant food of the home-stewed variety. A simple blend of onions and tomatoes, with naturally smothered chicken drippings contributing the main flavor, gives this recipe its integrity and popularity. If you like Italian, you'll make this often!

4 tbsp. extra-virgin olive oil
2 cups diced yellow onions
6 cloves garlic, minced
2 cans Contadina Tomato Paste
1 can Hunt's Stewed Tomatoes, diced
5 tomato-paste cans filled with chicken stock
2 tsp. Frank Davis Sicilian Seasoning
2 bay leaves
1 tsp. basil
4 tbsp. minced parsley
1 tsp. coarse-ground black pepper
10 skinless chicken thighs, bone-in
Salt to taste
1 lb. #4 spaghetti, cooked al dente
Shredded Parmesan cheese for garnish

In a large Dutch oven that has a tight-fitting lid—it could be anodized aluminum or Magnalite—heat the oil and fry down the onions until they soften and begin to brown. Then drop in the garlic, tomato paste, and tomatoes and stir everything together.

After cooking the mixture for 5 minutes or so, stir in the chicken stock. Then when the tomato base has taken on the texture of a velvety-smooth gravy, spice it up with the Sicilian seasoning, bay leaves, basil, parsley, and pepper. At this point you cover the pot and slow-simmer the savory concoction for about 15 minutes. While this is happening, skin, defat, and wash the chicken thighs.

Next, bring the gravy to a slow boil and immediately drop in the chicken thighs—*one at a time*—until they are all in the pot. Now tightly cover the pot, reduce the fire to low, and simmer the dish for 1-1½ hours (or until the chicken begins to show signs of falling off the bone).

When this happens, the dish is done. All that's left is to taste for salt and adjust the pepper if you so desire. Serve the chicken thighs piping hot over freshly prepared spaghetti, and cover with Parmesan cheese. A little homemade garlic bread and a frosty Italian mixed salad topped with garlic-Parmesan dressing on the side rounds out the feast.

Chef's Note:

1—This dish is like red beans—always better the next day after everything has had a chance to marry. Serving it the next day is also the best way to remove all the fat. Stashed in the refrigerator overnight, all the excess grease from the chicken will float to the surface as the gravy cools. It then becomes merely a matter of lifting if off and tossing it out!

2—It you're looking for a great red gravy recipe, this is it! You can use it to cook beef, pork, sausage, fish, shrimp, and other meats Italian style. Or it can be cooked and simmered meatless for a great vegetarian gravy. Oh—and if you ever get a hankering again to do hardboiled eggs in red gravy, this is the gravy you want to make!

3—Ordinarily, the recipe for keeping this gravy consistent time after time is "3 tomato cans full of water or broth to every one can of paste." But here's a trick—whenever you use chicken in a gravy, reduce the liquid addition by one "canful" because as it cooks the chicken throws off lots of natural liquids and resultantly will cause your gravy to end up too watery.

4—It is not necessary to brown the chicken before putting it into the gravy. Nor is it necessary to preseason the chicken. Much like a stew, the thighs as they cook will absorb seasoning from the red gravy. So what does that tell you? Overseason slightly!

5—Don't stir the pot once the chicken is added. The chicken will tenderize quickly and fall off the bone easily, losing the integrity of the poultry and taking on the semblance of a gumbo.

6—Add salt at the last minute, and only to your taste. There is salt in the chicken stock and salt in the cheese you'll sprinkle on top of the dish when you serve it. Adding salt too early in the cooking process could create a problem.

7—By the way, I know that you know how to cook pasta. But just for the record, you'll never go wrong if you (1) buy a good brand of pasta (preferably #1 semolina), (2) follow package directions, (3) use a lot of salted water in a large pot to give the pasta room to boil, (4) boil the pasta only until it's tender, not until it's soft (the Italians call it al dente), and (5) oil it down with extra-virgin olive oil after it's cooked to keep the strands from sticking together. But of course, you knew all that already, right?

Frank's Herbed-'n'-Roasted Chicken Thighs

Pick up a dozen plump chicken thighs, skin them, wash them, pat them dry, generously sprinkle them with a concoction of herbs and spices, and stash them in a 400-degree oven until they're honey brown and roasted to a "fall-off-the-bone tenderness." Then stack 2 per person atop a plate of hot ziti pasta, drizzle on the pan juices, and serve with a side of pan-braised, buttered spinach. It just don't get no better than this, no, bruh!

4 tbsp. extra-virgin olive oil
2 large onions, coarsely chopped
5 ribs celery, coarsely chopped
1 green bell pepper, coarsely chopped
6 medium carrots, coarsely chopped
½ cup coarsely chopped parsley (leaves and stems)
½ lb. baby bello mushrooms, thickly sliced
20-30 garlic cloves
3 bay leaves
12 chicken thighs, skinned and washed
2 tsp. Frank Davis Poultry Seasoning

1 tbsp. Frank Davis Grill-N-Broil Seasoning
1 tsp. Hungarian paprika
⅓ cup chopped fresh rosemary
¼ cup chopped fresh thyme leaves
½ cup chiffonade-cut basil
¾ cup white wine
2 tbsp. heavy cream
1 tsp. Kitchen Bouquet
4 tbsp. sweet cream butter, melted
6 cups ziti pasta, cooked al dente
½ cup shredded Romano cheese
1 tsp. coarse-ground black pepper

This is essentially an extremely easy "family" recipe that, when served, actually tastes as if you've been working on it for days on end! But if you never tell, then neither will I!

Start off by rubbing down the insides of a baking pan with the oil. Be sure to select a pan that will be large enough to comfortably accommodate all of the chicken thighs. Then, uniformly mix together the onions, celery, bell pepper, carrots, parsley, mushrooms, garlic, and bay leaves and distribute them evenly on the bottom of the pan, tossing them lightly in the oil. At this point, immediately slide the pan into a 400-degree preheated oven to start the "vegetable roasting" process, and begin seasoning the chicken.

To do that, place the skinned and washed thighs on a large sheet of freezer wrap (this protects the countertop from contamination) and pat them dry with a couple of sheets of absorbent paper towels. Then begin liberally sprinkling each one with the poultry seasoning, grill-n-broil, and paprika. You need to remember that these seasonings are crucial to the dish, but be careful not to overseason the chicken thighs, either. *It's the one single mistake most cooks make!*

When the thighs are seasoned, remove the baking pan from the oven with a pair of mitts (*be careful—it's gonna be hot!*) and set it on the countertop on a couple of trivets. Then place all the chicken pieces directly atop the roasted veggies, taking care that they do not touch each other. Then when the dish has been assembled, evenly place the rosemary, thyme, and basil into the baking pan. Finally, stir together the wine, cream, and Kitchen Bouquet and pour it, too, evenly over the chicken.

Now carefully and tightly cover the pan with a sheet of heavy-duty aluminum foil, return the pan to the oven, and continue to cook for 45 minutes. Then, when the allotted time has expired, open the oven, remove the foil, brush each thigh with the butter, and brown the chicken for 10 minutes more.

When you're ready to eat, ladle out plates of the hot ziti. Then scatter on each a fistful of Romano cheese, sprinkle on a touch of pepper, top with 2 roasted thighs, drizzle on some of the natural pan juices, and serve alongside a generous helping of pan-braised fresh spinach. This recipe should give you enough to feed 6 guests (or at least 3 real hungry chicken lovers!).

Chef's Note:

1—You can use a disposable aluminum pan to make this recipe if you want.

2—"Baby bellos" are small portabello mushrooms. Many of the finer supermarkets are carrying them these days.

3—Do you really need all that garlic? Probably not! But if you like good garlicky-flavored chicken and sauce (and especially if you like softened, creamy garlic pods), put them in just as the recipe suggests.

4—It is recommend that you allow the vegetables to roast alone for at least 15 minutes before placing the chicken on top of them. This sweetens them and begins the "sweating" process that produces the pan drippings.

5—If you don't have my seasonings on hand, you can substitute a couple of teaspoons of my homemade "Salt-n-Pepper" mix. To make this, you mix together in an airtight container equal parts of kosher salt and coarse-ground black pepper. If you want to "flavor" the mix, stir in a little onion powder, garlic powder, and celery salt to taste.

6—You can serve the pan drippings 1 of 2 ways: (1) simply spoon out the jus (pan gravy) and the softened vegetables together, or (2) strain out the softened veggies, serve them on the side or toss them out completely, and spoon just the jus over the pasta. Actually, there's another way, too—just pour the entire contents of the baking pan into a Vita-Mix, a blender, or a food processor and puree it into an emulsion. You talk about some good!

7—To make pan-braised fresh leaf spinach, take a chicken fryer with a tight-fitting lid, melt down 3 tbsp. unsalted margarine or bacon drippings, sauté 1/3 cup vegetable mirepoix from the produce department of your favorite supermarket, and stir in 2 bags pre-washed fresh spinach leaves. Then place the lid on the pan and allow the spinach to "braise" over medium-high heat for about 5 minutes or until it fully wilts. Finally, finish off the dish by sprinkling on 1 tsp. Frank Davis Vegetable Seasoning and a little extra melted butter or margarine.

Turkey Tetrazzini Rotini

Blend succulently roasted chopped turkey with a creamy sauce and ladle it over al dente rotini pasta and you have one of those classic dishes that's so good you just can't stop with one helping! This is such a simple recipe to prepare, you should do it often!

¼ stick butter or margarine
1 cup minced onions
⅔ cup minced celery
½ cup minced green bell pepper
4 cloves garlic, minced
1 cup thinly sliced mushrooms
½ cup cocktail sherry
1 can cream of chicken soup
1 can cream of shrimp soup
2 cups turkey pan drippings, as needed
2-3 tbsp. gravy flour (optional)

2 bay leaves
4-5 cups diced roasted turkey
1 tsp. Frank Davis Poultry Seasoning
½ tsp. crushed red pepper flakes
6 cups rotini pasta, cooked al dente
1 cup thinly sliced green onions
1 bunch parsley, minced
Grated Parmesan cheese for topping

In a heavy Dutch oven that has a lid, melt the margarine over medium heat and drop in the seasoning vegetables—the onions, celery, bell pepper, garlic, and mushrooms. When they have wilted and softened, slowly drizzle on the sherry, increase the fire to high, and cook the mixture for a few minutes until the alcohol burns off and leaves only its essence.

At this point, spoon in the soups and fold them uniformly into the seasoning vegetables. But here's where your creative judgment comes into play. Once again over medium heat, bring the mixture to a slow bubble and begin adding the turkey pan drippings a little at a time to give you the proper consistency. You don't want the sauce to be "pasty," but you don't want it watery, either. It should cling to and evenly coat the pasta when you ladle it over the top, not drain through it. Of course, if you get a little too liberal with the drippings and the sauce is a tad on the "thin" side, you can always whisk in a touch of the flour to re-thicken it (that's why it's there).

Finally, it's time to drop in the bay leaves, add the turkey, season the concoction with poultry seasoning, and spice everything up with red pepper flakes.

All that's left now is to put a lid on the pot, reduce the fire to low, and slow-simmer the sauce for about 15 minutes or until the turkey is piping hot.

When you're ready to eat, ladle a generous portion of the creamy mixture over each plate of hot rotini pasta, garnish it with green onions and parsley, sprinkle it with Parmesan cheese, and serve it alongside a chunk of hot buttered French bread. I promise you, one helpin' just won't do!

Chef's Note:

1—It is best if you roast about an 8-10-lb. turkey for this recipe. I suggest that you slice the breast meat to use for sandwiches and use the remainder of the bird for the pasta dish.

2—You can change the main ingredient in this recipe to create new dishes—for example, try substituting chicken, smoked pork, ham, shrimp, or possibly crabmeat for the turkey.

3—You shouldn't need added salt for this recipe. But if you find there's not enough in the cream soups for your liking, you can always add a little just before you serve the dish.

4—"Gravy flour" is a finely ground, powdery flour used almost exclusively for whisking into sauces to make instant, lump-free gravies. Pillsbury and Wondra are the principal manufacturers.

Sicilian Pasta d'Ova
(Classic Pasta with Eggs and Red Gravy)

Pasta and eggs is probably one of the oldest and most popular Friday Lenten dishes ever to be served in New Orleans (and everywhere else you find concentrations of Italians, for that matter). But it's a great dish whether you're Italian or not and whether it's Lent or not. So for that reason alone, I wanted to share it with you.

¼ cup extra-virgin olive oil
1 medium onion, minced
6 cloves garlic, minced
2 large cans Contadina or Hunt's Tomato Paste
6 large cans water or vegetable stock
½ cup Madeira wine
10 cloves garlic, peeled
2 bay leaves
1 tbsp. Frank Davis Sicilian Seasoning
½ cup minced flat-leaf parsley
6 anchovies, chopped and mashed
2 tsp. salt
1 tsp. red pepper flakes
½ tsp. coarse-ground black pepper
1 dozen eggs
1 lb. pasta, cooked al dente
½ cup thinly sliced green onions
1 cup grated Romano or Parmesan cheese
Loaves of French or Italian bread for dipping

Start off with a heavy-bottomed, 6-qt. Dutch oven or oval roaster that has a lid and heat the oil until it almost sizzles. Then drop in the onion and minced garlic and sauté the mixture until it wilts and softens (but be careful not to burn the garlic or it will turn bitter). When the onions have rendered out most of their water, stir in the tomato paste and fry it down—stirring continuously—for 1-2 minutes to "mellow out" the tomato acid.

At this point, pour in the water or stock, along with the wine, and work the liquid into the tomato paste until a smooth and silky gravy base forms. Then drop in the garlic cloves, bay leaves, Sicilian seasoning, parsley, and anchovies. When all the ingredients are in, season the gravy—Italians refer to it as a sugo—with salt and red pepper flakes, put the lid on the pot, reduce the fire to very low, and simmer for about 1 hour, stirring occasionally.

When you're ready to eat, transfer about a third of the gravy to a 12- or 14-in., high-sided fry pan or chicken fryer. Then bring the pan to a slow, slow boil and begin cracking the eggs directly into the hot gravy—*but you got to do this very gently or the eggs will "run" through the gravy and the yolks will break.* As long as the gravy is simmering, you can continue to add and cook eggs—just avoid stirring the pot! Incidentally, just so you'll know, it will take about 4 minutes for the eggs to harden and be ready to serve (since what you're really doing is poaching them in the hot flavored gravy).

The classic Sicilian way to serve this dish is to first plate up a helping of pasta. Then ladle some gravy from the Dutch oven over the top, crown it with a couple of eggs (removed from the gravy with a slotted spoon), sprinkle on some green onions and Romano, and top it off with a hefty piece of Italian bread hot from the oven!

I doubt that you could find an Italian family in New Orleans that hasn't dished this up as the mainstay meal on any Friday during Lent. And especially on Good Friday.

Chef's Note:

1—If you're going to make this recipe outside of Lent, you can make it with water, vegetable stock, seafood stock, or chicken stock. Chicken stock is recognized as "meat" and traditionally cannot be eaten on Fridays during Lent.

2—The recipe is traditionally made with #4 spaghetti, although you can use another pasta shape if you prefer. I can also tell you that whole-wheat pasta makes a nice substitute.

3—A nontraditional and nonauthentic variation is often served in New Orleans. Rather than cook the eggs in the gravy, some folks simply hard-boil the eggs, peel them, drop them into the gravy, and simmer them for 2 hours along with the gravy. Granted, this is good, and it's a shortcut, but it doesn't have the taste or texture of the classical dish.

4—The gravy that you don't use when serving this dish (in other words, the extra gravy you have left over after doing the eggs) can be cooled then refrigerated and used for other Italian recipes.

Pasta Buccatini d' Caesar

A greatly adorned version of the classic Roman *Alio e Olio* and one of the acclaimed dishes of the Caesars, this casserole could very well become one of your family's favorite ways to eat pasta. It's unbelievably tasty, it's simple to prepare, and it also makes a great meatless dish for diabetics. Make it once and you'll make it again and again! And you can make it according to your design.

1 lb. buccatini pasta (#7)
¾ cup + 4 tbsp. extra-virgin
    olive oil
1 small eggplant, diced
1 cup sliced mushrooms
1 cup sundried tomatoes
1 cup marinated artichoke
    hearts, drained and sliced
2 oz. anchovies (with oil),
    chopped

6 cloves garlic, minced
½ cup minced parsley
⅔ cup thinly sliced green onions
1 tsp. crushed red pepper
    flakes
2 tsp. Frank Davis Sicilian
    Seasoning
¾ cup grated Parmesan cheese
3 cups shredded mozzarella
    cheese

First, in a large stockpot, boil the buccatini in salted water until it becomes al dente—*cooked but still firm.* Then drain the pasta well in a colander, transfer it to a large mixing bowl, toss it well with 4 tbsp. oil, and set it aside.

Next, place 2 12-in. skillets on the stovetop. In the first, pour in ¼ cup olive oil, bring it to medium-high heat, and sauté the eggplant until it becomes soft (which should take 5-7 minutes). In the second skillet, pour in another ¼ oil, bring it to high heat, and sauté the mushrooms until they are golden brown. When both the eggplant and mushrooms are done, combine them in 1 skillet, toss them together, and set them aside as well.

Now take the skillet you just emptied, pour in the remaining ¼ cup oil, bring it to high heat, and sauté together the tomatoes, artichokes, anchovies, and garlic. This should take only a few minutes, but make sure you constantly stir the mixture to keep the garlic from burning.

At this point, put all the ingredients you just prepared into the mixing bowl containing the pasta and toss everything together well. Then drop in the parsley, green onions, red pepper flakes, Sicilian seasoning, and Parmesan cheese and toss everything together once again.

Finally, transfer the pasta to a large casserole dish (preferably glass) and top it with the mozzarella. All that's left is to slide the dish into a preheated 400-degree oven and bake it until the mozzarella melts (12-15 minutes) and turns a lightly toasted color.

I suggest that you serve the casserole piping hot from the oven with a cold tossed green salad and a generous piece of garlic bread on the side.

Chef's Note:

1—Pasta Buccatini d' Caesar is traditionally done as a meatless dish. But if you'd like to top it with some kind of meat, simply sauté about 1 lb. Italian sausage in a skillet and crumble it on top of the casserole at the same time that you sprinkle on the mozzarella.

2—The dish can be prepared in advance and kept in your refrigerator until you're ready to serve it. I do recommend, however, that you complete the preparation only up to the point of adding the mozzarella. Then when you're ready to eat, slide the casserole into the oven, toast the cheese, and serve it piping hot. Precooking the cheese and then reheating the dish results in a gummy, oily casserole.

3—If you wish to reduce the amount of olive oil in the casserole, simply use only the scant amount you'll need to accomplish the sautéing. In fact, if recommended by your physician, it is okay to reduce the quantities of all the other ingredients you personally need to cut back on. The basic cooking technique, however, should stay the same and you should see little difference, even with the alterations, in the final presentation.

4—To keep the eggplant from absorbing excess oil and to make sautéing easier, sprinkle the diced eggplant generously with salt and let it rest on the countertop for about 15 minutes. Then rinse off all the salt, dry the eggplant with paper towels, and sauté it as directed in the recipe.

5—I seriously suggest that you avoid buying the sundried tomatoes you find prepackaged in the grocery stores. They're usually hard as rocks, are impossible to soften even with hours of soaking, and lack any and all flavor. Instead, get your sundrieds from an Italian specialty store where they're sold in bulk. Nor-Joe Import Company off of Old Metairie Road has a primo variety so good you can eat 'em like candy!

Sicilian Pasta e Fagioli
(New Orleans Pasta Fazoole)

White cannellini beans, diced pancetta, chopped crushed plum tomatoes, and a rich chicken broth—spice it up Italian style, smother it down with tagliatelle noodles, and garnish with grated Pecorino Romano cheese. What you end up with is one of the classiest Sicilian dishes ever put together!

2 cups dried cannellini beans
3 cups water
9 cups canned chicken broth
2 bay leaves
2 garlic cloves, crushed
⅓ cup chopped sage
½ cup + 6 tbsp. extra-virgin olive oil
10 oz. pancetta or prosciutto, diced
10 oz. salt pork, diced
2 medium carrots, minced
1 large rib celery, diced
1 medium yellow onion, diced
4 garlic cloves, minced

5 plum tomatoes, peeled, crushed, and chopped
¼ tsp. crushed red pepper flakes
1 tsp. dried rosemary
1 tsp. ground thyme
2 tsp. Frank Davis Sicilian Seasoning
4 cups tagliatelle noodles, cooked al dente
¼ cup minced parsley
Coarse-ground black pepper to taste
½ cup grated Pecorino Romano cheese

To properly prepare pasta e fagioli, it needs to be done in 3 parts.
Part 1—Soak the cannellini beans.

First, wash the cannellini beans in cold running water and pick through them, taking care to remove any foreign objects or bits of gravel. Then place the beans into a large stainless-steel or glass stockpot that has a lid and generously cover them with plain cold water. Set the pot of beans in a cool place for at least 1 hour (but preferably overnight).

Part 2—Precook the cannellini beans.

Thoroughly drain off the soaking water and repeatedly rinse the beans under cold running water until the "foam" is completely gone (this will probably take 2-3 good washings). Then add to the stockpot 3 cups water, 3 cups chicken broth, the bay leaves, crushed garlic, and sage and bring the mixture to a rolling boil. At this point, continue to boil for exactly 10 minutes. When the allotted time is reached, once again thoroughly drain the beans in a colander and set them aside for a while.

Part 3—Cook the fagioli.

Now take the same stockpot in which you soaked and precooked the beans, place it over a medium-high fire, pour in 6 tbsp. oil, drop in the pancetta and salt pork (along with the carrots), and fry down the meats until they shrivel and begin to brown slightly. Then immediately stir in the celery, onions, and minced garlic and cook them until they totally wilt and clear (but do not let the garlic burn or it will become bitter).

When the seasoning base is done, add to the pot—*in order*—6 cups chicken broth, the beans, tomatoes, red pepper flakes, rosemary, thyme, and Sicilian seasoning. Then bring the entire mixture to a boil but *reduce it immediately to a simmer,* cover, and cook for about 2 hours altogether, stirring every now and then.

But here's the trick to authentic fagioli. About halfway through the cooking process, take approximately half of the beans out of the pot and puree them either by hand or in a food processor or blender. Then return them to the pot, stir them into the mix thoroughly, and continue to cook for the time remaining.

Finally, about 10 minutes before you're ready to eat, gently stir the cooked pasta into the beans. Then when you serve, drizzle a little oil over each bowl, garnish with parsley and pepper, and shower on the cheese.

The dish is best accompanied by hot garlic breadsticks, beets tossed with Italian olive salad, and a glass of chilled white wine.

Chef's Note:

1—Soak the beans only in stainless steel, glass, or plastic—no reactive metals!

2—All the Sicilian and Italian products you need for this recipe are available locally at Nor-Joe Import Company on Frisco Street in Old Metairie or at Central Grocery on Decatur Street in New Orleans.

3—If you live where you can't find the Italian products, white beans (Great Northerns) can be substituted for the cannellinis, broad egg noodles will take the place of tagliatelle noodles, hickory-smoked bacon will do well instead of pancetta, and Frank Davis Sicilian Seasoning can be ordered online from www.frankdavis.com or by calling 985-643-0027.

Mary Clare's Sicilian Butterbeans and Orzo

If you like the old classic Italian recipe for "pasta fazoole," where creamy white beans smother al dente pasta in a bowl to make a semi-soup, you're really going to love this dish. Large creamy lima beans, seasoned to mouthwatering perfection, are ladled over orzo, crowned with large pieces of poached sausage, and covered with Parmesan cheese. Mama mia! Few flavors are this satisfying!

2 lb. Camellia Brand large limas (butterbeans)
3 qt. tap water for soaking beans
3 cans Swanson's Low-Sodium Chicken Broth
3 broth cans filled with water
2 lb. smoked or Polish sausage
2 cups vegetable mirepoix
½ cup extra-virgin olive oil
3 bay leaves
¾ cup shredded basil

2 tsp. Frank Davis Sicilian Seasoning
Salt and coarse-ground black pepper to taste
1 lb. orzo, cooked al dente
1 cup grated Parmesan cheese
2 rounds of pull-apart garlic bread
Tomato, red onion, and avocado salad
¾ cup Italian olive salad

First and foremost, place the dried beans into a 5-qt. stainless-steel stockpot that has a lid. Then completely cover them with water, place the lid on the pot, and let them soak at room temperature for several hours (or in the refrigerator overnight). This is a prerequisite for making a good batch of Sicilian butterbeans! The soaking process puffs the beans and softens the hulls to make them super tender.

In the meantime, take a second 5-qt. stainless-steel stockpot that has a lid and add to it the chicken broth and cans of water. Then bring the mixture to a full boil. While the broth is coming up to heat, slice the sausage both lengthwise and crosswise into single-serving pieces. Then drop them into the boiling broth, reduce the fire to low, and simmer them until they puff up and become fork tender (which should take about 10 minutes). Remove them from the pot and set them aside.

Note: do not discard the sausage poaching broth! This will serve as the liquid in which you cook the butterbeans. It can be made in advance and refrigerated, along with the sausage, until ready for use. After it cools, you may also want to skim off the excess fat—it will collect and gel on the surface.

Now, when you're ready to cook the beans, pour out all of the soaking water and then add the beans to the sausage poaching broth that you saved. This is also the time when you add to the bean pot the vegetable mirepoix, oil, bay leaves, basil, Sicilian seasoning, salt, and pepper. Of course, you might want to hold off on adding any extra salt until you taste the seasoned sausage broth—there may be enough residual salt from the sausage to suit your taste.

At this point, bring the pot of beans to a boil, *but then instantly reduce them to low.* Then add the sausage to the pot, stir the ingredients thoroughly, put the lid on, and let the pot simmer for about 1 hour (or until the butterbeans are tender and creamy). When you're ready to eat, spoon a little of the hot orzo into each soup bowl and then ladle a generous helping of the butterbeans over the top.

All that's left is to crown the bowl with a piece of sausage and a helping of Parmesan cheese and serve it with a hearty piece of pull-apart garlic bread and a crisp tomato, red onion, and avocado salad topped with olive salad.

As I said at the beginning of the recipe . . . Mama mia!

Chef's Note:
1—A variety of smoked sausages may be used when making this recipe. Simply select the flavor of your choice and prepare it as instructed above.

2—If you'd prefer to mix the orzo and beans together in the same pot and serve the dish as a single item, fold in about half the amount of orzo to beans to get the right consistency. Ideally, it should be mixed just prior to serving.

3—Pull-apart garlic bread is a loaf of round bread found at many supermarket deli counters. Ask the bakery staff for it if you don't see it displayed. If you can't find it where you shop, however, a loaf of garlic bread (homemade or frozen) will suffice nicely.

Frank's White Beans, Pasta, and Pork Chops

You can use almost any kind of white beans you like for this dish, but I prefer the large, creamy, Italian cannellini beans. Spice them up with slices of fried prosciutto, simmer them down until tender, and ladle them over big hot bowls of pasta. Topped with golden roasted pork chops, this is a meal you'll serve your family often.

¼ cup extra-virgin olive oil
1 lb. prosciutto slices
2 cups minced onions
1 cup minced celery
½ cup minced green bell
  pepper
1 tbsp. minced garlic + 10
  cloves garlic, peeled
1 lb. dried cannellini beans
¼ cup minced parsley
1 tsp. thyme

1 tbsp. basil
4 bay leaves
6 cups chicken stock
2 cups bottled water
Salt and black pepper to taste
3 lb. thin pork chops
1 qt. skim milk
4 cups Frank Davis Chicken Fried
  Mix or seasoned flour
1 lb. canneroni pasta, cooked
  al dente

First, take a heavy 5-qt. Dutch oven that has a lid and put it on a high fire. Then, in the oil, sauté the prosciutto slices, onions, celery, bell pepper, and garlic until the seasoning vegetables soften and turn a honey brown (just don't let the garlic burn!). Next, toss in the beans, parsley, thyme, basil, and bay leaves and mix everything thoroughly (incidentally, the fire stays on high during this entire process).

Next, pour in the chicken stock and water and stir everything together again until uniformly combined. Add salt and pepper. Then bring the beans to a boil, but immediately reduce them to a simmer, cover the pot, and cook them until they become rich and creamy (about 3 hours). Stir the pot occasionally.

When the beans are done, preheat the oven to 450 degrees. Then dip the pork chops into the milk and dredge them lightly in the spicy chicken fried mix. Now shake off the excess and place them into a shallow sheet pan, which you've sprayed with nonstick cooking spray. One word of note here: *take care that the chops don't touch each other.* At this point, slide them into the oven and bake for 20-30 minutes or until golden brown and tender. *Do not overcook them, however.* If you do, they will turn out dry and rubbery.

When the meat is ready, place a helping of the pasta in each deep bowl, ladle out a generous portion of piping hot beans over the top, and serve with a couple of the pork chops and a chilled olive salad.

I gotta tell ya . . . this is the next best thing to being in Palermo eating pasta e fagioli!

Chef's Note:
1—The beans will cook much quicker and become much creamier if you soak them overnight before you cook them. However, it's not a requirement that you do so.
2—If you can't get to an Italian specialty store to buy cannellini

beans, you can substitute regular white beans, Great Northerns, or navy peas in their place. You can also substitute for the canneroni any kind and shape of pasta you prefer. By the way, canneroni is a shorter version of cannelloni. It's $^1/_2$ in. in diameter and $^3/_4$ in. in length.

3—For a richer base flavor, omit the water.

4—The preformulated chicken fried mix is already seasoned with all the spices you'll need to do this recipe. I encourage you not to add any more seasonings to the mix, especially pepper. If you make your own mix, however, you'll need salt, black pepper, white pepper, cayenne pepper, onion powder, garlic powder, and thyme to taste. The premixed coating is available online at www.frankdavis.com by clicking the Frank Davis icon.

5—To get a quicker cooking time and more uniform results with your pork chops, instead of placing them directly into the sheet pan, I suggest that you place a baking rack in the pan and lay the pork chops on the rack. This way the heat can circulate completely around the meat and delicately roast both sides of the chops at the same time.

Shrimp, Pasta, and Artichoke Hearts

This is real easy! My Pot-Cooked Artichokes recipe will help you get started.

4 tbsp. extra-virgin olive oil
4-6 anchovies, mashed
½ cup thinly sliced green onions
3 cloves garlic, minced
1 lb. peeled raw shrimp, chopped
2 artichoke hearts, coarsely chopped
Scraped pulp from artichoke leaves
2 cups salted artichoke water, as needed
⅓ cup heavy cream
½+ cup grated Parmesan cheese
Dash fresh-cracked black pepper
1 lb. small egg noodles, cooked al dente
Minced parsley for garnish

Just take a heavy 12-in. skillet and heat the oil over a high flame. Then stir in the anchovies, and quickly toss in and sauté the green onions and garlic. Then drop in the shrimp, artichoke hearts, and scraped artichoke pulp. When the shrimp turn pink (and be sure you don't overcook them or they'll turn rubbery), pour in a little of the artichoke water to create a sauce.

All that's left now is to whisk in the cream, $^1/_2$ cup cheese, and pepper. Then when you're ready to eat, drop the noodles into the shrimp and artichoke sauce, toss the pan a couple of times to uniformly blend everything together, and serve piping hot with a little parsley (and a little extra Parmesan) as garnish!

Chef's Note: If you don't have any fresh shrimp handy but you do have a couple of packages of sundried shrimp in the pantry, you can run them through the slicer blade of a food processor and simmer them in the cream to create an alternate pasta topping that's surprisingly tasty.

N'Awlins Shrimp-'n'-Macaroni Salad

Actually, you don't really need to use "macaroni"—you can make this dish with small shells, mini elbows, ditali, bowties, acini pepe, or any other pasta shape you like. You just want to make sure that the pasta is done al dente, the shrimp are poached to perfection, the seasonings are chopped superfine, the mayonnaise is rich and creamy, and you're extra hungry when you sit down to eat!

4 qt. salted water
2 qt. plain water
¼ cup Frank Davis Complete Seafood Boil
1 lb. small pasta shells
2 lb. small shrimp, peeled and deveined
1 cup Blue Plate Mayonnaise
½ green bell pepper, chopped superfine

1 rib celery, chopped superfine
½ medium onion, chopped superfine
2 tbsp. minced parsley
1 tbsp. apple cider vinegar
1 tbsp. Frank Davis Seafood Seasoning
Salt and black pepper to taste
1 bunch green onions, thinly sliced, for garnish

First, in a 6-qt. stockpot, bring the 4 qt. salted water to a rapid boil. At the same time, using a 4-qt. saucepan, bring the 2 qt. plain water to a rapid boil and flavor it by stirring in the seafood boil.

Now drop the pasta shells into the stockpot and cook them over high heat for 6-8 minutes until they are al dente (tender but not soft). I suggest that you stir the pasta occasionally as it boils to keep the shells from sticking together.

Meanwhile, when the seafood water begins boiling, go ahead and drop in the shrimp. But as soon as the water comes back to a boil, turn the fire off, remove the pot from the burner, and allow the shrimp to poach in the seasoned liquid for about 10 minutes to pick up all the spice.

When the pasta shells are cooked, pour them into a colander, wash them thoroughly in cold water, and set them aside momentarily to drain. *Note: it is very important to get all the water off the pasta; otherwise the mayonnaise dressing will become thin and watery and the dish will turn out unbelievably flat!* This is also the time when you take a slotted spoon, ladle the shrimp out of the seasoned water, and coarsely chop them with a chef's knife. Remember that they too must be dry when they go into the salad dressing.

Now you're ready to take a large mixing bowl and completely blend together the mayonnaise, bell pepper, celery, onion, parsley, shrimp, and vinegar. I suggest that you take your time and combine all the ingredients well so that they are uniformly mixed into the mayonnaise.

Finally, cover the mixture tightly with plastic film and set it in the refrigerator for about 1 hour so that all the flavors "marry." Then when you're ready to put the salad together, take a large bowl and a rubber spatula and fold the mixture into the pasta until every single shell is coated. All that's left is to go ahead and season the salad with the seafood seasoning, salt, and pepper.

Of course, you can serve the salad right away; but to make it the best it can be I suggest that you sprinkle on the green onions, tightly cover the bowl again with plastic wrap, and allow everything to rest overnight in the bottom of the refrigerator.

Y'all, this might very well end up being your absolute favorite dish of all time (or at least all summer long!). Go ahead—whip up a batch before the end of the day!

Chef's Note:
1—You can use those precooked tiny salad shrimp in this recipe— just poach them first in my seafood boil to add flavor to the finished dish.
2—To make this "sugar-watchers" compliant, you could substitute small whole-wheat shells for the semolina pasta in the original dish. But my mawmaw just wouldn't hear of it!

3—I suppose you could use almost any brand of mayonnaise you like, but the person who taught me how to do this recipe said I'd burn in hell when I die if I ever made it with anything other than Blue Plate! Oh, yeah—and using "diet" or "lite" mayonnaise is absolutely out of the question!

4—For a creamier salad, just stir in more mayo than I listed in the ingredients.

Granny's Bronzed Oysters and Pasta

Bronzing oysters is an exercise in pure simplicity. In fact it's quite possibly the easiest culinary technique you will ever do. But then, when you toss the bronzed oysters with freshly boiled thin spaghetti so that the pan drippings become the succulent sauce, you end up with quite possibly the best-tasting oyster dish you ever put in your mouth, too!

8 tbsp. extra-virgin olive oil
4 tsp. Frank Davis Bronzing Mix
4 tsp. Frank Davis Sicilian Seasoning
4 dozen shucked oysters with their liquor
4 tsp. minced fresh garlic
4 tbsp. chopped parsley
4 tsp. high-quality brandy
3 tbsp. cornstarch + ½ cup chicken stock

1 lb. #3 thin spaghetti, cooked al dente
1 cup shredded Italian cheese mix
4 tsp. coarse-ground black pepper
4 tbsp. thinly sliced green onions for garnish

Start off by putting a 12-in. nonstick skillet on top of the stove and turning the fire under it to medium high. Then after allowing the pan to heat for several minutes, pour in about 2 tbsp. oil and swish it around to evenly coat the pan.

Then when the oil just begins to smoke, start adding 1 dozen oysters to the skillet *one at a time* (leaving the excess oyster liquor behind as you add). Then lightly sprinkle the oysters with about 1 tsp. each of the bronzing mix and Sicilian seasoning—half on one side, and half on the other.

A note of caution here: you will have to cook the oysters on both sides, but you'll flip them over only once. This is best done by first dropping them into the skillet and seasoning them delicately. Then at the exact moment when you notice their edges beginning to curl (which should take about 1 minute), turn them over gently with a pair of tongs and season the other side. At this point you want to watch the pan closely—oysters cook very quickly and all you want is for their edges to curl. Overcooking them shrivels them up and turns them into tiny chewy blobs resembling knotted rubber bands.

As the batch comes ready, remove them from the pan with the tongs and place them on a warming platter momentarily. In the meantime, add to the skillet 1 tsp. garlic, 1 tbsp. parsley, 1 tsp. brandy, and a scant spoonful or 2 of the cornstarch/chicken stock mixture—you wanna be kinda stingy with the cornstarch, because all you want to do is slightly thicken the pan drippings so that the sauce will stick to the pasta.

Finally, when you're ready to eat, put the oysters back into the skillet, toss them in the sauce to reheat them, and top the skillet with about 1 cup spaghetti. Once more, toss the pan to combine the pasta and oysters thoroughly and then turn out the dish onto a heated dinner plate. Finish the dish by sprinkling it with ¼ cup Italian cheese, seasoning it with 1 tsp. pepper, and garnishing it with 1 tbsp. green onions.

Now repeat the procedure 3 more times and you got a dinner for 4! Oh, I almost forgot—a nice hot buttery pistolette right from the oven is the only thing missing!

Chef's Note:
1—If you can't find bronzing mix and Sicilian seasoning where you shop, you can order them directly from www.frankdavis.com.

2—This dish always comes out best if you can find unwashed oysters (oysters packed in their own liquor). For that reason, it might be worth your while to buy them in the shell and shuck them yourself.

3—Be careful not to puncture the oyster membranes as you add and remove them from the skillet (thus no meat forks, please!). This allows the oysters to remain plump and juicy instead of deflated and dry.

4—I suggest that you mix the cornstarch and chicken stock before beginning the recipe. The whole thing goes so fast that you won't have time to mix it as you cook.

5—You've probably figured out by now that this recipe is done on a "per-serving" basis. Oh, it could be fixed ahead, tossed together en masse, and then kept in a warm oven for a spell; but while it's edible done that way, it loses its character, its depth, and its richness. Cook it in batches for best results.

CHAPTER 8

Vegetables and Side Dishes

Frank's Vegetable Secrets

Here's a how-to guide to preparing corn on the cob, green beans, and cabbage without overseasoning and overcooking them. See if you know the secrets for perfect vegetables!

How to Cook Perfect Corn on the Cob:

1 gal. water	½ cup soft tub margarine or
2 tbsp. salt	sweet cream butter
8 ears yellow corn	¼ cup Frank Davis Sprinkling Spice

In an 8-qt. stockpot that has a lid, bring the water to a full and rapid boil. Then add the salt and stir until it is completely dissolved.

At this point, with the corn shucked, de-silked, and cut into halves, drop the ears into the water, *uncovered.* The boiling will stop. When it returns, time the ears for exactly 7 minutes. Then remove the pot from the burner, place the lid on the pot, and allow the corn to sit in the water for about 10 minutes to plump the kernels.

Serve them piping hot from the water bath, slathered with margarine and liberally seasoned with sprinkling spice.

Variation: Follow the exact cooking directions as above, only prior to dropping in the ears of corn, stir into the water ½ cup heavy cream and 10 oz. of hickory-smoked bacon. Allow the cream and bacon to boil in the water for at least 10 minutes to flavor the stock. Corn done in this manner turns out uniquely spiced and intensely flavored.

How to Cook Perfect Green Beans:

1 gal. water	⅓ stick butter, softened
2 tbsp. salt	8-oz. wedge herbed Brie
3 lb. fresh green beans, washed	cheese, sliced
and trimmed	
2 tbsp. Frank Davis Vegetable	
Seasoning	

In an 8-qt. stockpot that has a lid, bring the water to a full and rapid boil. Then add the salt and stir until it is completely dissolved. At this point, drop the green beans into the water, but leave the pot *uncovered.*

The boiling will stop. When it returns, reduce the fire to a slow bubble, cover the pot, and time the beans for exactly 10 minutes, stirring once or twice. Then, with the lid still in place, remove the pot from the burner and allow the beans to "poach" in the water for about 10 minutes or until they turn "tender crisp" (not hard and crunchy, but not mushy and overcooked either).

When they're done, drain off the water and place the beans in a very large mixing bowl. Then drop in the vegetable seasoning, butter (*in pats*), and cheese. Toss the beans over and over on themselves until the butter and Brie totally melt and adhere to the beans.

All that's left to do is serve the green beans piping hot alongside your favorite main dish. If done right, this vegetable could easily serve as a dessert!

How to Cook Perfect Cabbage:

12 oz. center-cut bacon, diced

1 cup coarsely diced onions

1 gal. water or diluted chicken broth

3 lb. smoked sausage, cut into half-links

2 medium heads green cabbage, quartered and cored

1 tbsp. Frank Davis Vegetable Seasoning

¼ cup soy sauce for garnish (optional)

1 bottle Gulden's Brown Mustard for dipping sausage

In a 12-in. Teflon or anodized aluminum skillet, sauté the bacon until it browns and the drippings render out. Then toss in the onions and sauté them as well until they begin to caramelize around the edges.

At this point, transfer the bacon and onions with a slotted spoon to an 8-qt stockpot that has a lid, pour the water into the pot, and bring the mixture to a rolling bowl. Then drop in the smoked sausage, cover the pot, and reduce the fire to medium low (you want the water at a slow bubble). Now cook the sausage for about 30 minutes to completely tenderize it and flavor the poaching stock.

When the links are done, remove them from the pot and set them on a warming platter temporarily. Then with the fire at a medium setting, place the cabbage wedges down into the stock so that they are completely submerged in the liquid. Once again put the lid on the pot and allow the cabbage to "poach" in the flavored broth for about 6 minutes. You'll have to watch it closely, though! Cabbage cooks and softens rather quickly.

When you can pierce the core portion of the wedges easily with an ice pick, finding only little resistance, remove the cabbage from the pot, immediately place it into a large mixing bowl, sprinkle on the vegetable seasoning, and serve it steaming hot alongside the smoked sausage.

Lightly sprinkle 1-2 splashes soy sauce over each cabbage wedge for a little added flavor if you so desire, and be sure to squeeze a hearty dab of brown mustard next to the sausage for dipping.

Lagniappe: The broth left in the stockpot makes a great clear soup to serve as a separate dish.

South Louisiana Indian Maquechoux

This is probably one of the tastiest things you can do with fresh corn in the wintertime. So essentially what you end up with is a traditional holiday gift recipe, compliments of the Houmas and the Choctaws, that's typically seasonal and typically Southern!

4 tbsp. butter or bacon drippings	1 large can diced tomatoes (1 lb. 12 oz.), with liquid
¾ cup minced onions	1 cup light cream
1 small green bell pepper, minced	1½ tsp. salt or Frank Davis Vegetable Seasoning
6 cloves garlic, minced	¼ tsp. red pepper flakes
6 large ears corn, with kernels cut from the cobs	¼ tsp. black pepper
3 tbsp. minced parsley	½ cup minced green onions

First, take a heavy 4-qt. Dutch oven that has a lid and melt the butter over medium heat. Then drop in your onions, bell peppers, and garlic and cook them together for about 5 minutes, stirring constantly and being careful not to let the garlic burn.

When the veggie seasonings are soft, stir in the corn kernels, parsley, tomatoes, cream, salt, red pepper flakes, and black pepper. I also suggest that you take a tablespoon, scrape the "corn cream" from the pulp on the cobs, and add that to the pot. Technically, it's nothing but cornstarch, but it lends a velvety smoothness and creaminess to the finished dish.

At this point, bring the maquechoux to a full boil, *but quickly reduce the heat to low, cover the pot, and let the dish simmer for about 15 minutes or until the corn is tender.* All that's left then is to whisk in the green onions, remove the Dutch oven from the heat, and let the maquechoux stand for about 10 minutes so that the combination of flavors can marry before you serve it

As a side dish, maquechoux can be served as a vegetable alone or over a bed of steamed rice as a complementary corn dressing.

Chef's Note: The trick to making a good maquechoux is to avoid overcooking it. Corn is a starchy vegetable that toughens when it is simmered too long. To get the right texture in a maquechoux, you want a slight crispness in every bite!

Green Beans Almondine

Do you like green beans? Then you're gonna love these! For a light yet delectable vegetable side dish, fix your green beans with slivered almonds and top them with a silky, buttery sauce. You'll find that they will complement almost any entrée!

2 cans French-cut green beans, drained and washed	1 cup concentrated chicken stock
½ stick sweet cream butter, lightly salted	½ cup minced onions
½ cup slivered almonds	3 tbsp. cornstarch + ¼ cup water
	Salt and black pepper to taste

First, liberally butter a 9x11 glass baking dish and place the green beans in it.

Then in a 10-in. heavy aluminum skillet, melt the butter over high heat, drop in the almonds, and quickly stir them until they lightly toast (watch the skillet closely—the almonds will burn quickly!).

When the almonds are ready, immediately pour in the chicken stock to stop the toasting process, and stir in the onions. Then reduce the heat to low and simmer the sauce for about 5 minutes or until the onions wilt.

At this point, bring the sauce back to a boil. Then slowly stir in the cornstarch and water mixture and cook the sauce until it reaches the consistency you desire—I suggest that you make it about the texture of melted ice cream.

When it's ready, season it to taste with salt and pepper and ladle it over the green beans, using a fork to *gently* work it into the layers.

All that's left is to place the dish (uncovered) into a preheated 350-degree oven and bake it for about 20 minutes or until everything is hot and bubbly.

Chef's Note:

1—If you want to use fresh or frozen green beans, just prepare them according to package directions or your favorite recipe before topping them with the almond sauce.

2—You may substitute 2 tsp. of my Frank Davis Vegetable Seasoning for the salt and pepper. It can be ordered directly from my Web site, www.frankdavis.com.

Cajun Pot-Fried Green Beans

The Cajuns refer to this cooking technique as *routee,* which best translates as "pot-frying." Over the years, I've done it with pork, venison, chicken, and a variety of other meats, but I'm convinced it lends itself best to the cooking of green beans! This is how all fresh green beans should taste.

12 oz. lean bacon, coarsely chopped
1 heaping cup coarsely chopped onions
1 tsp. minced garlic
3 lb. fresh green beans, washed and trimmed

1 tsp. Frank Davis Vegetable Seasoning
½ tsp. salt
½ tsp. coarse-ground black pepper
½ cup chicken stock
1 tbsp. Kitchen Bouquet

In a large cast-iron Dutch oven that has a lid, fry down the bacon pieces until they take on a crispy texture and render out most of their drippings. Then with a strainer spoon, remove the pieces from the pot and set them aside on a saucer. Immediately, though, replace the pieces with the onions and stir-fry them until they begin to brown. Once caramelizing has begun, you can drop in the garlic and stir it into the mixture (but keep it moving so that it doesn't burn and turn bitter!).

At this point, the green beans go into the pot—*all by themselves— no water, no liquid!* To start them cooking, all you do is take a spoon and thoroughly coat them with the hot bacon drippings, which are sizzling in the bottom of the pot. But this is not a recipe you can walk away from! You need to stand there for at least the next 5 minutes and stir, stir, and stir some more! It is important that you raise the temperature of the beans to the "pot-fry" level, which is high enough to actually fry the beans in the slight amount of drippings but not hot enough to burn them.

After the allotted sizzling time, toss the bacon bits back into the pot and sprinkle on the seasonings. Mix together the chicken stock and Kitchen Bouquet. Then, reduce the fire to medium low, pour on about 1 tbsp. of the stock/Kitchen Bouquet mixture, stir everything together, put the lid on the pot, and let the beans steam. It's just a matter of continuing to add the liquid a little at a time as needed, until the beans are cooked and tender.

Oh—if necessary, adjust the seasonings right before you serve the dish.

Chef's Note: This same technique can be used to pot-fry cauliflower, broccoli, asparagus, zucchini, yellow squash, cucuzzi, carrots, and mirliton.

Garbanzo Bean and Tomato Salad

A "crisp cold salad" doesn't always mean made with lettuce and tomatoes. It could be made with garbanzo beans, tomatoes, black olives, and avocados, tossed with an olive oil and balsamic vinaigrette. You're gonna love this one!

3 cans garbanzo beans, 15-oz.
size, drained
6 oz. feta cheese, crumbled
1 extra-large Creole tomato,
chopped
½ bunch green onions, coarsely
sliced
1 small red onion, coarsely
chopped
3 tbsp. chopped parsley
25 pitted black olives (the oily
kind)

2 ripe avocados, seeded and
cubed
1½ tsp. Frank Davis Vegetable
Seasoning
½ tsp. black pepper
3 tbsp. fresh-squeezed lemon
juice
2 tsp. aged balsamic vinegar
6 tbsp. extra-virgin olive oil or
pecan oil

Very simply, take a large bowl and gently combine all the ingredients. Then toss, toss, and toss some more, until every ingredient is fully distributed throughout the rest of the ingredients.

Then cover the bowl with a sheet of plastic wrap, place it in the refrigerator, and chill for 30-45 minutes before serving. You'll find that this salad will be among your family's favorites.

Chef's Note: If you'd like to cook your own garbanzo beans (chickpeas) from scratch, you will need 6 cups chicken or vegetable broth and 2 cups dried chickpeas. Bring the broth to a boil, stir in the beans, cover, and simmer the pot slowly for about 1 hour or until the beans yield readily to gentle pressure between your fingers.

Frank's Secret-Recipe Cole Slaw

1 small green cabbage, finely
shredded, core removed
1 small red cabbage, finely
shredded, core removed
6 carrots, peeled and shredded

3 ribs celery, minced
1 green onion, thinly sliced
1 medium onion, grated and
drained

Go ahead and combine everything uniformly in a large stainless-steel mixing bowl. Then, before adding the dressing, take time to ensure that all of the veggie liquids are removed, so that only dry veggies get coated with the dressing. A great way to do this is with a salad spinner. If you don't have one, wrap the veggies in a large towel and wring them dry.

The Dressing:

4 tbsp. high-quality vegetable oil	1 tsp. Dijon mustard
¾ cup Blue Plate Mayonnaise	1 tsp. kosher salt
¾ cup Miracle Whip Salad Dressing	1 tsp. coarse-ground black pepper
¼ cup sugar (optional)	1 can crushed pineapple, drained and squeezed through cheesecloth
4 tbsp. apple cider vinegar or tarragon vinegar	

In a large stainless-steel mixing bowl, whisk together all of the ingredients, except the pineapple, until the mixture is silky and creamy. In fact, overwhisk if you have to, in order to create a smooth emulsion. Then when the blend is perfect, gently fold in the pineapple pieces until they are evenly distributed through the dressing.

If you find that the final mixture turns out a tad dry, simply spoon in a little extra mayonnaise.

Finally, allow the dressing to stand at room temperature for about 30 minutes before folding it into the slaw vegetables. Then chill the slaw for at least 1 hour before serving.

Variation: Pour the dressing immediately over the slaw veggies, toss everything completely, cover, and refrigerate for at least 4 hours before serving. The finished slaw will also hold nicely overnight in the refrigerator, provided that the shredded veggies are well drained before mixing them with the dressing.

Or chill both the shredded veggies and the dressing separately. Then toss together just before service, sprinkle very lightly with paprika for garnish, and crown with some fresh-ground black pepper at the table.

Grandmaw's Greens

It just wouldn't be Grandmaw's kitchen without something nice and green cooking on the stove! And nothing is more fitting in Grandmaw's kitchen than a big ol' pot of collards smothered with pickled pork and topped with sliced red onions. Talk about making a meal special! Not only that, it serves as the perfect accompaniment to just about anything you plan on cooking for the entrée.

¾ lb. pickled pork
1 qt. rich chicken stock
2 qt. bottled water
½ tsp. fresh-cracked black pepper

3 bags frozen collard greens, 16-oz. size, thawed
1 medium red onion, thinly sliced
¼ cup melted butter for topping

First, cut the pickled meat into $1/4$-in. strips. Now bring the meat, chicken stock, water, and pepper to a boil in a large Dutch oven that has a lid. Then immediately reduce the heat to low, cover the pot, and simmer the stock for about 1 hour (this is an important step, since it allows sufficient time for the flavoring stock to develop).

At this point, drop in the greens and cook them over a gentle flame for about 20 minutes or until they become sweet and tender.

When you're ready to eat, serve the collards using a slotted spoon, sprinkle on the onions, and top with the butter. Of course, a little pot liquor drizzled over the top is hard to beat, especially if you're a country boy!

Real Eggplant Parmigiana

This is the authentic taste of old Sicily—the lightly fried eggplant, the cheeses, the homemade *sugo.* This eggplant dish isn't like the one the short-order cook attempts to fix down at the neighborhood restaurant. This is the kind of eggplant dish you only get in your Italian grandma's kitchen! *Ciao, paisano!*

2 medium eggplants, cut in
¼-in.-thick slices
3 eggs
4 tbsp. water
2 cups Italian seasoned breadcrumbs
½ cup extra-virgin olive oil
½ cup peanut oil
3 cups homemade tomato gravy
(*sugo*)

1 cup ricotta or cottage cheese
2 tsp. Frank Davis Sicilian
Seasoning
1 tsp. coarse-ground black pepper
2 cups shredded mozzarella
cheese
1 cup shredded Parmesan
cheese

The first thing you want to do, long before you even begin to think about cooking, is to take the sliced eggplant and soak the pieces for about 20 minutes in a glass bowl filled with cold, heavily salted water. This does 2 things: (1) it removes the oxalic acid from the eggplant (which is the stringent substance in the vegetable that gives eggplants their notorious "bite") and (2) it seals the pores and fibers of the eggplant (which prevents the vegetable from acting like a sponge and soaking up oil as it fries).

Once the soaking process is done, remove the eggplant slices from the water and drain them well (in fact, for best results, I suggest that you even pat the slices dry with paper towels). Then, *in order,* (1) beat the eggs and the 4 tbsp. water together to make a wash and place it into a shallow plate; (2) place the breadcrumbs into a shallow baking pan; and (3) dip the eggplant slices first into the egg wash and then into the breadcrumbs.

Be sure you take your time and coat each slice thoroughly, because it's the "coating" that actually binds the other ingredients—*the gravy and the cheeses*—to the eggplant slices. Then when all of the slices have been done, set them aside on a sheet of waxed paper for about 5 minutes (you want to give the crumbs a chance to adhere to the egg; otherwise they will fall off the eggplant when it fries).

In the meantime, mix together the olive oil and the peanut oil, pour it into a sauté pan, and bring it up to medium-high heat. Then, a few slices at a time, begin browning the eggplant. As you remove them from the pan, place them on several layers of paper towels to drain.

In an 11x14x2 glass casserole dish, first ladle in a base layer of tomato gravy (about ½ cup). Then lay in about half of the eggplant slices and top that layer with dollops of the ricotta. Next, sprinkle the dish lightly with some of the Sicilian seasoning and black pepper, follow that with a uniform sprinkling of both the mozzarella and

Parmesan, and then ladle on some more of the gravy. Then merely repeat the whole layering process once again and end up crowning the casserole with a healthy handful of Parmesan.

All that's left is to slide the dish into a preheated 350-degree oven and bake it covered for 50 minutes and then uncovered for another 10 minutes—to brown the crust. I suggest you serve it hot from the oven as an entrée or ice cold from the refrigerator as an appetizer. There's no way you can serve it that's not *fantastico, molto bene!*

Chef's Note:
1—It isn't necessary to peel the eggplants. Actually, I personally think the flavor is richer and better if the skin is left on.
2—It would be a shame to make this dish with ordinary ol' bottled commercial tomato sauce. But if you absolutely must use the bottled stuff, then by all means try to find a high-quality local gravy such as Sal & Judy's Original Tomato Gravy.

Tender Smothered Cucuzzi
(In a Shrimp Courtbouillon)

Cucuzza is probably one of the lightest and most flavorful vegetable side dishes served at home in New Orleans, regardless of whether you happen to be Italian or not. And what's so nice about it is that it essentially goes with anything. Cucuzza is simple to prepare, readily reheatable, and easily done in advance. Be warned, though, that if you fix this once, you'll be asked to fix it again and again!

½ lb. acini pepe pasta
4 tbsp. extra-virgin olive oil
1½ cups minced onions
4 cloves garlic, minced
1 can diced tomatoes with liquid (303 size)
1 cup canned chicken broth
2 bay leaves
¾ tsp. Frank Davis Sicilian Seasoning
½ tsp. basil

2 cucuzzi
2 lb. raw shrimp, peeled and deveined
Salt, cayenne pepper, and black pepper to taste
2 tbsp. minced parsley
½ cup thinly sliced green onion bottoms
Grated Parmesan cheese for garnish

Before you begin preparing the cucuzzi, take a 3-qt. stockpot and boil the pasta only until it is *al dente.* Then drain it thoroughly in a fine-mesh colander. Set it aside to cool.

Meanwhile, in a 5-qt. Dutch oven with a tight-fitting lid, heat the oil to medium high, drop in the onions and garlic, and sauté them only until the onions turn clear—*do not let the onions caramelize and do not let the garlic burn.*

Next, toss the tomatoes into the pot along with the chicken broth, bay leaves, Sicilian seasoning, and basil. Then stir everything together well, cover the pot, and simmer the mixture over low heat for about 15 minutes.

While the tomato stock is cooking, take a potato peeler and a paring knife and strip the green skin from the outside of the cucuzzi. Then cut the cucuzzi pulp into 1-in. dice (4-6 cups). When the tomato stock is ready, drop the pieces into the stock, stir everything together well, cover the pot once more, and cook the cucuzzi over medium-high heat until it softens (which should take 20-30 minutes).

One of the last steps in preparing this recipe is to build the shrimp courtbouillon. When the cucuzzi pieces are tender, stir the shrimp into the pot and allow them to cook—*uncovered this time!*—for about 5 minutes or until they turn pink. Then quickly drop in the pasta, cover the pot again, and let the dish simmer once more for about 4 minutes to come to full heat. Then season it with salt and pepper.

When you're ready to eat, quickly stir in the parsley and the green onions and serve the cucuzzi piping hot in small bowls as a separate vegetable side dish, generously topped with grated Parmesan cheese.

Chef's Note:
1—A cucuzza is a long Italian squash with a delicate sweet taste that's rich in vitamin C and high in nutritional fiber. It cooks easily without a lot of added moisture.

2—If you can't find cucuzzi for this dish, you can substitute mirliton instead.

Frank's Creole Mirliton Casserole

Tender young pieces of mirliton, gently seasoned with a vegetable mirepoix, simmered in butter, succulently smothered with sausage and chopped shrimp, covered with a crunchy cornflake and Parmesan cheese topping, and baked to a hot bubbly consistency—that's a Creole mirliton casserole, y'all!

6 medium mirlitons
4 tbsp. butter, softened
1 medium yellow onion, minced
4 green onions, thinly sliced
½ green bell pepper, minced
½ red bell pepper, minced
2 ribs celery, minced
6 cloves garlic, minced
1 medium tomato, seeded and diced
1 cup coarsely chopped mushrooms
2 lb. raw shrimp, peeled and chopped
1 lb. Polish sausage, small diced

¼ cup minced parsley
½ tsp. thyme
½ tsp. rosemary
1 tsp. salt
½ tsp. black pepper
½ tsp. red pepper flakes
4 cups homemade French-bread crumbs
1 can chicken broth (optional)
1 egg, well beaten
½ cup crumbled cornflakes
1 tbsp. butter, melted
½ cup shredded Parmesan cheese

First, take your mirlitons and boil them whole in lightly salted water until an ice pick will pierce them all the way through without using excessive pressure. Then remove them from the pot and set them aside to cool (you can discard the water).

In the meantime, in a 5-qt. Dutch oven, melt the 4 tbsp. butter over medium heat and sauté the onions, bell pepper, celery, garlic, tomato, and mushrooms until everything is soft (which should take about 5 minutes).

While the seasonings are simmering, slice the cooked mirlitons in half lengthwise, remove the center seedpods, and throw them away. Then take a paring knife and carefully peel the outer skin away from the pulp. Once the skin is removed, dice the pulp into small pieces and set it aside.

At this point, preheat the oven to 325 degrees. Then turn the fire under the Dutch oven up to high and drop in the shrimp and sausage. Within 2-4 minutes, the shrimp will turn pink, which is exactly the way you want them—*just pink, not cooked*—and the sausage will brown slightly around the edges.

When this happens, add to the mixture the mirliton pulp. Then stir the pot constantly for 10-15 minutes, cooking everything together over medium-high heat until a chunky paste forms (it may turn slightly watery, but don't worry about it). When the texture is just the way you want it, remove it from the heat and drop in the herbs and spices—the parsley, thyme, rosemary, salt, black pepper, and red pepper flakes. Be sure to fold them well into the mirliton, shrimp, and sausage blend.

Now it's time to begin working the French-bread crumbs into the casserole mixture (and this is best done a little at a time). When all the bread is added, you should end up with a rather dry paste that tends to stick to the spoon. If it is still too moist, add a few extra bread-crumbs, because if the mixture is too wet, it will run during the baking process. If on the other hand your mix turns out too dry, simply moisten it to your liking with a little chicken broth. Then when you're satisfied with the final consistency, and the mixture has cooled down a bit, quickly stir in the egg to bind everything together.

Finally, transfer the mixture to a large casserole dish (I find that a buttered glass dish works best). Then combine the cornflakes with the butter and liberally top the casserole with the mixture, slide the dish into the oven on the center rack, and bake it uncovered for 25-30 minutes or until the topping turns a toasty brown. All that's left is to spoon out the hot casserole on warm dinner plates, garnish with a little Parmesan cheese, and serve it piping hot right from the oven.

Chef's Note:

1—You'll notice that no chicken broth is added to the mixture until after the mushrooms, shrimp, sausage, and mirliton have had a chance to cook for a while. These ingredients will release a certain amount of liquid as they simmer. All in all, you don't want the final concoction to be too watery, or you'll have to add too much bread to the casserole.

2—When adding the egg, stir it into the mixture quickly. If the casserole hasn't cooled enough when it goes in, it could actually scramble the egg instead of incorporate it as a binder.

3—For a little extra enhancement, liberally sprinkle the casserole with shredded Parmesan cheese when it has 10 minutes left to bake in the oven. This will form a nice crusty topping on the dish.

4—A mirliton casserole goes well with creamed peas, buttered carrots, and a crisp lettuce salad topped with French dressing.

N'Awlins' Favorite Rice Pilaf

So, okay—I could be wrong! Maybe this isn't N'Awlins' favorite rice pilaf! But I do know that it's easy as heck to whip up and it tastes great and it goes with almost everything. So whatcha thinking?

2 cups raw long-grain rice
2 tbsp. extra-virgin olive oil
1 stick + 3 tbsp. butter
1 cup minced onion
⅔ cup minced celery
⅔ cup minced green bell
  pepper
½ cup minced carrots
½ lb. sliced mushrooms
3 plum tomatoes, seeded and
  diced

½ cup chopped parsley
1 cup crumbled vermicelli,
  uncooked
1 tsp. Frank Davis Vegetable
  Seasoning
½ tsp. coarse-ground black
  pepper
½ tsp. kosher or sea salt
4 cups vegetable broth
1 cup slivered almonds

First, preheat the oven to 375 degrees. Then wash the rice in a colander several times under cool running water until all the excess starch is gone. When it's done, let it stand in the sink and drain for a few minutes.

Next, heat the oil and 4 tbsp. butter in a heavy skillet, and sauté the onion, celery, bell pepper, carrots, and mushrooms until they begin to wilt. Then drop in the tomatoes and ¼ cup parsley and continue to cook the ingredients over medium heat for about 6 minutes until tender.

At this point, brown the vermicelli lightly along with the veggie mirepoix (for about another 5 minutes). Now add the rice; sprinkle the pan with the vegetable seasoning, pepper, and salt; and toss everything until fully combined. Then transfer the contents of the skillet to a large buttered baking pan or casserole dish.

Meanwhile, in a separate saucepan bring the vegetable broth to a rolling boil and pour it evenly over the rice mixture. At this stage, all that's left to do is to cover the pan tightly with aluminum foil and bake the pilaf in the oven for 45 minutes-1 hour (I suggest that you stir the rice once after 30 minutes then again after 45 minutes). Finish up the dish by removing the pan from the oven and allowing the rice to rest for 15 minutes before serving.

When you're ready to eat, fluff the pilaf with 2 serving forks, top the casserole with 4 tbsp. butter so that it melts evenly into the rice, then garnish with the remaining parsley and butter-toasted slivered almonds (the easiest way to do that is to brown them quickly in 3 tbsp. sizzling butter—but watch them carefully so that they don't burn!).

This pilaf is best when served piping hot . . . and it goes with almost any entrée!

Frank's Famous Rice Cooker Casserole

This is one of those dishes you can actually start and finish in your automatic rice cooker! Just follow the directions step by step and it will be there, moist and full of flavor, whenever you're ready to eat. It is a perfect side dish for almost any entrée, but it goes especially well with turkey, or duck, or goose, or pork roast!

2½ cups raw long-grain rice
4½ cups Swanson's Chicken
    Broth
½ tsp. turmeric
1 tsp. basil
1½ tsp. sea salt
1 tsp. freshly ground black
    pepper
¼ stick margarine

¾ cup minced onions
½ cup minced celery
1 cup medium-diced mush-
    rooms
½ cup thinly sliced green onion
    tops
⅓ cup minced parsley
4 tbsp. melted butter

The first thing you want to do is make certain you rinse all the excess starch off the uncooked rice. The best way to do this is by repeatedly washing the grains under cool running water in a large mixing bowl, then each time straining off the water in a fine-mesh colander.

Now, place the drained rice into your rice cooker and pour the chicken broth over it. This is also the time for you to stir in the turmeric, basil, salt, and black pepper. Go ahead and turn the rice cooker on.

Meanwhile, in a small nonstick skillet on medium high, heat the margarine and quickly sauté the onions, celery, mushrooms, and green onions. When they've softened and begin to show signs of browning, take the lid off the cooker and evenly blend—*actually, you might want to "fold" instead of blend*—into the rice the sautéed veggies and all but about 2 tbsp. parsley. Then put the cover back on the device and allow it to continue cooking.

When the rice is almost done, remove the lid once more and pour on the melted butter. Then with a meat fork, "fluff" the rice so that the grains separate.

All that's left to do now is to check the casserole every once in a while to refluff the rice.

When you're ready to eat, remove the insert from the rice cooker, garnish the rice with the remaining parsley, and serve it piping hot alongside your entrée, whatever it might be. Oh—and if you're fixin' something that yields a gravy, be sure to spoon lots of it over the rice when you serve it. Mmm!

Chef's Note:

1—If you don't have an automatic rice cooker, you can cook the dish in an aluminum Dutch oven on the center rack of your oven, set at 350 degrees, for about 40 minutes.

2—The amount of moisture you add to this dish is critical if the rice is to come out fluffy instead of sticky and gummy. Be sure to drain all the excess water off the rinsed rice! And be sure to carefully measure the chicken broth! You'll find you'll have exactly the amount you need once the juices render out of the onions, celery, and mushrooms.

3—If you'd care to add more flavoring to the rice as it cooks, feel free to drop in minced rendered-out bacon, precooked smoked or breakfast sausage, diced roast pork, chopped poached shrimp or crawfish tails, lump crabmeat, or anything else for which you have a personal taste. The versatility of this dish is limited only by your imagination.

CHAPTER 9

Lagniappe

Frank's Heretofore Guarded Secrets!

Keeping the Red Stuff Potent!

You probably already knew that if you stored your herbs and spices in a cool place away from direct heat they'd last longer, right?

But did you know that if you put your "red spices"—such as chili powder, paprika, cayenne—in the refrigerator, they will keep their color and potency twice as long as if you stored them on the spice rack? So put down the book now and go move them!

Don't Pit the Avocado!

If you're going to use only half of an avocado when you cut it, leave the pit in the unused half and wrap it tightly in plastic film. Guess what? The pit will keep the second half from turning yucky and brown! Of course, you have to store it in the refrigerator. But with the pit in, it can keep perfectly for a couple of days.

Dispelling the Roux-Mers!

A real Cajun roux is a mixture of flour and oil cooked in a heavy skillet until it turns a beautiful brown and takes on a nutty aroma. When you leave out the oil and brown the flour in a microwave, you have *browned flour—not a roux!* Oh sure, you can use it to thicken liquids and you can justify that it's healthful for you because it's fat free. But please don't call it a roux. It doesn't look like a roux and it certainly doesn't taste like a roux!

Chopping Fruit Is Easy!

Getting ready to chop up some dried fruit for special desserts or holiday fruitcakes? It doesn't have to be hard to do. Try this. Put the fruit in the freezer for a couple of hours. Then chop them with a chef's knife. They'll cut so quick and clean you won't believe it! And just in case your knife starts sticking, dip it in hot water every few minutes or so to liquefy the sugar.

No More Soggy Bottom Crusts!

Are you constantly complaining that the bottom crusts on all your pies turn soggy, especially when you make custard pies and quiches? Well, try this guarded secret and your problems are over!

Brush a slightly beaten *egg white* on the uncooked pie shell and bake it at 425 degrees for about 5-10 minutes. Then add your filling and bake it according to the recipe directions. I promise you the crust will be so flaky you'll call all your friends and tell them about it!

And Picture-Perfect Top Crusts, Too!

You know that rich, brown glaze you see on top of the pies they make at your favorite bakery? Know how you can do that at home?

Simple! Just brush the top crust lightly with milk—*yep, milk!*—just before you bake the pie. Works every time!

A Little Bit of Egg-ology!

Whenever you want to separate egg whites from egg yolks easily, do it while the eggs are still cold right from the refrigerator. But . . . if you want to get the maximum volume when you're beating egg whites for a meringue, let the eggs come to room temperature first. Got it? Separate cold; beat warm!

Cookie Crumbs to Ice-Cream Toppings!

Next time the kids leave a half-dozen half-empty bags of cookies stashed in the pantry, don't rant and rave. And by all means don't throw them out!

Mix them all together—the macaroons, Oreos, vanilla wafers, animal crackers—and run them through the pulse cycle of a food processor until they're coarsely chopped. If you turn them into cookie crumbs, they make excellent toppings for ice creams and puddings! Oh—and you can stash them in your freezer!

Speaking of Toppings for Ice Cream!

Take some of those quick-cooking oats—like Quaker or Aunt

Jemima—and brown them real fast over high heat in a small amount of butter in a nonstick skillet. You'll be surprised just how crunchy and crispy they'll get. And it's a real cheap (as well as healthful) substitute for chopped nuts when you're baking cookies or looking for a sprinkling to put over an ice-cream sundae.

Cutting Back on the Butterfat?

I don't care what anybody says, the best-tasting milk in the whole wide world was the milk delivered to your door in glass bottles by the milkman! Remember how the cream came to the top? And it had that crimped paper cap over the mouth? And it was sealed with a little cardboard tab that you had to lift out of the recessed slot?

Well, those days are long gone. And so are the days of drinking the cream—the butterfat—off the top of the milk. Today, doctors say all that stuff is detrimental to your health and they want you to reduce your intake of butterfat to help lower your cholesterol.

So just in case you need to know the percentages of butterfat in dairy products, here's your chart:

heavy cream: 42 percent
cream cheese: 32 percent
table cream: 28 percent
ice cream: 12 percent
whole milk: 3.5 percent
low-fat milk: 1 percent
skim milk: .5 percent

Frank's Study Sheet for Wok Cooking

Invest in and learn to use a good wok. It requires only small quantities of oil, cooks quickly, seals in natural juices and flavor, *and is excellent for cooking for 2.*

The best wok you can buy is one that is designed to go on top of the stove and made from low-carbon steel. These woks need to be seasoned, just like cast iron, but they focus the heat only on the bottom, where the real cooking takes place. Just for the record, if you have an electric range, *no wok will work well.* Woks require a high degree of heat to cook properly—you can't get that kind of heat from an electric element! If all you have is an electric stove, use a nonstick skillet instead of a wok. You can still do stir-frying!

You're going to find that a *heat ring* (a circular device with holes in the sides) comes packed as an accessory with most woks. *Don't use them to cook on!* They're made for use in other countries, not in the good old U.S.A. They will burn the finish off most stoves and keep your wok from getting hot enough. But they can be placed inside the wok and used for steaming vegetables.

Electric woks are also available to the home cook, but they don't perform nearly as efficiently as top-of-the-stove models because their thermostats don't keep the temperature standard and they can't recycle quickly enough to get the job of stir-frying done. Yet if you prefer to buy electric, go ahead. Just keep the quantities you cook very small so that the heat tends to remain more constant.

It is also important that you invest in a good set of wok tools. Standard and slotted spoons are okay in a pinch, but nothing beats the *ladle and chan, the brass strainer, the spatula, and the bamboo brush.* (A chan is the spatula or "shovel" that is used in combination with the ladle for wok cooking. It is not to be confused with the "Chan pan," a specialized, rounded wok named after the person who devised it.)

Note: as is the case with cast iron, once a low-carbon steel wok is seasoned, use only the bamboo brush or a nylon scrubber to clean it! Avoid using soap in the wok—it will literally absorb into the steel pores and give your dishes a detergent taste. And never use a Brillo or SOS pad! After each use, brush out the wok with clean hot water (if something sticks, rub it off with a little salt), dry it immediately, and reapply a very light coat of vegetable oil to prevent it from rusting . . . *because a good wok will rust!*

How to Cook in a Wok

What can you do in a wok? Well, you can stir-fry, sauté, steam, poach, deep-fry and boil! Here are specific tips, tricks, and techniques.

Place it on your stove's burner or an outdoor propane fryer. Remember, to get a wok to cook properly, you have to concentrate the heat *just on the bottom.* You want the sides to remain only warm, because that's where you are going to stack the cooked food to keep it at serving temperature—in other words, you cook on the bottom then push the food up the sides to keep it heated.

Use only small amounts of oil—just enough to lightly coat the meat and vegetables. And keep the food moving all the time! Never stop stirring! Stir-fry from the bottom, push it up the sides, and let it fall back to the hot bottom again. The constant agitation seals in all the natural flavor and keeps the food from scorching. Hint—use the chan to push the food away from you and the ladle to pull it back (you actually roll the food over on itself using this technique).

To steam in a wok (or to finish a dish with a sauce), push the food up the sloped sides and add the poaching or steaming liquids (preferably flavored stocks!) to the bottom. Then cover the wok with the domed lid and let only the steam finish cooking the food. Don't let the food become submerged in the liquid—that's boiling! It will give you nothing but blah-tasting meats and nasty soggy vegetables.

To season meat and vegetables in a wok, use any of a variety of flavorings. I've included a list of Asian ingredients that I recommend you keep on hand. Feel free to experiment with each of them to find which ones you like best. Remember—you don't use salt in wok cookery! The rich Asian flavorings make it unnecessary; and if you use soy sauce, it already contains sufficient salt for most tastes. I also recommend that you use only white pepper when you stir fry, if for no other reason than uniform flavoring.

Beef or chicken stock are the recommend liquids for poaching or creating a sauce. Thicken your sauces by slowing stirring into the liquid small quantities of cornstarch mixed with cold water. I suggest about 4 tbsp. cornstarch dissolved in 1/2 cup water. But here's the trick: to get the cornstarch mixture to thicken your sauce, the sauce must be cooking at a rolling boil. Oh—and a touch of sugar takes the edge off any bitter taste.

To stir-fry meats in a wok (beef, chicken, shrimp, veal, pork), cut the meats into small julienne strips, preferably on a diagonal bias, and coat them with the white of an egg, sprinkle on a few drops of soy sauce and sesame seed oil, dust them with some cornstarch, and drop them a few pieces at a time into hot oil in the bottom of the wok. Remove the meats when they're cooked (and believe me, they'll cook quickly!), drain them on paper towels to remove any excess fat, and return them to the wok when the vegetables are done.

To get the absolute best flavor and texture out of your wok-cooked vegetables, try to cut them so that they're all the same size and learn to cut them on a bias so that you expose as much of the cooking surface as possible. Oh—and to reduce wok-cooking time even further, either blanch the cut vegetables in boiling water for 1-2 minutes, or microwave them in a few tablespoons of stock before adding them to the wok. Both methods tenderize the veggies and reduce the actual cooking time. Just be sure you don't over-tenderize!

Recommended Stir-Frying Ingredients

Chicken stock—The #1 wok-flavoring agent! Homemade is always best; canned as a broth is okay.

Beef stock—Homemade in a Crockpot is best; canned as a broth or consommé is okay.

Vegetable stock—Homemade in a Crockpot is best; canned as a broth is okay.

Acini pepe pasta—An alternate to rice, this is the tiny pasta found in most soups. Supermarkets have it.

Chinese noodles—They come in a can and you sprinkle them on your dish after cooking for added crunch.

Soy sauce—A primary flavoring for wok cooking. But buy only the best you can!

Teriyaki sauce—A primary sweet flavoring you can use in wok cooking.

Chili sauce—Sometimes mixed with garlic for added spice.

Black bean sauce—Good stuff. Learn to cook with it.

Oyster sauce—Another primary ingredient for wok cooking. You can add oyster sauce to anything.

Hoisin sauce—A rather sweet bottled Asian sauce that's great for specific dishes, namely pork.

Cornstarch—Your standard Asian thickening agent, your "Chinese roux."

White pepper—The recommend pepper for wok cooking. Black pepper burns and turns bitter.

Eggs—Except for fried rice, you usually use only the whites of eggs (which cuts down the cholesterol).

Sesame-seed oil—Add only a few drops at the end of the cooking process to intensify flavors.

Peanut oil—Recommended for stir-frying because it can take the high heat required for wok cooking.

Water chestnuts—These give your dishes a crunchy texture. Drain and wash them well before using.

Bamboo shoots—These are a little more tender than water chestnuts. Good flavor; but wash them too before using.

Snow peas—A great vegetable for stir-frying.

Cabbage—An essential vegetable and a crunchy substitute for bok choy. Shred it to cook it in a wok.

Onions—Use either yellow and green onions in wok cookery, depending on the recipe. Bias cut them.

Celery—Cut the ribs in diagonal bias pieces. They should be in almost every Asian dish.

Bell peppers—Cut them in uniform pieces for cooking in a wok, but use them sparingly in most dishes.

Broccoli—Outstanding in a wok, but use only the florets and don't let them get mushy.

Zucchini—Either julienne them or chunk them on a bias. Again . . . don't let them overcook!

Cauliflower—Like broccoli, keep them tender crisp and use only the florets. Lightly poach them first.

Mushrooms—You can use the Asian dried ones after rehydrating them, or use the supermarket kind.

Ginger—An essential for Asian cooking! Use the fresh stuff and grate it for best results. Use sparingly.

Baby canned corn—Tiny ears that you drop in when the dish is almost cooked. Wash before using.

Sugar—A teaspoon or so takes the bite off bitter sauces in wok cooking. Granular sugar is the right kind.

Dry cocktail sherry—The wine of choice in wok cooking. You don't need to buy rice wine.

Plum jelly—Mix it with soy sauce and a little sherry to make a super plum sauce for meats and egg rolls.

Rice—Keep some cooked rice in the refrigerator all the time. Either steam it before serving or stir-fry it in the wok.

Cooked pasta—#4 or vermicelli is best for wok cooking. Stir-fry for a great chow mein or lo mein.

Stir-fry meats—
  Chicken: Usually skinned breasts, julienned in thin strips.
  Beef: Usually flank steak or roast, stripped of all fat and sliced extremely thin on a bias.
  Pork: Usually fillets, rib roast, or Boston Butt, stripped of all fat and sliced extremely thin on a bias.
  Ground beef or pork: You can use ground meats when you're in a real hurry!
  Ham: Always fine dice and stir-fry with the vegetables to impart the greatest flavor.
  Sausages: Be sure you slice them thinly and fry them from the outset with the vegetables.

Shrimp: Always butterfly the large ones, but the tiny ones cooked whole work best.

Crawfish: Add them to whatever dish you're cooking directly from the package. Great for woks!

Fish: Always cut in cubes no larger than 1 in. for best results in stir-frying.

Alligator: Cut the meat the same as you'd cut fish, but the thinner the better for stir-frying.

MSG—Monosodium glutamate. Don't buy it; don't use it! You don't need it in good Asian food!

Crowning Condiments New Orleanians Put On Their Red Beans!

Maybe Yankees can eat beans plain-like! In fact, maybe even folks living north of LaPlace, east of Pearl River, and west of Covington can eat their beans unadorned! But if you were born and raised in the Crescent City and you religiously had your red beans and rice every Monday, then you had a secret and specialized topping, a crowning touch, that you added to the plate minutes before the first bite. Check out the list below and see if your favorite ingredient is on my list!

Liquid smoke
Catsup
Mayonnaise
Louisiana Hot Sauce
Vinegar
Olive oil
Lea & Perrins Worcestershire
  Sauce
Yellow or Creole mustard
Chopped fresh hot peppers
1 tbsp. Blue Plate Mayonnaise
Vinegar-based slaw
Banana peppers (minced)
Chopped Vidalia onions
Canned chili con carne
Chopped kosher dill pickles

Sliced green onions
Tabasco
Diced Ma Brown pickles
Diced raw white onions
Juice from pickled onions
Homemade whole or diced
  pickled onions
Minced jalapeno peppers
Holland Onions
Dill or sweet pickle relish
Italian salad dressing
Rotel tomatoes
Shredded cheddar cheese
Raw spinach + pearl onions
Slice of chocolate cake
Granular sugar

Pepper vinegar
Jalapeno juice
Extra-soft peanut butter
Banana (mashed)
Vinegar from Crystal Pickled
  Peppers
Chow Chow

Chili powder
Melted butter
White vinegar
A splash of Tiger Sauce
Shredded American cheese
Pace Piquante Sauces

CHAPTER 10

Desserts

New Orleans Bananas Foster

Combine bananas with a rich, buttery, brown-sugar syrup that is laced with dark rum and banana liqueur and flavored with cinnamon, and pour it all over creamy vanilla ice cream, and you've got yourself a classic Southern dessert that you don't have to go to a fancy French restaurant to get.

1½ sticks sweet cream butter
1 cup loosely packed dark
  brown sugar
⅓ cup dark rum
½ cup banana liqueur

1 tsp. ground cinnamon
2 tsp. vanilla extract
6 ripe bananas, peeled and
  sliced lengthwise
French vanilla ice cream

First, take a 12-in. heavy aluminum skillet, preferably one that's nonstick, and melt 1 stick butter over medium-high heat until it begins to foam. Then slowly add in the brown sugar and briskly whisk it into the butter until it thoroughly dissolves. (You'll know when it's ready because all of the butter will be absorbed into the sugar and the syrup will turn smooth.)

Next, *carefully* stir in the rum (it will splatter all over the stove—*and you!*—and flame up if poured in too quickly!) and mix it well into the syrup. Then pour in the banana liqueur (*again, slowly!*) and blend it in, too. All this time, your fire is still set at medium high.

At this point, drop in the remaining butter in small pats and gently cream the pieces into the syrup. When the pats have completely melted, add the cinnamon and vanilla, whisk everything together once again, reduce the heat to low, and cook the sauce for about 4 minutes—*stirring constantly*—until it turns shiny and silky.

Finally, cut the sliced bananas crosswise into 4 pieces, drop them into the sauce, and simmer them for a couple of minutes until they soften. Then serve the bananas right from the skillet, along with a generous helping of the sauce, over a heaping scoop of French vanilla ice cream.

And don't skimp—make it Häagen-Dazs or Blue Bell. Count calories tomorrow!

Old-Fashioned Creole Rice Pudding

This is what your mawmaw made with every little bowl of rice she ever had left over from supper the night before. Over the years, you've tried it in expensive restaurants, and as the featured dessert at some of your best friends' houses, and even at some fairs and festivals. But nobody ever made rice pudding like your mawmaw, huh? Guess what? Here's her recipe from the "old days."

3 eggs, slightly beaten
¾ cup brown sugar
1 cup heavy cream
1 cup half-and-half
2 tbsp. pure vanilla extract
4 tbsp. butter, softened
1 tsp. ground cinnamon
⅛ tsp. ground nutmeg
⅛ tsp. ground mace
⅛ tsp. salt

2½ cups cooked long-grain rice
1 cup golden raisins
½ cup chopped pecans and almonds
½ tsp. grated lemon zest
2 tsp. fresh-squeezed orange juice
Pinch grated orange zest
2 tbsp. granulated sugar for frosting

Start off by preheating your oven to 350 degrees. This is critical, because the pudding just won't come out right if the oven isn't at the correct temperature when the mixture goes in.

Then, in a large mixing bowl, whisk together the eggs, brown sugar, cream, and half-and-half. Take a little extra time to do this using a real whisk—this is the step that forms the basic custard, which will hold the rice together. Then when the mixture is rich and creamy, add the vanilla, butter, cinnamon, nutmeg, mace, and salt. Once again, whisk together all of the ingredients until thoroughly combined.

Now, ever so gently, fold in the rice, raisins, nuts, lemon zest, orange juice, and orange zest. This step, too, is critical because it is at this point that each grain of rice becomes "seasoned" with the spices. Then when the blend is right, transfer the mixture to a buttered 2-qt. casserole dish. Then place the dish into a larger pan filled with water to create a water bath (bain marie). Baking in this manner tempers the custard, helping to keep it light and preventing it from burning.

All that's left, then, is to bake the pudding—*uncovered*—on the center rack in the oven for approximately 1 hour or until the pudding is set and a toothpick inserted into the center comes out clean. Evenly sprinkle the granulated sugar lightly over the top of the pudding about 5 minutes before you take it out of the oven, so that the sugar will brown and crystallize on the surface.

Creole rice pudding can be served piping hot right from the oven or ice cold right from the refrigerator. It's outstanding as is, but some New Orleanians like to drizzle a little cane syrup over the top!

Christmas Praline Pecan Cake

Of course you can go with fruitcake or sugar plums or even old-fashioned Figgie Pudding, but when it comes to the ultimate dessert for Christmas dinner, this one ranks as one of my all-time favorites! For some reason it just exemplifies the spirit of the holiday season . . . and it's so Southern, too!

2 tbsp. shortening or softened margarine
¾ cup pecan meal or graham-cracker crumbs
1 box Duncan Hines Deluxe Yellow Cake Mix
3¾-oz. box Jell-O Vanilla Instant Pudding

4 large eggs, room temperature
½ cup Crisco oil
¼ cup dark Karo syrup
¾ cup praline liqueur
¾ cup chopped pecans
¾ cup Heath's Bits-O-Brickle Chips or cracked Butterfinger

First, preheat your oven to 350 degrees. Then grease a 10-in. tube or Bundt pan with either the shortening or margarine and liberally coat the insides and bottom with the pecan meal or graham-cracker crumbs.

Next, combine and blend the cake mix and pudding mix in a large bowl, and add to it the eggs, oil, syrup, and liqueur. Then, with an electric mixer, start beating the ingredients at low speed until they are thoroughly blended (this should take about 1-2 minutes). Then immediately increase the beater to medium speed and whip the mixture for 3-4 additional minutes—*this serves to bring it to the proper consistency.*

Finally, when the mixture is silky smooth, fold in the pecans and Bits-O-Brickle until they are uniformly dispersed in the batter. Then pour the batter into your prepared pan, place the pan on the middle rack of the oven, and bake for 45-50 minutes (or until a tester inserted into the cake comes out clean).

When it's done, cool the cake first in the pan on a rack for about 20 minutes; then remove it from the pan and cool it for another 20 minutes or so before you glaze and garnish it.

The Glaze:

2 cups Domino Confectioners
   10X Powdered Sugar
2 tbsp. softened butter
6 tbsp. praline liqueur

Chopped pecans for garnish
Heath's Bits-O-Brickle Chips,
   or cracked Butterfinger for
   garnish

To make the glaze, simply combine the sugar and butter in a small bowl. Then beat with an electric mixer until velvety smooth, adding the liqueur gradually to achieve the desired consistency. When it's ready, drizzle it over the cake and garnish with a few chopped pecans and a handful of Bits-O-Brickle or Butterfinger. Oh—be sure to leave a slice out for Santa!

Chef's Note: To make pecan meal or graham-cracker crumbs, simply put either pecan halves or graham crackers (or a combination) into a food processor and chop them with the steel cutting blade until you get a fine consistency.

Mary Clare's Sugar-Free Pumpkin Pies

Here's another fantastic holiday dessert that you can make sugar free. Never thought pumpkin pie could be made to taste wonderful with an artificial sweetener? Well, I want you to try this! I mean, you gotta have pumpkin pie for the holidays, right?

2 cans Libby's pumpkin,
   15-oz. size
2 cans Pet evaporated milk
4 eggs, slightly beaten
10 tsp. Equal Recipes
2 tbsp. all-purpose flour

1 tsp. salt
3½ tsp. pumpkin-pie spice
2 frozen preformed pie shells,
   deep 9-in. size
1 large Cool Whip Free

First, preheat the oven to 450 degrees—it is important that you make sure the thermostat reaches that temperature before you attempt to bake these pies.

In the meantime, take a large mixing bowl and thoroughly blend together with a wire whip all the ingredients, except for the pie shells and the Cool Whip. Then when the mixture is nice and smooth, gently pour it into the unbaked pie shells and level it off. Now follow the next steps closely:

1—Slide the pies onto the center rack of the oven and bake them initially for 20 minutes.

2—Reduce the temperature to 350 degrees and continue to bake for 40 minutes longer or until a butter knife inserted into the filling comes out clean.

Finally, when the pies are done and the fillings are set, remove them from the oven and cool them completely on a rack. After they come to room temperature, you can either plop a dollop of Cool Whip over each slice of pie as you serve it, or pipe the Cool Whip in a decorative manner over each entire pie with a pastry bag.

A slice goes real good with a glass of cold milk after all the entrées are gone!

Chef's Note:

1—You just might want to have an extra pie shell handy. Oftentimes, the quantities called for in this recipe will make you a third pie.

2—If you'd like to trim a few extra grams of fat, as well as the sugar, from the pie, you can use Pet evaporated skim milk in place of the regular variety. The difference in taste will be practically unnoticeable.

3—Equal Recipes is the granular aspartame product made exclusively for baking and cooking. It is available at most supermarkets on the artificial sweetener shelf.

Creamed Frangelico Strawberries in
Decadent Chocolate Sauce

Nothing beats a flat of fresh Ponchatoula strawberries! Unless, of course, you cover them in sugar and grenadine, top them with a Creole cream cheese dip laced with Frangelico, and stack them in a tall soda glass between layers of decadent chocolate sauce! That beats fresh strawberries, I guarantee!

The Berries:

4 pt. fresh strawberries,   2 cups granulated sugar
   destemmed, washed, and   2 cups grenadine syrup
   halved

Toss the berries thoroughly with the sugar and grenadine in a large plastic bowl and let them macerate in the bottom of the refrigerator at least overnight until a rich syrup forms. In the meantime, make a batch of dip.

The Creole Cream Cheese Dip:

3 cups Creole cream cheese   ¾ cup granulated sugar
1 cup sour cream   ¼ cup Frangelico liqueur

In a half-gal. plastic container, blend together all the ingredients with a hand mixer until the dip is creamy and silky. When it's ready, place it in the refrigerator and allow it to chill for at least 3 hours.

The Decadent Chocolate Sauce:

2 cups granulated sugar   ½ cup light corn syrup
½ cup Hershey's cocoa   1 tsp. vanilla extract
1½ cups heavy cream   Whipped cream for garnish
1 stick unsalted butter   Strawberries for garnish

In a heavy 3-qt. saucepan, mix together the sugar, cocoa, cream, and butter. Then, over low heat so that the sugar and chocolate don't burn, melt everything into a smooth sauce. Note: you're going to have to stir the mixture continuously, but the sauce should smooth out in about 15 minutes. When it does, pour in the corn syrup and stir the sauce for another 5 minutes until a sheen forms.

At this point, remove the pot from the heat and quickly stir in the vanilla.

When you're ready to build your dessert, take a tall soda glass or Pilsner beer glass, spoon in a few strawberries and syrup, top with a couple of tablespoons of the Creole dip, and pour on a couple tablespoons of chocolate sauce. Then repeat the layering effect until the entire glass is filled to the brim! To dress it off, pile on a big dollop of whipped cream and garnish the top with a fresh strawberry.

Don't even ask how many calories are in this! You don't want to know!

Chef's Note:

1—The Creole dip can be made in advance, as it will keep in the fridge for at least 5 days. I suggest that you keep some handy all during the strawberry season!

2—The chocolate sauce should be served warm, but it, too, can be made in advance and stored in a Mason jar in the refrigerator for up to 7 days. I suggest that you reheat it in a heavy saucepan over very low heat, stirring constantly until smooth, before using it. I'd also keep a batch of this on hand all during the strawberry season, in case you feel like dipping a handful of berries just in the sauce.

A Summertime Blueberry Bonanza

Throughout the middle of summer, you can find pints and flats and buckets of blueberries almost everywhere! And many farms will even let you come and pick your own. So it's only fitting that I pass along to you three of my absolute favorite blueberry treats. Choose one or all of them to prepare for your family next time you're feeling "blue."

Blueberry Sherbet:

2 cups fresh-picked blueberries
1½ cups whole milk
¾ cup light Karo syrup

3 tbsp. fresh-squeezed lime juice
2 tbsp. Triple Sec or other
  orange-flavored liqueur

All you do is place the blueberries, milk, syrup, and lime juice in a food processor and puree the mixture until totally smooth. The pour the puree through a fine-mesh strainer and press out all the juice. Then discard the berry skins.

At this point, go ahead and add the liqueur to the strained mixture in a small bowl, cover it, and refrigerate it until it is ready to freeze. Then transfer the ice-cold mix to the freezing tub of your ice-cream maker and freeze it to the sherbet stage.

When you're ready for a special taste of summer, serve up the icy concoction with a heaping dollop of whipped cream or Cool Whip.

Blueberry Dumplings:

2½ cups fresh-picked blue
  berries
⅓ cup + 2 tbsp. granulated
  sugar
Salt
1 cup water

1 tbsp. fresh-squeezed lemon
  juice
1 cup all-purpose flour
2 tsp. baking powder
1 tbsp. ice-cold butter
½ cup whole milk

First thing you do is place the blueberries, ⅓ cup sugar, dash salt, and water into a medium-size, heavy-bottom saucepan that has a tight-fitting lid. Then, while stirring, bring the combination to a boil; but immediately reduce the heat to low and simmer the fruit mixture—*uncovered*—for 5 minutes. After the allotted cooking time, stir in the lemon juice and cover the pan.

In the meantime, make your dumplings by sifting together the flour, 2 tbsp. sugar, baking powder, and ¼ tsp. salt. Then with a pastry blade cut in the butter until the mixture turns the consistency of coarse meal. At this point, add the milk all at once and stir the batter just until the flour is dampened.

All that's left to do now is drop the dumplings by tablespoons into the simmering blueberry mixture, cover the saucepan tightly, and cook everything over low heat for 10 minutes without removing the cover. The end result is dumpling perfection!

These are best served in dessert bowls, each topped with a scoop of French vanilla ice cream.

Old-Tyme Blueberry Cobbler:

1 cup all-purpose flour
½ cup + 3 tbsp. granulated
   sugar
1½ tsp. baking powder
1¼ tsp. ground cinnamon
Salt
1 egg, beaten

1 cup milk
2 tbsp. cornstarch
3 cups fresh-picked blueberries
4 tsp. fresh-squeezed lemon
   juice
1 tsp. lemon zest
½ cup melted butter

This summertime blueberry dessert is nothing less than sinful!

First, preheat your oven to 375 degrees. Then, in the meantime, make the cobbler topping by thoroughly stirring together the flour, 3 tbsp. sugar, baking powder, ¼ tsp. cinnamon, and ¼ tsp. salt. Then combine the egg and milk and stir that into the dry ingredients just until the mix is moistened. Now set it aside for a while.

Next, to make the fruit mixture, first combine ½ cup sugar and the cornstarch in a saucepan. Then add the blueberries, lemon juice, lemon zest, 1 tsp. cinnamon, and dash salt, stir everything together, and cook it over medium heat—continuing to stir—for 4-6 minutes or until thickened.

At this point, pour half of the butter into an 8x8-in. glass baking dish, place the berry mixture on top of the butter, spoon the cobbler topping over the fruit, and drizzle the topping with the remaining butter. All that's left to do, then, is to slide the dish into the oven and bake the cobbler at 375 degrees for 15-20 minutes or until the topping is a crispy golden brown.

I suggest that you serve this dessert warm, crowned with ice cream or whipped cream.

Frank's Homemade Funnel Cakes

Next to beignets and café au lait, funnel cakes are probably the most popular dessert items served at Louisiana fairs and festivals. And while they're Amish in origin and the pride of Pennsylvania Dutch country, these sugary, crispy confections have become as Cajun and as Creole as they can get.

3 large eggs
2¼ cups whole milk
½ tsp. pure vanilla extract
4 cups all-purpose flour, sifted
1 tbsp. double-acting baking
  powder

½ tsp. salt
1 cup lightly packed light brown
  sugar
2 cups vegetable oil for frying
1½ cups powdered sugar
1 tbsp. ground cinnamon

In a bowl, whisk together the eggs, milk, and vanilla until frothy. In a second bowl, sift together the flour, baking powder, and salt (don't just mix it—it must be sifted). Then stir the brown sugar into the flour mixture until uniformly combined.

Next whisk the dry ingredients into the egg mixture, then beat with a rotary hand mixer until smooth and lump free.

Test the batter to make sure it flows easily through the funnel or funnel cake pitcher. If it is too thin, add a tad more flour; if it is too thick, add a little more milk. When you reach the consistency of heavy pancake batter, you have the perfect mix.

If you're making the cakes without a "ring mold," pour about 1 in. oil into a heavy cast-iron or nonstick 8-in. skillet and heat the oil to 375 degrees. If you're going to use a funnel cake ring, pour about 2 in. oil into a cast-iron or nonstick 12-in. skillet, place the ring into the center of the pan, and heat the oil to 375 degrees.

When you're ready to cook, hold your finger over the bottom of the funnel or use a funnel cake pitcher and fill it with the batter.

Hold the funnel spout over the hot oil and remove your finger. Then immediately start to drizzle the batter into the oil, moving the funnel around to make a crisscross or squiggly design. I suggest that you first make a circle around the outside edge of the pan or the ring, then crisscross back and forth to tie the circle together. You will need to move the funnel spout continuously to keep the batter from forming "dough balls" in the oil. In short, once the flow starts, keep it moving until you have the cake formed. Also remember that the batter will swell as it cooks, so don't "overflow" it into the pan.

Fry the cake for about 3 minutes on one side until golden brown, then flip it over with a pair of tongs or a wide spatula and fry the other side for about 1 minute. (If you are using a ring, lift the ring off of the funnel cake as soon as the batter takes shape and remove it from the pan.)

When the cake turns a rich golden brown, remove it from the oil with a slotted spoon, chef's hook, or tongs and drain it on several layers of paper towels.

Finally, mix the powdered sugar with the cinnamon, transfer it to a shaker can, and sprinkle the finished funnel cake heavily with it while still hot. Continue making funnel cakes one at a time until all of the batter is used.

Serve immediately. This recipe will make about eight 8-in. cakes.

Chef's Note:

1—If you don't have a funnel cake pitcher or rings and want to add them to your kitchen arsenal, you can get them in New Orleans at Gold Medal Concessions (504-733-7348) or by going to the Pennsylvania Dutch Company at www.funnelcakes4u.com. If you'd like to use a premixed batter instead of making your own, you can also order it in 5-lb. bags.

2—Never fry lower than 375 degrees! The cakes will absorb too much oil. Somewhere between 375 and 400 degrees is ideal.

3—To reach the correct frying temperature, you can heat the oil until it just begins to smoke slightly. But the proper way to reach the correct oil temperature is to use a fry thermometer. They can be purchased at all kitchen shops and most grocery stores.

4—For a nice variation when you serve the cakes, instead of sprinkling them with cinnamon sugar, drizzle them generously with either Louisiana cane syrup or homemade molasses, or spread them liberally with canned apple pie filling that has been warmed.

5—Extra leftover batter may be stored in the refrigerator for up to 3 days. In fact, for a large "Funnel Cake Party," you might choose to make the batter in advance and stash it in the refrigerator until ready to use. Just remember to take it out of the refrigerator so that it can come to room temperature before dropping it into the hot oil.

Original Amish (Cajun) Friendship Bread

Lord only knows how, amongst the Pennsylvania Dutch people, this recipe really got started, but folks in Southeast Louisiana will tell you that they're surely glad it made its way down to the swamps and bayous. While it is said to be Amish, I can promise you that it will be absolutely relished as a crowning-touch dessert bread after anything you fix that's Cajun or Creole! You need to get a batch brewin' today!

1 pkg. active dry yeast	2 cups sifted flour
2½ cups warm water (110 degrees)	1 tbsp. granulated sugar

First you make the starter. Begin by dissolving the yeast in 1 cup warm water in a glass bowl (do not use any kind of metal, neither spoon nor bowl, when making this recipe). Now let the yeast stand for abut 10 minutes. Next, stir in the remaining water, the flour, and the sugar. At this point, beat the mixture with a wooden spoon until it is smooth.

When thoroughly combined, place the dough on the countertop or table, not in the refrigerator. This version of the bread starter contains no milk products, so it doesn't need to be chilled. Now cover the bowl with a clean dishtowel and allow the starter to begin the fermentation process.It will be a full 10 days before you use the starter for making bread or for giving batches away to your friends (and it is normal for the batter to thicken and bubble).

Here is the processing procedure and schedule. *Note: whenever air gets in the bag, let it out!*

Day 1   This is the day you make your starter. Do nothing!
Day 2   Transfer to a gal.-size Ziploc bag and squeeze the bag to mix.
Day 3   Squeeze the bag to mix.
Day 4   Squeeze the bag to mix.
Day 5   Squeeze the bag to mix.
Day 6   Add 1 cup flour, 1 cup sugar, and 1 cup milk to bag. Squeeze.
Day 7   Squeeze the bag to mix.
Day 8   Squeeze the bag to mix.
Day 9   Squeeze the bag to mix.
Day 10 This is baking day!

Transfer the batter to a large glass bowl. Then blend into the batter

1 cup flour, 1 cup sugar, and 1 cup warm milk (110 degrees). Stir thoroughly with a wooden spoon, pour 1 cup starter dough into a gal.-size Ziploc bag, and seal it up. Repeat this until you have 4 packets of starter dough. You will give a bag to 3 of your best friends or neighbors (along with this recipe), but keep 1 bag for yourself. Then to the remaining batter in the glass bowl, add the following:

1 cup oil	1 large box vanilla instant
2 cups flour	pudding
1 cup sugar	1½ tsp. baking powder
½ cup milk	2 tsp. ground cinnamon
2 tsp. vanilla extract	½ tsp. salt
½ tsp. baking soda	1 cup chopped pecans
3 large eggs	¾ cup raisins

When everything is thoroughly mixed, pour the batter into 2 large, well-greased and sugared loaf pans (use a mixture of granulated sugar and cinnamon). You can also sprinkle some extra cinnamon and sugar on top of the bread.

All that's left is to bake the loaves at 325 degrees for 1 hour. They can be sliced and served piping hot or cooled and served later at room temperature. Warning—this stuff can be addicting!

Chef's Note: Of course, don't forget that the process starts all over again at Day 1 with the extra bag of starter you kept for yourself! So as Sonny and Cher once sang, "The beat goes on!"

Frank's Sicilian Fig Cookies

I don't care what anybody says, this recipe makes fantastic cookies, whether you're Sicilian or not! They're super crispy on the outside, moist and figgy on the inside, and bursting with pure Mediterranean flavor. But the best part is they're so darn easy to make!

8 cups all-purpose flour	2 cups granulated sugar
2 tsp. baking soda	½ cup milk, scalded
2 cups melted Crisco shortening	2 tsp. vanilla extract
2 eggs, beaten	

To make the dough, first mix together the flour and baking soda in a large bowl. Then, in an electric mixer, whip the shortening, eggs, sugar, milk, and vanilla until smooth and fully blended. Now, a little at a time, add the flour to the egg mix and knead it into a resilient "dough ball." *Hint: dough hooks or a good processor do an excellent job of kneading and save you considerable time.*

When the dough is ready, wrap it in plastic film and set it aside while you make the fig filling.

The Fig Filling:

1 ½ lb. dried figs	½ lb. brown sugar
½ lb. dates	½ tsp. ground nutmeg
½ lb. raisins	½ tsp. ground cinnamon
½ lb. mixed walnuts and pecans	½ tsp. ground cloves
½ orange (peel and all)	1 jigger whiskey
Juice of ½ lemon	

In a food grinder, fine-grind all the dried fruits and nuts, as well as the orange (or mince them with the cutting blade of your food processor). Then, in a large bowl, mix in the remaining ingredients and stir everything together well (again, the dough hook attachment on your mixer will save you a lot of time and elbow grease because the paste turns thick once the brown sugar is added).

Then, when everything is uniformly mixed, set the paste aside for about 10 minutes to "cure."

At this point, preheat your oven to 400 degrees. Now, in small batches, roll out the dough and cut it into thin strips about 2 in. wide by 12 in. long. Then spread a bead of the fig filling directly down the center of each dough strip and wrap the sides of the dough around the stuffing. Seal in the filling by rolling the dough back and forth, like a rolling pin, with your fingertips a couple of times. Then cut the dough into cookies about 2 in. long, place them on a greased cookie sheet, and bake them at 400 degrees for 15-18 minutes or until they turn a honey brown.

Chef's Note:
1—Here's a little Italian lagniappe. If you want to make real Sicilian sesame cookies, just make the dough, roll it out with your fingertips into a ³/₄-in.-diameter tube shape, cut the tube into 2-in. cookies, top

each with toasted sesame seeds, and bake them on a greased cookie sheet at 400 degrees for 10-12 minutes. You'll think you're sitting in a piazza in Palermo when you're eating these!

2—Note: this is the guarded fig cookie recipe of the late Nina Scalia Bruscato, who gave it to me because I married her youngest daughter. There are no better Italian cookies anywhere! Thanks, Mom!

Index